Delivery of Goods under Bills of Lading

Probably *the* core characteristic of a bill of lading [illegible] lading must be presented at the port of destination for a consignee to be entitled to delivery of the goods and for the carrier to get a good discharge of its delivery obligation by delivering the goods to said consignee. This notion is accepted virtually worldwide, but the more precise content of the "presentation rule" differs from jurisdiction to jurisdiction. Furthermore, and of importance, the legal basis establishing the "presentation rule" differs.

With the technological advances in maritime transport as well as in communications technology and the emergence of more complicated trading patterns, a system where a specific tangible piece of paper issued at the port of loading has to be presented at the port of discharge to obtain delivery of the goods seems almost archaic and can obviously create problems. Thus, in practice very often – especially in some trades such as the oil trade – the bill of lading is not available at the port of discharge when the ship is ready to deliver the cargo.

The book will first analyse the "presentation rule", its finer contents and its legal basis. It will then go on with (legal) analyses of three developments and responses to the problems that the bill of lading system gives rise to in practice, viz. the commercial, the international legislature's, and the technological response. The commercial response analysed here consists of contractual exemption or limitation clauses in the bill of lading set up as a defence against claims for misdelivery. The international legislature's response denotes the adoption of the Rotterdam Rules which as the first international convention on carriage of goods by sea includes elaborate rules on delivery of the goods. Finally, the technological response denotes the possibility of using electronic (equivalents of) bills of lading. The analyses will include a comparative approach examining both English and Scandinavian law to elucidate the issues with greater clarity.

Dr Anders Møllmann is an Associate Professor in Maritime Law at the University of Copenhagen, Denmark.

Delivery of Goods under Bills of Lading

Anders Møllmann

Routledge
Taylor & Francis Group
LONDON AND NEW YORK

First published 2017 by Routledge

2 Park Square, Milton Park, Abingdon, Oxfordshire OX14 4RN
52 Vanderbilt Avenue, New York, NY 10017

Routledge is an imprint of the Taylor & Francis Group, an informa business

First issued in paperback 2018

British Library Cataloguing in Publication Data
A catalogue record for this book is available from the British Library

Library of Congress Cataloging-in-Publication Data
Names: Møllmann, Anders, author.
Title: Delivery of goods under bills of lading / Anders Møllmann.
Description: Abingdon, Oxon ; New York, NY : Routledge, 2017. | Includes bibliographical references and index.
Identifiers: LCCN 2016027954 | ISBN 978-1-138-68832-2 (hbk) | ISBN 978-1-315-54189-1 (ebk)
Subjects: LCSH: Contracts, Maritime. | Bills of lading. | Delivery of goods (Law) | Rotterdam Rules (2008)
Classification: LCC K1178 .M65 2017 | DDC 346.02/5—dc23
LC record available at https://lccn.loc.gov/2016027954

ISBN: 978-1-138-68832-2 (hbk)
ISBN: 978-0-367-07553-8 (pbk)

Typeset in Baskerville
by FiSH Books Ltd, Enfield

To Lisa, Erik, and Nils

Contents

Acknowledgements

This book has been written as part of a project which was generously funded by the Danish Maritime Fund for which I am thankful.

The project has been ongoing for quite some years and many people deserve (and hopefully have felt) my gratitude for their help and support. Rather than a long list here, I will, however, only mention a few people.

Throughout the years I have had the good fortune of having the companionship of my colleague, mentor, and friend, Professor Vibe Ulfbeck. Her continuing encouragement, advice and faith in me have been invaluable.

The good people at the Scandinavian Institute of Maritime Law at the University of Oslo have always shown interest in my project and offered to discuss various issues. Particular mention should be made of Professor Erik Røsæg who (amongst other things) was so kind as to organise a seminar at the institute where we could discuss a previous draft of Chapter 4. I am grateful to all the people there.

I was also fortunate to be invited to present a part of the project at an Oslo-Southampton-Tulane Colloquium in Romsey where I received much valuable response. I am grateful to Professor Filippo Lorenzon for inviting me.

The book is dedicated to my partner and sons whose everyday lives have been affected far too much for far too long by the writing of this book.

I have strived to state the law as it was in mid-May 2016.

Anders Møllmann
Copenhagen, 10 June 2016

1 Introduction

1 Theme

Maritime transport plays a significant part in international trade. With the parties situated in different countries, physical delivery of the goods does not happen directly between seller and buyer, but rather with a carrier as "middleman". Thus in its most simple form, the sold goods are handed over from the seller to a carrier who in turn hands them over to the buyer. From a business perspective this raises several practical and legal questions. Who has to procure and pay for the carriage of the goods? When does the risk for and property in the goods pass from seller to buyer? Who controls the goods while they are in transit? Who can claim them from the carrier and how is the simultaneous exchange of the goods and the purchase price ensured, that is how is it ensured that the goods are not handed over to the buyer without payment of the purchase price when the seller is not in physical possession of the goods? Such issues are of utmost importance in the sales contract relationship. It is in this context that the contract of carriage and the law regulating it must function.

The latter questions above relate to the delivery of the goods from the carrier when they arrive at their destination. Delivery of the goods to a receiver is obviously an inherent part of any contract of carriage. From a maritime (and other transport) law perspective the question is who can claim delivery of the goods from the carrier and to whom can the carrier deliver the goods in order to obtain a good discharge of its obligations. For centuries one of the main ways to regulate these issues has been to use the transport document known as a bill of lading. When under a contract of carriage a bill of lading is issued, important legal consequences occur which inter alia make the tangible bill of lading an indispensable part of the delivery of the goods. Thus, as is well-known, once a bill of lading is issued, that same physical, original bill of lading must be presented to obtain delivery of the goods, a function which has given the bill of lading the metaphorical designation "the key to the floating warehouse". In this capacity, the bill of lading may be used in the sales contract relationship to ensure payment of the purchase price before parting with control over the goods.

Despite its importance in both the sales contract and the contract of carriage context, the issue of the delivery of the goods covered by a bill of lading is surprisingly superficially treated in most textbooks on the carriage of goods by sea. This book is therefore devoted to this subject.

The basic principle that delivery must – and must only – be made against presentation of the bill of lading can, however, not always be adhered to. Local laws may force the carrier to deliver goods to authorities, e.g. customs authorities, and not to the bill of lading holder, and trade restrictions such as embargoes may make it illegal for the carrier to deliver the goods to the bill of lading holder. The carrier may be met by fraudsters who present a forged bill of lading or may be faced with a genuine bill where an indorsement turns out to be invalid. The question then arises who must bear the risk of such incidents.

The bill of lading system is also under pressure. This is largely due to technological advances both in terms of communication technology and maritime technology, i.e. faster and safer ships, as well as certain trade practices. In this day and age, the fact that the consignee has to produce a unique tangible piece of paper to obtain delivery of goods, the carriage of which will almost certainly have been contracted using digital means, seems almost archaic. The speed of maritime transport, even when slow-steaming, is high and getting the bill of lading to the destination before the goods arrive is often a problem, especially if the payment modality is one that requires several parties to handle the bill of lading such as in a documentary credit.

As a result, situations very often arise where the bill of lading is not available at the destination and the person claiming delivery therefore cannot present the bill. These situations obviously occur more often in trades where the maritime carriage is short or the goods are sold, often more than once, while in transit, thus creating a chain of sales and possibly documentary credits that the bill of lading must pass through before reaching the final buyer. This is for instance the case in the North Sea and Persian Gulf oil trades.[1] There are no reliable statistics available showing the extent of the problem but an educated estimate by a long-time practitioner has been forwarded stating that the bill of lading is not presented in 15 per cent of all cases in liner trade, 50 per cent in bulk trades, and close to 100 per cent in oil and related trades.[2]

1 Steven J. Hazelwood and David Semark, *P & I Clubs Law and Practice* (London: Lloyd's List, 2010), para 10.95. The authors in fn 77 note that some masters engaged in the Gulf oil trade will say that they have rarely, if ever, enjoyed the luxury of delivering their cargoes in exchange for a bill of lading.

2 Gertjan van der Ziel, "Delivery of the goods, rights of the controlling party and transfer of rights", in *A New Convention for the Carriage of Goods by Sea – The Rotterdam Rules*, ed. D. Rhidian Thomas (Lawtext Publishing Limited, 2009), p. 248.

This problem is not new and the industry has dealt with it in various ways. The predominant way is for the carrier to deliver the cargo to the person whom it believes to be entitled to it against that person (or the charterer) providing a letter of indemnity, preferably backed by a bank or other financial institution, for the liability the carrier exposes itself to by delivering the goods without the presentation of the bill of lading.[3]

Even if some practitioners will say that the system of delivering against a letter of indemnity works, it is undesirable. From a practical perspective it leads to administrative burdens and uncertainty as well as producing unnecessary costs of ensuring the backing of a financial institution. From a more principled perspective, it undermines the bill of lading's status as the central transport document, identifying the person entitled to delivery of the goods, i.e. its function as a document of title or legitimation paper depending on the legal terminology applied.

Another way carriers have attempted to avoid liability after delivering goods without presentation of an original bill of lading has been to rely on exemption or limitation of liability clauses in the bill of lading.

These problems may be seen as a sign that the public regulation of bills of lading no longer fully corresponds to the practical needs of the business reality. The above-mentioned measures can then be regarded as the private actors in the sector's attempt at overcoming this inconsistency. The question is to what extent it is possible for these private actors to avoid or remedy the conceived defects of the public regulation through the use of contract. The answer to this question heavily relies on what the basis of the regulation is.

In recent years, interesting developments have also taken place which could influence or perhaps even solve some of the problems of the bill of lading system. In 2008, the United Nations adopted the Rotterdam Rules[4] which for the first time set out positive rules at the international level regulating the delivery of the goods. These rules include an attempt at alleviating the problems outlined above. The Rotterdam Rules can thus be seen as the international lawmakers' response to (inter alia) the problems related to the bill of lading system.

Another solution which has been promoted to the problems involved in the use of paper bills of lading is a change to electronic communication and documentation. The use of electronic alternatives to bills of lading has, however, met substantial legal obstacles which have been sought solved in

3 Another device has been to keep one original bill of lading on board the ship which the master could then give to the person claiming delivery who would then immediately give it back to the carrier. This practice has rightfully been called "a mockery of the normal system", Hazelwood and Semark, *P & I Clubs Law and Practice*, para 10.135.

4 United Nations Convention on Contracts for the International Carriage of Goods Wholly or Partly by Sea, see *infra* Chapter 5, part 1, for an introduction to the Convention and its creation.

various ways. The constant evolution in computer science consistently enhances the technical possibilities of producing a practical, user-friendly system for using electronic bills of lading. Yet at the international level, no rules have previously regulated the use of electronic bills of lading ensuring any legal status of such electronic bills. The Rotterdam Rules have introduced rules which are aimed at facilitating the use of electronic transport documentation. The introduction of electronic bills of lading is thus industry driven, but for it to become a fully viable solution, the participation of lawmakers seems to be necessary.

In this book, the rules regarding the delivery of the goods carried under bills of lading and the basis of these rules will be examined. This will lead to an analysis of the commercial response to some of the conceived problems in the system through the use of exemption clauses.[5] These analyses will then form the basis of an assessment of the viability of the possible solutions offered by the Rotterdam Rules and the use of electronic transport documents. To set the context in which the analyses must be performed, the book will commence with an introductory chapter on the role of the bill of lading in international trade.

The legal issues pertaining to delivery of the goods fall in a border zone between several legal disciplines, namely contract law, property law, tort law and the law on negotiable instruments. Further, while the content of the main rules on the delivery of the goods are largely the same, their bases differ quite a lot in different legal systems. The same applies to other key aspects of using bills of lading such as the precise implications of the negotiability of the bill. Bills of lading often include choice of law and jurisdiction clauses, but it is not as widespread as in charterparties and normally arbitration clauses are not used. Also, many jurisdictions do not (at least not fully) recognise such clauses in relation to bills of lading or specifically to claims for misdelivery. English law therefore does not play as significant a role as in relation to charterparties. When analysing the law pertaining to delivery of goods and particularly when assessing possible developments in the field, it is therefore relevant to compare English law with other legal systems. As will become apparent, the basis of the rules pertaining to delivery of goods has a substantial impact on the viability of the developments in the field. For reasons that will be expanded upon in the following part, the Scandinavian countries are an interesting object of comparison. For these reasons the analyses in this book will be of both the law of England and of the Scandinavian countries.

5 The problems relating to the commercial response in the form of using letters of indemnity when delivering without presentation of an original bill of lading regard mainly the enforceability of the letter of indemnity, i.e. of a separate contract, and not directly the delivery obligations under the contract of carriage. Though an interesting subject, it falls outside the main scope of this book and will therefore not be dealt with here. See instead e.g. Felipe Arizon and David Semark, *Maritime Letters of Indemnity* (Abingdon: Informa Law from Routledge, 2014).

2 Some methodological remarks

2.1 English and Scandinavian law

English law plays a dominant role in relation to bills of lading and has done so even more in previous times when much of the law as it stands today developed. It has been the traditional choice to insert English law and jurisdiction if a jurisdiction and choice of law clause has been included in the bill of lading. The effect of such clauses has, however, been limited by mandatory legislation in many countries. English law represents the common law tradition with its focus on case law.

English maritime law has indeed developed in the common law although especially the carriage of goods has been supplemented in important respects by statute, of most importance in this context the Carriage of Goods by Sea Act 1992 and Carriage of Goods by Sea Act 1971. The treatment of bills of lading has very much taken its starting point in the bill of lading being in essence a contract and unresolved issues have thus to a large extent been dealt with using contract law principles. However, in relation to delivery issues common law actions, especially bailment and the tort of conversion, have also played important parts, although more so prior to the passing of the COGSA 1992.

The Scandinavian countries'[6] legal systems are normally considered mixed legal systems meaning that they are rooted in the civil law tradition but leave a wider discretion to the courts and place more emphasis on case law than the traditional continental civil law systems.

For well over a century, Denmark, Sweden and Norway have had an extended cooperation in the field of private law. Important pieces of legislation in this field are results of joint commission works which have led to virtually identical acts as well as virtually identical or at least very similar travaux preparatoires. After World War II, Finland has joined in this tradition for cooperation. Of particular relevance to the present topic is the fact that the countries have virtually identical Merchant Shipping Acts, Acts on Instruments of Debt, and Contracts Acts. The same was the case with the Sale of Goods Acts, but when Finland, Sweden and Norway changed their Sale of Goods Acts in the 1980s, Denmark chose not to do so.

The first Swedish, Norwegian and Danish Merchant Shipping Acts[7]

6 Throughout used to denote Denmark, Norway, Sweden and Finland, see *infra* part 2.4. on the terminology.

7 The Merchant Shipping Acts are also often referred to as the Maritime Code or the Nordic Maritime Code. Throughout this book the term Merchant Shipping Act will be applied. English translations (not legally valid) of all four countries' Merchant Shipping Acts are available. For Denmark: www.dma.dk/SiteCollectionDocuments/Legislation/Acts/2014/LBK-75-17012014-merchant%20shipping%20act.pdf. For Norway: http://folk.uio.no/erikro/WWW/NMC.pdf. For Finland (only Chapter 13 which is the

resulting from the above-mentioned collaboration were passed in the early 1890s. The current acts are from the 1990s with later amendments.

As a result of the cooperation between the countries in this field there is a tradition for including sources, such as travaux preparatoires, case law and literature, from the other countries when interpreting the legislation. The sources from the other countries, of course, have no formal status in the forum country, but they may nevertheless influence the interpretation. This tradition is perhaps particularly strong within the field of maritime law. Here, quite a lot of emphasis is placed on not least the case law of the other countries. This has for a very long time been helped by a joint Nordic law reporter for maritime cases having been in existence for over a century.

The focus of this book, the law regarding delivery of the goods, must be analysed using several disciplines of law, as stated above. This involves the application of especially the Merchant Shipping Acts and the Acts on Instruments of Debt as well as contract law principles partly found in the Contracts Acts. As already stated, these all have their roots in the collaboration between the four countries. However, there are, unsurprisingly, discrepancies between the countries also in this field stemming from other legislation, principles, case law or traditions. Despite this fact, the similarities are so extensive that this book will deal with Scandinavian law as one with the inherent risk of minor imprecisions that this choice entails. Of course, where larger differences exist this will be pointed out. The choice to deal with Scandinavian law must not be misunderstood to mean that Scandinavian law exists as a "law" which is applicable in any jurisdiction or that a Scandinavian Merchant Shipping Act exists. Any case must be decided under the law of one of the countries.

The Scandinavian approach has, unsurprisingly, also been to approach the bill of lading as a contract, but a contractual relationship which is heavily regulated by mandatory legislation. This includes analogous application of the legislation applicable to negotiable instruments of debt. Finding answers to unresolved issues, thus, often is a question of legislative interpretation rather than applying principles of contract. This makes for an interesting contrast with English law which, as will be shown, has significant

relevant chapter for the topic of this book): www.helsinki.fi/oikeustiede/oppiaineet/sopimusoikeus/materiaali/FinnishMaritimeCode,chp%2013EEW.pdf. The Swedish translation is available in book form, *The Swedish Maritime Code Sjölagen 1994 – In Swedish and English*, Skrifter utgivna av Axel Ax:son Johnsons institut för sjörätt och annan transporträtt (Stockholm: Juristförlaget, 1995). Translations used in this book will be from the Danish version unless otherwise noted. Due to legislative tradition, the sections of the Acts (not called section in the original languages, but paragraphs (§)) are in Norway and Denmark consecutively numbered while in Sweden and Finland the numbering starts from 1 again in each chapter. In the text, the Danish/Norwegian numbering will be used. A table "translating" the numbers to the Swedish/Finnish numbering can be found in Annex 1.

impact on how challenges to the bill of lading system can be sought overcome.

2.2 Comparative method

The analysis of each legal system must, of course, apply the accepted legal methods of that system with some adjustments which enhance the comparative analysis. This may give rise to surprises to readers when reading about the "other" system than their own. Thus, a Scandinavian lawyer may find that the analysis of English law places a surprising amount of emphasis on specific quotes from case law and performs a surprisingly literal interpretation of statutes (although Scandinavian lawyers are probably more often subjected to English law than vice versa) while an English lawyer may be surprised to see the emphasis placed in Scandinavian law on the travaux preparatoires of statutes, the wide analogous application of certain statutes and the scarceness of judicial support for some of the submissions made. That must necessarily be so when comparing two such relatively different legal systems.

The adjustments that have been found useful to enhance the comparative analysis include the above-mentioned choice of focusing on Scandinavian law rather than the law of one of the four countries. Another choice with respect to English law is to refer more than is usual for English law books to legal literature instead of listing the full line of authorities from which the rule, principle or assertion in question has been derived. This (it is submitted) heightens the readability and makes the comparative analysis more accessible.

As will be shown, English and Scandinavian law apply quite different concepts in attributing the various functions to bills of lading. Therefore, the comparative analysis cannot take such concepts as its starting point. Instead, the analysis will be made on the basis of the functions of the bill of lading in relation to delivery of the goods as well as on various typical problems in practice. The comparison will also be performed at this level, rather than applying a Länderbericht method, but the comparisons must, of course, be read in the context of the entire analysis.

The functional approach, thus, means asking questions based on the functioning of the bill of lading rather than trying to derive all the functions from a classification of the bill of lading. This means, for instance, that the recurring questions in Chapter 3 are who can claim delivery of the goods from the carrier and to whom the carrier can deliver the goods in order to obtain a good discharge of its delivery obligation. Conversely the analysis does not take as its starting point the fact that a bill of lading is a document of title under English law and a negotiable document under Scandinavian law. The effects of the approach may, however, appear more clearly in relation to English law because many of the answers under Scandinavian law must in fact be derived using the concepts and principles especially associated with negotiable documents.[8]

2.3 The Rotterdam Rules

A large part of this book is devoted to analyses of the Rotterdam Rules.[9] The Rotterdam Rules is a United Nations Convention not yet in force. This has various implications on the interpretation thereof. First, an obvious consequence is that no case law exists on the Rules.[10] Second, the convention is not at a stage where the interpretation is one which must be made in a dispute between private parties. It is at a stage where national governments must decide whether to ratify the convention and, if so, how to implement it in its national legal order. When interpreting the convention in that context, limitations on the use of travaux preparatoires which would normally apply when courts interpret international conventions, e.g. the fairly narrow possibilities of English courts to seek recourse to the travaux preparatoires, do not apply. In this regard, it is worth noting that detailed and comprehensive reports have been produced and formally adopted by the Working Group and the Commission of UNCITRAL of all its deliberations. These reports and the formal Working Papers which were submitted during the six years of negotiations are publicly available in all United Nations languages at the website of UNCITRAL.[11] These reports, and to a lesser degree the Working Papers, constitute the travaux preparatoires of the convention and may, it is submitted, be given quite some weight in the interpretation.[12] Finally, it should be noted that the Rotterdam Rules themselves include an article, article 2, setting out that in the interpretation of the convention "regard is to be had to its international character and to the need to promote uniformity in its application and the observance of good faith in international trade".

8 Charles Debattista, *Bills of Lading in Export Trade*, 3rd ed. (Haywards Heath: Tottel Publishing, 2009), p. 25 et seq., also chooses to apply a functional approach because of the lack of a unanimously accepted definition of "document of title". Hugo Tiberg, "Legal qualities of transport documents", *Tulane Maritime Law Journal* 23 (1998), performs an analysis of the legal qualities of transport documents using only Continental notions and explains his choice with the, slightly provoking, statement; "Because only the continental instruments are sharp enough to distinguish the many real issues involved", p. 2.

9 Chapters 5 and 7.

10 The Rules have been noted in various cases internationally, including by the US Supreme Court, but have obviously not been part of the ratio decidendi.

11 www.uncitral.org.

12 The present author was the Danish representative to the negotiations from November 2006 to the adoption of the convention in 2008. However, any intentions behind and negotiations of the rules will, of course, only be taken into account to the extent they have been reproduced in the official reports and working papers.

2.4 Terminology

A distinction is sometimes made between misdelivery and wrongful delivery. In this book, no such distinction will be made and the terms will be used interchangeably, but preferring misdelivery.

Scandinavia comprises Norway, Sweden and Denmark, while "the Nordic countries" comprise the three as well as Finland and Iceland. As already noted, the private law collaboration which has led to virtually identical Merchant Shipping Acts is between Norway, Sweden, Finland and Denmark. In this book "Scandinavia" and "Scandinavian" is used to refer to all four countries.

English law denotes the law of England and Wales.

The carrier is for obvious reasons a recurring party throughout the book. Nowadays, a carrier is almost invariably a company. Therefore the personal pronoun "it" will be used rather than "he" or "she".

3 Structure of the book

After this introductory chapter, Chapter 2 will provide a brief, general introduction to the bill of lading and its role in international trade to serve as a basis for diving into the specific issue of the delivery of the goods.

Chapter 3 will then provide a detailed analysis of the law as it is with regard to the requirement to deliver the goods only against presentation of an original bill of lading.

Chapters 4–7 are dedicated to analyses of the industry's response to some of the problems inherent in the bill of lading system and other developments aimed at (inter alia) relieving some of those problems.

Chapter 4 deals with exemption clauses in bills of lading and their applicability to claims for misdelivery. Chapter 5 takes on the Rotterdam Rules as they deal with the delivery of the goods.

Chapters 6 and 7 both deal with the use of electronic bills of lading. While Chapter 6 analyses the use of electronic bills of lading[13] under current law, Chapter 7 looks at the same under the Rotterdam Rules. Both chapters take a wider approach than only focusing on the specific issue of the delivery of the goods. The reason for this is that while the use of electronic bills of lading may alleviate some of the problems associated with the requirement that delivery must only be made against presentation of an original bill of lading, the problems currently inhibiting the use of such electronic bills are only partly related to the issue of the delivery of the goods.

Finally, Chapter 8 contains some concluding remarks.

13 As to the use of the term "electronic bill of lading" see Chapter 6, fn 1.

2 The bill of lading in international trade

1 Introduction and the basic functions of the bill of lading

The focus of this book is on the legal position of the parties involved in contracts for the carriage of goods covered by a bill of lading and more specifically the law pertaining to the obligation on the carrier only to deliver the goods against presentation of an original bill of lading – "the presentation rule".

Before diving into this specific aspect of the use of bills of lading, in this chapter a brief introduction of the bill of lading's functions and especially the bill of lading's role in international sales will be provided. It is in this context that the bill of lading must function and with this context in mind that the analyses in this book must be performed. Thus, for instance alternatives to the current legal regimes and documentary practices which would deprive the bill of lading any of its key features in relation to international trade would most likely not be viable.

A bill of lading is generally said to have three basic characteristics; it is a receipt for goods shipped or received by the carrier, it contains or evidences the contract of carriage of the goods by sea, and it gives an exclusive right to claim delivery of the goods. The third function is under English law often described by stating that the bill of lading is a document of title. However, this terminology is not used in all jurisdictions and, as will be shown, even under English law the precise content of this term is not completely clear and the presentation requirement does not necessarily apply only to bills of lading which are documents of title at common law.[1]

It is (mainly) the third function that distinguishes the bill of lading from other transport documents, such as the sea waybill, and which gives the bill of lading its distinct role in international trade. It is this third function that is the focus of this book.

1 See *infra* Chapter 3, parts 2.2 and 3.2.

2 Basic function of bills of lading in international sales

One of the fundamental principles in the law governing sales of goods is that the goods sold and the payment therefore must be exchanged simultaneously. This principle is set out in both the Danish Sale of Goods Act § 14,[2] the English Sale of Goods Act 1979, s. 28, and the United Nations Convention on Contracts for the International Sale of Goods (CISG), article 58(1). In international sales (and national distance sales), the buyer and seller will normally not meet to exchange the goods. Instead the goods will be shipped to the buyer most often using a third party carrier.

In such circumstances, the buyer will not want to pay the purchase price until it receives the goods and can ascertain that they comply with the agreed specifications. Likewise, the seller will not want to part with the goods until it is certain that the purchase price will be paid, thus running the risk of incurring costs and possibly having unpaid goods placed in a distant port where they may be difficult to resell or even control. Furthermore, the buyer may wish to resell the goods before they arrive at the destination. It is therefore necessary to establish some other way of exchanging possession of the goods and the purchase price and this is where the bill of lading is the key.

As the bill of lading is necessary to obtain delivery of the goods at the destination (and elsewhere) and a transfer of the bill of lading transfers constructive possession of the goods, the bill of lading can function as a representative of the goods and can thus be used to ensure the concurrent performance of the parties' obligations. The buyer in fact pays the purchase price not against delivery of the goods, but against documents representing the goods. This is normally termed "Cash Against Documents" or simply "CAD".

The bill of lading, thus, plays an important part in the performance of the sales contract, but this fact also highlights the fact that the bill of lading is part of a number of contracts involved in a sale of goods, of which the sales contract sets the frame as between buyer and seller. Any international sale of goods will normally contain at least three contracts, namely the sales contract, governing the sale between buyer and seller, the contract of carriage, governing the relationship between carrier and shipper (the identity of whom will be further set out below) as well as subsequent holders of the bill, and the letter of credit, governing the payment of the purchase price etc. as well as the relationship with the banks involved. Furthermore, a contract of insurance of the goods to be shipped will normally be made.

2 See also the Norwegian, Swedish and Finnish Sale of Goods Acts § 10(1) and § 49(1).

3 The sales contract

The sales contract is the first out of the abovementioned contracts that the buyer and seller will enter into. It therefore sets the frame for the entire transaction, including (if diligently made) the nature and content of the shipping documents (for the purposes of this book; the bill(s) of lading) to be tendered by the seller and the terms of the letter of credit to be opened by the buyer.

Many aspects of the transaction may be decided by the parties simply by the choice of shipping terms. Most commonly used, at least in the commodity trades, are the terms FOB and CIF which trigger a whole series of legal consequences and obligations on the parties. These include many aspects of the contract of carriage to be concluded. These terms are regulated in national law, but also – perhaps more importantly – in the INCOTERMS, a very widely used set of standard (trading) terms developed by the International Chamber of Commerce (ICC). These must be incorporated in the sales contract to apply. Many of the specifics of the contract of carriage, the insurance contract, and the letter of credit to be entered into as well as the documents to be tendered must, however, be set out in the sales contract.

In an FOB, Free On Board, sale, the seller must deliver the goods free of cost to the buyer in the hold of a ship nominated by the buyer at the port designated in the sales contract. It is thus the buyer who must contract with a carrier for the carriage of the goods and thereby the buyer who will be privy to that contract.[3] The FOB term has been known for over 200 years.[4]

In a CIF, Cost Insurance Freight, sale, the seller must ensure the carriage of the goods to the specified port and carry the cost of said carriage, i.e. the freight, as well as obtain and pay for insurance of the goods up to that point. It is thus the seller who contracts with the carrier and becomes privy to the contract of carriage.[5]

3 See however the following part as to the variety of types of FOB contracts.

4 Filippo Lorenzon, *Sassoon on C.I.F. and F.O.B. Contracts*, 5th ed., British Shipping Laws (London: Sweet & Maxwell, 2012), para 9-002.

5 A separate issue is the passing of the risk of the goods. In either type of sale the risk of the goods has traditionally passed from the seller to the buyer when the goods pass the ship's rail at loading (under English law often stated as "on shipment"), although the wording of the INCOTERMS has been changed in the 2010 edition which may cause confusion, see ibid., para 2-006. Thus, the division of risk and the division of cost does not apply the same dividing point. Nor does the obligation to take out insurance necessarily lie on the party bearing the risk. The passing of the risk means that for damage to goods occurring during their carriage, the buyer will most often not have a claim against the seller, but only against the carrier. Thus, while the passing of the risk is not as such tied with the issuance or tendering of a bill of lading, the bill of lading still plays an important role in two respects. First, it will be an important piece of evidence as to the quantity and condition of the goods at the time of shipment. Second, it will often form the basis of the buyer's title to sue the carrier for loss of or damage to the goods. It may also be noted that with the rise of containerisation the very firm principle of the risk of

3.1 The bill of lading in relation to the sales contract

In sales on CIF or FOB terms, or other shipping terms, the seller's performance of the sales contract is two-pronged; that is a physical performance and a documentary performance. The physical performance, in essence, consists of the physical delivery of goods conforming to the contract at an agreed place. The subject of physical performance falls outside the ambit of this book.

The documentary performance is where the bill of lading plays a central role. The documentary performance denotes which documents the seller has to tender under the contract of sale to trigger the payment obligation of the buyer. The precise content of the documentary performance will depend on the shipping term employed and the individual terms modifying or supplementing said term. It will, however, almost always include a bill of lading as this is how the buyer can ensure that the seller cannot after the payment of the purchase price control the goods.

In a CIF sale, the seller under English law is obligated to tender a shipped, negotiable bill of lading, unless the parties have expressly agreed otherwise.[6] Under Danish law, the seller must tender a bill of lading, unless otherwise agreed, but this may be a straight bill of lading or a received-for-shipment bill.[7] Under INCOTERMS 2010, the seller must tender "the usual transport document for the agreed port of destination".[8] Although "the usual transport document" will most often be a bill of lading, it is a broader term and may be something other than a bill of lading. However, the rule goes on to state that the document must enable the buyer to sell the goods in transit by the transfer of the transport document,[9] which strongly indicates the need for a bill of lading, but could also be fulfilled by a delivery order. Further, the rule does not state what type of bill of lading, if any, the seller must provide other than it must be "the usual".

the goods passing at the ship's rail has become somewhat less appropriate as the procedures in the carriage of containers mean that the seller (and the buyer) is not involved in the loading operations in any way. For that reason the ICC encourages that the FOB and CIF terms only be used in sales of commodities while FCA, Free Carrier, or CPT, Carriage Paid To, or CIP, Carriage and Insurance Paid to, should be used for containerised goods, see Jan Ramberg, *International Commercial Contracts*, 4th ed. (Norstedts Juridik, 2011), p. 57f. With all three terms, the risk of the goods passes with the handing over of the goods to the first carrier (unless otherwise agreed).

6 Michael Bridge, *The International Sale of Goods*, 3rd ed. (Oxford University Press, 2013), para 4.12. Lorenzon, *Sassoon on C.I.F. and F.O.B. Contracts*, para 5-001.

7 The Danish Sale of Goods Act § 64, cf. §§ 63, 16 and 71. The rule is not set out as an obligation on the seller to tender a bill of lading, but rather as an obligation on the buyer to pay against such document. A received-for-shipment bill is only acceptable if the sales contract does not set a last date for shipment or that shipment must be on a particular ship, see discussion in Henry Ussing, *Køb*, 4th ed. (7th print run (1985)) (Copenhagen: Jurist- og Økonomforbundets Forlag, 1967), p. 50 (with further references).

8 Rule A 8.

9 Ibid.

Thus, the fall-back rules on the transport document to be tendered are not the same which emphasises two points. First, although it seems almost trite to say that a CIF seller must as part of its documentary performance tender a bill of lading, this may not even be correct and leaves substantial room for variation depending on the applicable fall-back rules. Second, as a result, it is advisable to include a detailed specification of the documents to be tendered despite any "common understanding" of what CIF means in this respect.[10]

Above it was stated that it is the buyer in an FOB sale who contracts with the carrier for the carriage of the goods. This is, however, not an accurate statement as FOB contracts come in several varieties which in some leave it to the seller to contract with the carrier for the buyer. Thus, the FOB contract is a "flexible instrument".[11] An upshot of the flexibility is that the parties may have difficulty in finding guidance in the authorities as to the precise content of the parties' respective obligations.[12] In some instances the obligation of the seller will not be to obtain and tender a bill of lading, but rather to assist the buyer in obtaining a bill of lading. However, in most cases the seller must obtain and tender a bill of lading. In these cases basically the same considerations in relation to the type of bill required as mentioned above in respect of CIF contracts apply. The greater variety of FOB contracts as compared with CIF contracts only exacerbate the need for a clearly drafted "documents" clause in the FOB sales contract.

The bill of lading as the central document to be tendered bears with it three main consequences that are of great importance to the buyer, but also to the seller. It can aid both parties in raising finance for the transaction. It gives the buyer the possibility to sell on the goods while they are in transit. And it gives the buyer a number of rights against the carrier, namely the right to sue for loss of or damage to the cargo, the right to rely on statements about the goods as they were at the time of shipment, and – the topic of this book – the right to claim delivery of the goods from the carrier.[13] Under some jurisdictions, including English law, another important consequence is the bill of lading's ability to transfer property in the goods if so intended by the parties.[14]

10 Debattista, *Bills of Lading in Export Trade*, p. 12f, stresses the importance of a clearly drafted "documents" clause listing and describing the documents to be tendered.

11 So termed by Devlin J. in the often-cited case *Pyrene Co. Ltd. v. Scindia Navigation Co.*, [1954] 2 QB 402, p. 424.

12 Lorenzon, *Sassoon on C.I.F. and F.O.B. Contracts*, para 9-011. The newest edition of INCOTERMS, INCOTERMS 2010, has changed the rules on FOB to reflect this flexibility, see rule A 3(a), and ibid., para 9-010.

13 Debattista, *Bills of Lading in Export Trade*, p. 13.

14 *Infra* Chapter 3, part 2.2.

4 Documentary credits

Above, the tendering of documents was described in relation to the seller performing its obligations under the sales contract and thereby triggering the buyer's obligation to pay the purchase price. The documents, and especially the bill of lading, also play an important part in securing that the purchase price is in fact paid. Thus, as stated initially, the seller will not wish to part with possession of the goods, or even ship the goods to the buyer's country, without being certain that the purchase price will be paid. Such concurrent performance of the parties' obligations is often secured by using the system of letters of credit.

In very simple terms the system works in the following way. In accordance with the terms of the sales contract, the buyer will open a letter of credit with a bank typically in the buyer's own country. This bank, the issuing bank, undertakes to pay the purchase price on presentation of certain documents, including a bill of lading, in accordance with the instructions of the buyer. The issuing bank instructs a bank typically in the seller's country to advise the seller of the credit opened in the seller's favour. This bank, the advising bank, can also confirm the letter of credit whereby it gives its own undertaking to pay against presentation of the documents. It is then called the confirming bank. When the seller has shipped the goods and obtained a bill of lading from the carrier he will then tender the bill of lading and the other prescribed documents to the advising/confirming bank. The bank will then check that the documents conform to the instructions given under the letter of credit and if they do, pay the purchase price. The bank will then send the documents to the issuing bank that will perform their own check of the documents and in turn pass the documents on to the buyer who can then use the bill of lading to obtain delivery of the goods from the carrier. In this way the seller ensures that it does not part with the control over the goods without obtaining the purchase price and the buyer knows that the purchase price will not be paid without the seller giving up its control over the goods.

The sales contract will (should) stipulate by when and possibly with which bank the letter of credit is to be opened as well as other aspects of the letter of credit. The letter of credit will be governed by the terms and conditions therein and almost invariably the Uniform Customs and Practice for Documentary Credits (UCP). The UCP, like the INCOTERMS, is a set of rules developed by ICC to govern documentary credits. It must be – and almost always is – incorporated into the letter of credit by the parties. The current version is the UCP 600. It contains inter alia important provisions as to the required contents of bills of lading and to what extent the bank will examine the documents.[15]

15 See especially article 20.

It is important to note that the letter of credit is a contract separate from the sales contract. It is thus the instructions given by the buyer when applying for the opening of the credit with the issuing bank and not the documentary requirements as specified in the sales contract that the bank will act upon. If there is a discrepancy between the two, the seller may end up in a situation where he tenders documents that comply with the requirements of the sales contract and yet is denied payment under the letter of credit. Needless to say this creates various problems and possible claims.

The bill of lading also plays a role in the relationship between the buyer and the issuing bank. The issuing bank will often have provided some sort of financing of the purchase price. As security, the buyer will often pledge the bill of lading to the bank and even without a pledge the bank by physically holding the bill of lading ensures that the buyer cannot obtain the goods until he has paid the bank.

5 Summing up

As shown above, the bill of lading plays a very important role in various other contractual relationships quite separate from the contract of carriage and not involving the carrier. These contracts will have an impact on what is required of the bill of lading at a point in time when the contract of carriage has not yet been entered into and the bill of lading not yet been issued. It is in this context that the bill of lading will have to work to fulfil its role in international trade while at the same time fulfilling its role in the contract of carriage. The remainder of the book which focuses on the contract of carriage relationship must be read bearing this context in mind.

After this brief, general introduction of the bill of lading's role in international trade the focus will now be turned specifically to the rule that delivery of the goods must only be made against presentation of a bill of lading.

3 The law of delivery

1 The English and Scandinavian systems

The core notion when using a bill of lading in connection with carriage of goods is that the original bill of lading must be presented at the place of destination to obtain delivery of the goods and the carrier who delivers without the bill of lading being presented subjects itself to a liability for misdelivery.

The basis of the law pertaining to the delivery of goods under bills of lading follows the general differences in the legal systems of England and Scandinavia. Thus in Scandinavia, the rules on delivery are mainly set out in statute while in England, they are developed mainly in the common law, but supplemented by statutes.

In Scandinavia, the rules on delivery are included in the Merchant Shipping Acts,[1] Chapter 13, which regulates carriage of goods in general. These rules have been interpreted in a relatively small number of cases. In England, the law pertaining to bills of lading has developed over the centuries in common law and has in the past century and a half been supplemented by legislation, of which COGSA 1971 and COGSA 1992 are particularly relevant.

This chapter will explore the current law pertaining to the delivery of goods carried under a bill of lading. It will focus on the basis of the requirement to only deliver the goods against presentation of a bill of lading and to which documents the requirement applies. It will go on to analyse what the more precise content of the obligation is. Also, a brief survey will be made of to what extent the Hague-Visby Rules deal with the subject as both the Scandinavian countries and the United Kingdom are parties to these.[2]

1 See *supra* Chapter 1, at fn 7, on the "Scandinavian nature" of the Merchant Shipping Acts. The Acts are: in Denmark; Consolidated Act no. 75/2014 with later amendments. In Norway; Act no. 39 of 24.06.1994 with later amendments. In Sweden; Act no. 1994/1009 with later amendments. In Finland; Act no. 15.7.1994/674 with later amendments.

2 However, the Rules have been incorporated into the law of England and the Scandinavian countries in vastly different manners, cf. *infra* part 5 and Chapter 6, parts 3.1 and 3.2.1.

The chapter will go on to explore possible exceptions and modifications to the main obligation as well as the carrier's options as to how to deal with undeliverable goods. The consequences of breaching the obligation will be examined including the coverage of Protection and Indemnity (P&I) insurance. As will be shown, many aspects of these questions depend on the status of bills of lading as documents of title or negotiable documents. Therefore the analyses will commence with an examination of the basic status of the bill of lading in this respect under English and Scandinavian law respectively.

2 Basic status of bills of lading as negotiable documents and documents of title

Order bills of lading are said to be "negotiable" under both English and Scandinavian law. Under English law order bills of lading are also said to be documents of title.[3] Before going into deeper analyses of the presentation requirement, it is therefore relevant to look at the meaning of these terms and to what extent bills of lading as a starting point fall under these categories.

2.1 Scandinavian law

The Merchant Shipping Act does not specifically define bills of lading as negotiable documents. However, in the Danish travaux preparatoires to the 1892 Merchant Shipping Act,[4] which was the first to be made in collaboration between Norway, Sweden and Denmark, it is clearly stated that the bill of lading is a negotiable document. Thus, the explanation to § 132(2),[5] clarifies that this was already, i.e. prior to the Act, the case in Norway and Denmark, but that the subsection which introduced some requirements as to form was necessary to bring Swedish law in alignment with the law of the other two countries ensuring uniformity in this respect.[6] Accordingly, the Act (both the 1892 and the current) contains several provisions that regulate effects of the issuance of a bill of lading in a manner similar to the regulation of negotiable instruments of debt,[7] cf. §§ 302–306. These concern both the "legitimation" function and the effects of a transfer of the bill of lading.

The "legitimation" function denotes the question to whom the debtor may and must perform its obligations. In the law pertaining to negotiable

3 The status of other types of bills of lading in relation to presentation being required to obtain delivery will be dealt with in part 3.
4 Landstingstidende A 1891, column 2229.
5 Now contained in § 296 while subsection 1 is contained in §§ 292 and 294.
6 Landstingstidende A 1891, column 2496.
7 As will be explained immediately below a bill of lading is not an instrument of debt.

documents the legitimation function is normally divided into the "active" legitimation and the "passive" legitimation.[8] The passive legitimation entails that the debtor is discharged from its obligation by performing in good faith to the person legitimated by the document while active legitimation entails that the rightful holder may demand exact performance of the obligation. This function is obviously of crucial importance in connection with delivery of the goods carried under a bill of lading and will thus be analysed throughout this chapter.

The Merchant Shipping Act, however, only regulates some of the issues regarding the effects normally associated with negotiability of documents. Thus, for a bill of lading to have a truly negotiable nature, i.e. that a transferee may get a better title than its transferor, and to establish the finer details of the legitimation function the Merchant Shipping Act must be supplemented by other rules or principles.[9]

The general rules on the negotiability of documents are set out in the Scandinavian Acts on Instruments of Debt.[10] These acts regulate instruments of debt generally and contain a chapter specifically regulating negotiable instruments of debt. The rules of this chapter correspond to a large degree to the rules in the Merchant Shipping Act regarding the effects of a transfer of a bill of lading, but further rules are set out. As indicated by the title, the Act only applies to instruments of debt.[11] The term is not defined in the Act, but in the travaux preparatoires it is stated that the term "should only connote a written declaration that entitle to a principally unconditioned, unilateral claim for a sum of money".[12] This definition has become widely accepted as authoritative.[13] The travaux preparatoires go on to state that inter alia bills of lading fall outside said definition.[14] Thus, a bill

8 See for a brief general introduction in English Tiberg, "Legal qualities of transport documents", p. 6 et seq.

9 The fact that the rules of the Merchant Shipping Act must be supplemented by the generally applicable rules for negotiable documents was specifically stated in the Danish travaux preparatoires to the 1937 Merchant Shipping Act where the current § 302 (then § 156) was given its present wording, cf. Rigsdagstidende A 1936–37, column 4243 (the passage is set out in connection with § 159 (now § 305), but is of general applicability).

10 These acts came about as a result of a collaboration between Denmark, Sweden, Norway and Finland in the 1930s. This led to the passing of acts in 1936 in Sweden, in 1938 in Denmark, in 1939 in Norway and in 1947 in Finland. There is a high degree of uniformity between the acts on the issues of relevance to the topic of this book. The acts currently in force are for Sweden Act 1936:81, for Denmark consolidated Act no. 669/1986 with later amendments. For Norway Act 1939:1, and for Finland Act 1947:622.

11 In Danish "gældsbrev", in Norwegian "gjeldsbrev" and in Swedish "skuldebrev" all translating literally into "debt letter".

12 "Udkast til Lov om Gældsbreve med tilhørende Bemærkninger" (Copenhagen: 1935), p. 18 (my translation). This quote is taken from the Danish travaux preparatoires; similar statements are found in the travaux preparatoires of the other countries.

13 Lennart Lynge Andersen, Peter Møgelvang-Hansen, and Anders Ørgaard, *Gældsbrevsloven med kommentarer*, 2nd ed. (Copenhagen: Thomson, 2007), p. 32.

14 Fn 12.

of lading does not entitle to a claim for a sum of money, nor is it necessarily unconditioned as freight and charges may have to be paid. The question is whether the rules of the Act may still have an impact on the effect of a transfer of a bill of lading and the legitimation function.

When passed in the late 1930s, the Acts on Instruments of Debt were to a great extent a codification of the existing law applying to claims while at the same time introducing important changes and novelties.[15] Large parts of the Act therefore have analogous application to claims not covered by an instrument of debt.[16] Chapter 2 on negotiable instruments of debt is not considered to have such general analogous application.[17] However, the travaux preparatoires mention the possibility that these rules may be applied by analogy to other documents that are considered to be negotiable.[18] Such application is relevant for bills of lading.[19] This has two important consequences. First, rules in the Act which are not reflected in a corresponding rule in the Merchant Shipping Act may have analogous application. Second, when interpreting rules in the Merchant Shipping Act reference may be had to the principles in and interpretations of the Act on Instruments of Debt.

It may then be asked whether these rules may be derogated from by contract. The relevant rules of the Merchant Shipping Acts are mandatory.[20] Chapter 2 of the Act on Instruments of Debt is mandatory in relation to instruments of debt.[21] The question is whether this mandatory nature also extends to the analogous application to bills of lading. Obviously, if there is inconsistency between the rules of the Merchant Shipping Act and the Act on Instruments of Debt the former will prevail as the lex specialis in relation to bills of lading. The consideration underlying the mandatory nature of Chapter 2 is that it does not regulate the relationship between the original parties to the instrument of debt, but rather between one of the

15 "Udkast til Lov om Gældsbreve med tilhørende Bemærkninger", p. 17. Interestingly, in Denmark and Norway before the act was enacted all instruments of debt were considered negotiable unless clearly marked otherwise. In Sweden it was not so.

16 Ibid.

17 Bo von Eyben, Peter Mortensen, and Ivan Sørensen, *Lærebog i Obligatiosnret II – Personskifte i skyldforhold, Fordringers ophør, Hæftelsesformer*, 4th ed. (Copenhagen: Karnov Group, 2014), p. 62.

18 Fn 12.

19 B. von Eyben, P. Mortensen, and I. Sørensen, *Lærebog i obligationsret II, Personskifte i skyldforhold, Fordringers ophør, Hæftelsesformer*, 2nd ed. (Copenhagen: Thomson Reuters, 2005), 125. The passage on bills of lading has been deleted in the 3rd and 4th editions of this book due to the subject's "limited practical importance"(!). Jørgen Bredholt *et al.*, *Søloven med kommentarer*, 4th ed. (Copenhagen: Jurist- og Økonomforbundets Forlag, 2012), p. 460. Preben Lyngsø, *Gældsbrevsloven*, 3rd ed. (Copenhagen: Jurist- og Økonomforbundets Forlag, 1989), pp (especially) 82, 102, 21 and 47. Kurt Grönfors and Lars Gorton, *Sjölagens bestämmelser om godsbefordran* (Stockholm: P A Nordstedt & Söners förlag, 1982), p. 293.

20 § 254.

21 Lyngsø, *Gældsbrevsloven*, p. 84.

original parties and a third party or indeed between two third parties.[22] The same consideration is present in relation to bills of lading. On the other hand it could be submitted that the underlying consideration of negotiable instruments as such is that an acquirer of the instrument should be able to rely on the content of the instrument without having to look into outside factors and therefore a derogation contained in the instrument itself should be valid. There does, however, not seem to be any reason to differentiate between instruments of debt and bills of lading in this respect. Furthermore, such a derogation might change the negotiable nature of the document altogether. With some uncertainty, it is therefore concluded that the analogous application of the relevant parts of Chapter 2 of the Act on Instruments of Debt is mandatory.[23]

As stated, the Merchant Shipping Act and the Act on Instruments of Debt regulate the effects of a transfer of a negotiable bill of lading both between the debtor and the transferee and between the transferor and transferee.

As between transferee and debtor, i.e. the carrier in a bill of lading context, the Act on Instruments of Debt makes a distinction between so-called "strong" and "weak" objections. The debtor can only object to the validity of the instrument of debt or the content thereof on the grounds that it is forged, falsified, signed without authority or signed under threat or use of violence, § 17. These are the "strong" objections.[24]

§ 15 sets out the "weak" objections, which cannot be asserted by the debtor against a third party who has acquired the negotiable document in good faith. These include non-violent coercion, fraud, exploitation, that it would go against common decency to uphold the contract (unconscionability), that the document has been given up without the debtor's acceptance, that the debtor has not received the agreed remuneration, that payment had already taken place before the transfer of the document, or that the obligations under the document had been changed by agreement. Any such objections will be extinguished.[25]

22 Ibid.

23 Hugo Tiberg, "Liability for wrongful delivery", in *Cargo Liability in Future Maritime Carriage*, ed. Hugo Tiberg, Svenska Sjörättsföreningen Skrifter 73 (Stockholm: Jure AB, 1998), p. 165, states that "The rules of negotiable documents are so settled that the courts would probably refuse to have them set aside by contract." However, Tiberg suggests that the court may use other vehicles than the mandatory nature of the rules of negotiable documents to achieve this result, e.g. the Contracts Act § 36 by which the courts can set aside unreasonable contract terms.

24 § 17 also mentions invalidity as a result of incapability, that the instrument of debt has been declared null and void through the process known as mortification, *infra* at and in fn 139, or that the claim has been changed or no longer exists as a result of the legislation on limitation, preclusion or debt-restructuring. These are of less importance in the case of bills of lading.

25 These rules are obviously also of importance in relation to other effects of a transfer of a bill of lading than those related to delivery of the goods. Some of these issues will be touched upon in Chapter 6, part 3.1.2.

Further, §§ 13 and 19 set out the legitimation rule for negotiable instruments of debt. It is particularly these rules of the Act on Instruments of Debt which are relevant to consider in relation to the Merchant Shipping Act's rules on legitimation in regard to bills of lading, and thus the issue of delivery of the goods. As stated, they will be included in relevant parts of the analyses throughout the chapter.

As between transferor and transferee or other competing right holders, § 306(1) of the Merchant Shipping Act sets out the priority between transferees of different original copies of a bill of lading issued in a set while § 306(2) sets out that a person who in good faith has acquired an order or bearer bill of lading is not obliged to give it up to a person from whom it has been lost.[26] Thus, even a person from whom the bill of lading has been stolen cannot vindicate (i.e. reclaim) the bill. This is supplemented by the rule in the Act on Instruments of Debt § 14 which in essence establishes that any right that another person claims to have in the instrument of debt is extinguished if the holder has acquired the instrument of debt from a person who had legitimation qua the instrument of debt and has received the instrument of debt in good faith. Of some importance, § 14 specifies that when a transferor of an instrument to order bases his right on previous transfers the transferee need not check their validity unless specific circumstances give him reason to doubt them.

These rules combined with the relevant sections of the Merchant Shipping Act mean that the transferee can get a better title than the transferor thus giving the bill of lading its true negotiable character in a continental European sense.

2.2 English law

Bills of lading are very often referred to as being documents of title and indeed the only type of document recognised as a document of title at common law. Further, they are often described as either negotiable or non-negotiable. Yet there is surprisingly little agreement as to what the precise meanings of the terms are in relation to bills of lading.

The term "document of title" is not a term of art and even when the term is qualified by stating that it is "at common law" there is no authoritative definition.[27] The issue is subject to much analysis in the literature.[28]

26 See also *infra* parts 7 and 8.

27 Michael Bridge, ed. *Benjamin's Sale of Goods*, 9th ed. (London: Sweet & Maxwell, 2014), para 18-007.

28 Sir Guenter Treitel and F.M.B. Reynolds, *Carver on Bills of Lading*, 3rd ed., British Shipping Laws (London: Sweet & Maxwell, 2011), p. 323 et seq. Debattista, *Bills of Lading in Export Trade*, p. 25ff. Richard Aikens, Richard Lord, and Michael Bools, *Bills of Lading*, 2nd ed. (Abingdon: Informa Law, 2016), para 6.2 et seq. Michael Bools, *The Bill of Lading – A Document of Title to Goods; An Anglo-American Comparison* (London: LLP, 1997), analyses several aspects of bills of lading as documents of title.

The standard works Benjamin's *Sale of Goods* and *Carver on Bills of Lading* (the relevant parts of both are written by Sir Guenter Treitel) both define the traditional common law meaning of the term as a document relating to goods the transfer of which operates as a transfer of the constructive possession of the goods and can operate as a transfer of the property in them if so intended.[29] As can be seen, this definition of a document of title involves both questions of the right to possession and ownership.

The term is, however, also used in a wider sense, viz. to denote documents which have to be produced to obtain delivery of the goods without the transfer of the document necessarily being able to transfer property in the goods.[30]

Further, the Factors Act 1889, s. 1(4), contains a definition of documents which are documents of title with respect to that Act. This includes "any bill of lading". The Act regulates the effects of a transfer of a document of title (as defined in s. 1(4)) between transferor and transferee, i.e. the issues which in part 2.1 using the continental European terminology were said to give the document its negotiable character.

In the relationship between buyer and seller as well as the banks financing the transaction it is obviously of significant interest whether the transfer of the bill of lading can also transfer ownership in the goods, i.e. whether they possess the characteristics embedded in the traditional sense of document of title at common law. In *Lickbarrow v. Mason*[31] it was recognised that a bill of lading was a document of title as a result of a custom of merchants. This custom regarded order bills of lading and thus the quality as document of title attached to this type of bills of lading. The same has not been recognised for other types of bills of lading. Yet such bills of lading may also have to be presented to obtain delivery of the goods and thus be documents of title in the second sense mentioned above. This book concerns the delivery of the goods in the relationship between carrier and cargo side, that is in the context of the contract of carriage. It is therefore this second meaning of the term document of title, i.e. referring to documents which must be produced to obtain delivery of the goods they represent, which is relevant. As this concept is not very well defined it is perhaps better to take a functional approach asking the two basic questions whether the cargo side must present the bill of lading to claim delivery of the goods and whether the carrier can only obtain a good discharge of its delivery obligation by delivering against such presentation.[32]

29 Treitel and Reynolds, *Carver on Bills of Lading*, p. 323 et seq. Bridge, *Benjamin's Sale of Goods*, para 18-007.

30 Treitel and Reynolds, *Carver on Bills of Lading*, p. 324 et seq.

31 (1787) 2 T.R. 63; reversed (1790) 1 H.Bl. 357; but restored by the House of Lords (1793) 2 H.Bl. 211; (1794) 5 T.R. 683 (venire de novo) and (1794) 6 T.R. 131 (costs).

32 Such a functional approach, including other aspects than delivery as well, is also taken in Debattista, *Bills of Lading in Export Trade*, p. 28 et seq.

A different issue is what the exact meaning is when it is said that the bill of lading is negotiable which in some instances seems to be used interchangeably with transferable. The question is whether the bill of lading is negotiable in the same sense as in Scandinavia and continental Europe, i.e. meaning that the transferee may get a better title than the transferor had, or whether "negotiable" simply means that the right to claim delivery of the goods may be transferred by transferring (and delivering) the bill of lading duly indorsed, if relevant. The answer to this question is to be found in the Factors Act 1889[33] and the Sale of Goods Act 1979.[34]

It has often been said in both case law and the literature that a bill of lading is not negotiable in the strict sense.[35] These observations seem to take as the starting point the fact that the transferee only acquires the interest that the transferor had and thus defects in the transferor's title are not set aside (extinguished) as a result of the transfer.[36] This starting point is, however, subject to several modifications both at common law and through statute. Thus, a transferee may in certain circumstances defeat a seller's right of stoppage in transit, and possibly other equitable rights such as equitable liens, as well as another buyer's rights in a double sale situation and the ownership of the seller's (transferor's) seller if the seller (transferor) were in possession of the bill of lading. As compared with the situation in Scandinavia, it is worth noting that a transferee cannot defeat a previous holder's title if the bill of lading has been stolen from him.[37]

Negotiability as a concept is not one clearly defined group of legal characteristics that a document must possess in order to be deemed negotiable. Rather, it is a concept denoting that the transferee of a document may get a better title than the transferor had. The precise boundaries of to what extent the transferee gets a better title must be established by the law. As shown, the bill of lading in certain situations possesses that quality. The negotiable effects, however, do not stretch as far as those relating to bills of exchange, nor as far as the effects given to bills of lading in Scandinavia. Under the sales contract it may be important to establish whether a bill of lading is truly negotiable or "simply" transferable. With regard to the delivery of the goods in the carriage of goods relationship, as will be shown, contrary to the situation in Scandinavia, the finer details of the presentation rule do not depend on the law pertaining to negotiable documents. It is therefore sufficient for the present purposes to note that the bill of lading under English law possesses certain qualities as a negotiable

33 Especially ss. 8–10.
34 Especially ss. 24–25 and 47.
35 Treitel and Reynolds, *Carver on Bills of Lading*, p. 369 (with references to illustrative case law).
36 Ibid., p. 369 et seq.
37 Ibid. who cites Lord Campbell C.J. in *Gurney v. Behrend*, (1854) 3 El. & Bl. 622, p. 633f.

document without having to draw a firm conclusion on whether a bill of lading is a negotiable document senso strictu.[38]

Instead the issues pertaining to the delivery of the goods are normally dealt with using the terminology "document of title" in the second sense described above – a concept which is not very clearly defined. Therefore a functional approach will be taken. First, it will be analysed which documents (types of "bills of lading") the presentation rule applies to.

3 The relevant documents – "bills of lading"

It is probably *the* core notion of using a bill of lading as opposed to using other transport documents that the original bill must be presented to obtain delivery of the goods it represents. Having noted in the previous section that this requirement cannot simply be said to be a result of the bill of lading being a negotiable document the question arises which documents are in fact considered bills of lading and whether this core notion applies to all types of bills of lading. Especially the use of straight bills, i.e. bills to a named consignee and not to order, and recta bills, i.e. bills containing a specific ("recta") clause stating "not to order", have caused problems.

3.1 Scandinavian law

When Chapter 13 of the Merchant Shipping Acts, regulating the carriage of goods, was amended in 1994 (again) in a joint Scandinavian effort it was decided to include as much of the Hamburg Rules as possible without breaching the international obligations under the Hague-Visby Rules.[39] Chapter 13 thus incorporates the Hague-Visby Rules mixed with parts of the Hamburg Rules and a number of rules which are not convention based. In line with the principle of the Hamburg Rules the application of Chapter 13 is not dependent on the issuance of a bill of lading. The general rules on liability etc. apply to all carriage of goods by sea (including cabotage). These are supplemented by specific rules regarding bills of lading regulating documentary issues, liability for misdescription, delivery of the goods, etc. The specific issues relating to bills of lading are regulated in §§ 292–309 and §§ 302–304 deal specifically with delivery of the goods. It is important to note that most of the rules of Chapter 13 cannot be derogated from by contract to the detriment of the cargo side.[40]

38 Debattista, *Bills of Lading in Export Trade*, p. 79, concludes (like here) that bills of lading are negotiable in the sense that the title of the holder can prevail over that of the true owner

39 Sølovsudvalget, "Betænkning 1215 Om befordring af gods", (1991), p. 33.

40 § 254. It will be noted in the text if a rule can be derogated from.

§ 292 defines a bill of lading as a document which 1) is evidence of a contract of carriage by sea and that the carrier has received the goods, and 2) on its face is called a bill of lading (in Danish, Swedish and Norwegian: "konnossement") or contains a provision that the carrier undertakes only to deliver the goods against surrender of the document.

Pursuant to subsection 2, a bill of lading is considered an order bill even if it is made out to a named person unless an appropriate reservation such as "not to order" has been made. It is thus not necessary to add wording such as "or to order" for the bill of lading to become negotiable, that is transferable. The bill of lading simply must not include a so-called recta clause, i.e. a clause stating "not to order". This means that a document which under English law would be deemed a straight bill of lading could under Scandinavian law be considered an order bill of lading.

As can be seen from the definition, it is not a requirement that the document is transferable to be deemed a bill of lading. A recta bill is also a bill of lading in terms of the Merchant Shipping Act.

Pursuant to § 302, a person who presents a bill of lading and appears to be the rightful holder of it shall be entitled to take delivery of the goods (the "legitimation" function, cf. *supra* at fn 8 and *infra* part 4.1). § 304 sets out that the consignee may only demand the goods to be delivered by depositing the bill of lading and providing a receipt as the goods are being delivered. Neither of the two provisions distinguishes between order and recta bills of lading or between a "received-for-shipment" bill and a "shipped" bill. Thus, the core notion that the bill of lading must be presented to obtain delivery of the goods applies to all these documents.[41]

3.2 English law

The concept of a bill of lading is not as clearly defined in English law. The notion of bill of lading has evolved in common law in a piecemeal manner, in part on the basis of "the custom of merchants". In addition, legislation has been passed which has had an impact on the notion. It is safe to say, though, that one authoritative definition does not exist.

As for legislation, the preamble to the Bills of Lading Act 1855 stated that by custom of merchants "a bill of lading of goods [is] transferable by endorsement", but did not otherwise define the term.

Likewise, the Factors Act 1889 refers to bills of lading, but does not include a definition thereof. From the Factors Act it may however be assumed that an essential attribute of a bill of lading is its status as a document of title.[42]

41 With regard to recta bills this is specifically set out in the Danish travaux preparatoires to § 302, Rigsdagstidende A 1936–37, column 4240. See also Grönfors and Gorton, *Sjölagens bestämmelser om godsbefordran*, p. 293 (re recta bills) and p. 74 (re received-for-shipment bills).

42 Aikens, Lord, and Bools, *Bills of Lading*, para 2.102.

The Carriage of Goods by Sea Act 1971 (COGSA 1971) incorporated the Hague-Visby Rules into English law by giving them the force of law with some additional rules. Thus, the definition in the Hague-Visby Rules, article 1(b), of "contract of carriage" as a contract of carriage covered by "a bill of lading or any similar document of title" also became part of English law. The Hague-Visby Rules do, however, not include an actual definition of bill of lading and the application of COGSA 1971 has been the subject of several cases, with regard to the definition of bill of lading most notably in the House of Lords' decision in the *Rafaela S.*[43]

The Carriage of Goods by Sea Act 1992 (COGSA 1992), replacing the Bills of Lading Act 1855, includes a partial definition of bills of lading in section 1(1)–(3). Section 1(1) makes the Act applicable to "any bill of lading", but pursuant to section 1(2)(a) bills of lading do not include documents "which [are] incapable of transfer either by indorsement or, as a bearer bill, by delivery without indorsement". Consequently, both straight and recta bills of lading are not considered bills of lading under COGSA 1992, but rather constitute sea waybills. This was based on the fact that the Law Commission and the Scottish Law Commission did not consider straight bills to be documents of title at common law.[44] Section 1(2)(b) further sets out that the term bills of lading also includes "received-for-shipment" bills. Section 5(5), however, states that the Act shall have no prejudice to the application of the Hague-Visby Rules.

The conclusion which can be drawn from this is that the precise definition of which documents are bills of lading depends on the context in which the question is raised. Thus for instance, what may be a bill of lading in relation to COGSA 1971 may not be so in relation to COGSA 1992, as the case is with straight bills of lading. Consequently, the question of which documents must be presented to obtain delivery of the goods cannot be answered by reference to a definition of bill of lading. As stated in part 2.2, the issue is normally discussed by reference to which documents are documents of title – not in the traditional common law sense, but rather in the sense that they must be presented to obtain delivery. The discussion thus becomes circular if the presentation rule is simply said to apply to documents of title the definition of which is that the document must be presented to obtain delivery. Instead the question must be answered looking at the various types of bills of lading one at a time.

First of all, the presentation requirement applies to traditional order bills of lading.[45]

43 *J.I. MacWilliam Co. Inc. v Mediteranean Shipping Co. S.A. (Rafaela S.)*, [2005] 1 Lloyd's Rep. 346.

44 Law Commission, "Rights of Suit in Respect of Carriage of Goods by Sea," (London: The Law Commission and The Scottish Law Commission, 1991), p. 25f.

45 *Herman Carlberg v. Wemyss Coal Company Ltd.*, 1915 S.C. 616, p. 624. *Sze Hai Tong Bank Ltd. v. Rambler Cycle Co. Ltd.*, [1959] 1 A.C. 576, p. 586. See also *infra* at fn 64.

In the *Rafaela S*, the question was whether a straight bill of lading was a bill of lading or similar document of title within the meaning of the Hague-Visby Rules. The House of Lords concluded that it was and in doing so further stated that the report of the Law Commissions from 1991 could not govern the meaning of Rules given statutory force much earlier.[46] In determining this question the Law Lords, however, also considered whether the straight bill would have to be presented to obtain delivery of the goods. The straight bill in question contained an express provision requiring the surrender of an original bill of lading in exchange for the goods or delivery order. However, as obiter dicta both Lord Bingham and Lord Steyn stated that they would hold that the bill would have to be produced to obtain delivery even if there was no express provision to that effect.[47]

With regard to "received-for-shipment" bills of lading, the leading cases have revolved around whether such bills are in fact bills of lading for various purposes but there is very little case law on whether such documents must be presented in order to obtain delivery of the goods. This may be because the problem usually does not arise as the "received-for-shipment" bill will normally be converted into a "shipped" bill once the goods are in fact so shipped. However, in *The Marlborough Hill*[48] the "received-for-shipment" bill of lading stated that at the request of the shipowner one bill of lading must be surrendered on delivery of the goods. Lord Phillimore delivering the judgment of the Privy Council placed emphasis on this fact stating;

> [...] it is evidently contemplated by the document that the shipper will assign his rights and that the assignee or holder of the bill of lading will present the document at the port of delivery, and that his receipt and not that of the shipper will be the discharge to the shipowner.[49]

Also in *The Ines*,[50] the received-for-shipment bills stated in the attestation clause that one of the bills of lading must be surrendered in exchange of the goods. Clarke J. held that it was a breach of contract that the goods were delivered without presentation of the bill of lading.[51]

It is also worth noting that COGSA 1992 specifically acknowledges "received-for-shipment" bills as bills of lading in respect of that Act, s. 1(2)(b), and rights of suit in respect of the contract of carriage will thus

46 *J.I. MacWilliam Co. Inc. v Mediteranean Shipping Co. S.A. (Rafaela S.)*, [2005] 1 Lloyd's Rep. 346, at p. 354 per Lord Bingham of Cornhill and at p. 60 per Lord Steyn.

47 Ibid., p. 354 para 20 per Lord Bingham and p. 59 para 45 per Lord Steyn.

48 *The Ship "Marlborough Hill" v. Alex. Cowan and Sons Ltd. and others*, [1921] 1 A.C. 444.

49 Ibid., p. 453.

50 *MB Pyramid Sound NV v. Briese-Shiffarts GmbH & Co KG ("MS Sina") and another*, [1995] C.L.C. 886.

51 Ibid., p. 893. The issue was not really contested by the carrier.

transfer to the lawful holder in the same manner as with shipped bills of lading.[52] On that basis it seems clear that a "received-for-shipment" bill which includes a clause requiring its presentation to obtain delivery of the goods must be so presented. It is, however, not clear whether such requirement also applies to bills which do not include such a clause.[53]

In conclusion, the core notion that the bill of lading must be presented to obtain delivery of the goods certainly applies to order and bearer bills of lading as well as straight bills with an appropriate clause requiring the presentation of the bill. Most likely, it also applies to straight bills of lading without such a clause.[54] Further, it applies to "received-for-shipment" bills of lading with a clause requiring its presentation, whereas it is unclear if it applies if the bill does not contain such clause.

4 The main principles regarding presentation and their basis

The core notion when using a bill of lading that the original bill of lading must be presented to claim delivery of the goods and that the carrier is only discharged from its obligation by delivering against such presentation applies in both England and Scandinavia. However, the precise content of these principles and their foundation vary to some extent. This is important to establish as a basis for assessing possible solutions to the problems associated with the use of bills of lading and other possible future developments, especially the possibility of using electronic documentation.

4.1 Scandinavian law

The main provision regarding delivery in § 302 of the Merchant Shipping Acts sets out two conditions for a person to be entitled to delivery of the goods. The consignee must present the bill of lading and must appear to be the rightful holder of it. The person may appear to be the rightful holder either from the text of the bill of lading or from an uninterrupted

52 The act does, however, not define a received-for-shipment bill. These can vary to quite an extent and it is left to the courts to decide which documents in fact fall under s. 1(2)(b). Bridge, *Benjamin's Sale of Goods*, para 18-046.

53 Both Michael Bools and Sir Guenter Treitel discuss whether received-for-shipment bills could be documents of title at common law which would include, but is not necessary for, a requirement that the bill must be presented to obtain delivery of the goods. Bools argues that there is no logical reason why it should not be regarded as a document of title at common law, originally in Bools, *The Bill of Lading – A Document of Title to Goods; An Anglo-American Comparison*, p. 186 et seq., and repeated in Aikens, Lord, and Bools, *Bills of Lading*, para 6.12 et seq. Treitel argues that it should not be considered so unless a custom to that effect can be established to the satisfaction of the court, Treitel and Reynolds, *Carver on Bills of Lading*, p. 361, and in Bridge, *Benjamin's Sale of Goods*, para 18–106.

54 Stephen Girvin, "Bills of Lading and Straight Bills of Lading: Principles and Practice", *Journal of Business Law* (2006): p. 112.

series of indorsements or a blank indorsement, cf. § 302. If these conditions are fulfilled then the consequence as set out in § 302(1) is, directly translated, that the person is legitimated as consignee of the goods.[55] The provision thus applies the concept of legitimation which is a well-known concept in civil law in relation to negotiable documents.

As explained in part 2.1, in the law pertaining to negotiable documents the legitimation function is normally divided into the "passive" legitimation, denoting that the debtor is discharged from its obligation by performing in good faith to the person legitimated by the document, and the "active" legitimation, denoting that the rightful holder may demand exact performance of the obligation. With respect to bills of lading, the active legitimation thus entails that the person who appears to be the rightful holder can claim delivery of the goods. This flows directly from § 302. The passive legitimation entails that the carrier who in good faith delivers to the person who appears to be the rightful holder is discharged from its obligation to deliver the goods under the contract of carriage. This must be inferred from the rules on delivery in §§ 302–305 and follows from the rule in the Act on Instruments of Debt, § 19, which must be taken to have analogous application to bills of lading.[56] The legitimation function does not in itself entail that the document must be presented, however. Such a requirement attaches to what is (suitably) termed presentation documents and the obligation to present a bill of lading also flows directly from the wording of § 302 and the fact that § 304 requires the surrender of the bill duly receipted.

§ 302 raises the question to what extent the carrier must check the identity of the person claiming delivery and the validity of the indorsements, if applicable. This question relates to the passive legitimation function of the bill of lading, i.e. can the carrier be discharged of its delivery obligation if it delivers to a holder of a bill of lading which contains a false or non-valid indorsement? In practice, checking the indorsements can be a difficult task as there may be a whole series of more or less legible indorsements. The answer must be found in § 302 supplemented by an analogous

55 In U 2004.1142 S, the consignee in the bill of lading was named as "JAN KATKJAER, C/O SE-GROUP (AUST.) PTY LTD [address]". The notify party was stated as "SAME AS CONSIGNEE". The bill of lading was sent to SE Group (Aust.) Pty Ltd, but without indorsement to said company. The carrier delivered the goods to the company in Brisbane, Australia, upon presentation of the bill of lading. Jan Katkjaer who was an attorney-at-law and had guaranteed payment of the purchase price to the seller of the goods sued the carrier for wrongful delivery. The Maritime and Commercial Court of Copenhagen found in favour of Mr. Katkjaer stating that he was the named consignee and that the provision of "c/o" in the bill of lading was merely supplying an address and did not constitute an affiliation with the company or an agency. The receiver (SE Group) was thus not legitimated by the bill of lading in lack of an indorsement and the carrier therefore did not obtain a good discharge.

56 *Supra* part 2.1, at fn 9 et seq.

application of § 19 of the Act on Instruments of Debt.[57,58] The person claiming delivery must "appear" to be the rightful holder; § 302. § 19(2), second sentence, of the Act on Instruments of Debt supplements this by setting out that if the claimant supports its legitimation on previous indorsements then the debtor (i.e. the carrier) need not test their validity or authenticity unless the circumstances give reasons to do so. This is often seen as a requirement of good faith on behalf of the debtor. It is assumed that a carrier is not obliged to take a very active approach to checking the indorsements unless there are specific reasons to do so.[59] Such circumstances could be seen to exist, it is submitted, if the indorsements are illegible or close thereto.[60] If the bill of lading is an order bill indorsed to a named consignee or a recta bill then the carrier must also make a reasonable check of the identity of the person claiming delivery to ensure that it is the person named as consignee or an agent thereof.[61] If the carrier does check the indorsements and finds out that one of them is not authentic or invalid then the passive legitimation ceases and the carrier will not be discharged from its delivery obligation if it delivers to the person presenting the bill of lading.

As a starting point, the active legitimation function does not arise in relation to a holder to whom the bill is indorsed if one of the indorsements in the chain is invalid or not authentic.[62] However, both in this respect and in relation to the passive legitimation the question is whether such legitimation may re-arise despite the fact that the carrier (and the holder) has obtained knowledge of the lack of authenticity or validity. The question arises because the holder may be entitled to extinguish as against the

57 A bill of lading is not an instrument of debt in respect of the Act on instruments of debt, but the Act is given analogous application to other instruments which resemble such instruments, see *supra* part 2.1. This is assumed to be the case with § 19 in relation to bills of lading, cf. Preben Lyngsø, *Negotiable Dokumenter* (Copenhagen: Juristforbundets Forlag, 1972), p. 293.

58 In the Danish travaux preparatoires to the 1892 Merchant Shipping Act, § 134(2) – now § 302(1) – forgery or falsification (the Danish word "falskneri" can mean both) is given as an example of a situation where a person presenting a bill of lading may be legitimated by it so that the carrier will be discharged by delivering against it, Landstingstidende A 1891, column 2499. The 1892 Act was passed before the adoption of the Act on Instruments of Debt. Nevertheless, it seems correct to interpret the current § 302 with analogous application of the Act on Instruments of Debt, see also *supra* at and in fn 9.

59 Lyngsø, *Negotiable Dokumenter*, p. 294. Grönfors and Gorton, *Sjölagens bestämmelser om godsbefordran*, p. 296, states that the carrier is not entitled to examine the material validity of the transfers. This statement must presuppose that the indorsements or circumstances do not give cause for uncertainty.

60 Tiberg, "Legal qualities of transport documents," p. 18, seems to suggest the same as he states this as a requirement for ostensible title (his term for what is here called legitimation) to exist.

61 Ibid.

62 § 302(1) e.c. and the principle of *nemo dat quod non habet*.

previous holders the objections to the validity of the previous transfers and thus have a good title to the bill of lading despite the invalidity or lack of authenticity of the indorsements. Thus, § 306(2) of the Merchant Shipping Act sets out that a person who in good faith has acquired an order or bearer bill of lading is not obliged to give it back to a person from whom it has been lost. This must be interpreted in the light of § 14 of the Act on Instruments of Debt. § 14 deals with the transfer of negotiable instruments of debt and sets out that a transferee gets a good title to the instrument if the transferee in good faith obtains the instrument from the person who is legitimated, i.e. that the transferee extinguishes any objections to the transferor's title to the instrument. § 14(2), second sentence, contains a rule similar to that of § 19(2) setting out that if the transferor supports its legitimation on previous indorsements then the transferee need not test their validity or authenticity unless the circumstances give reasons to do so. Despite the wording being the same, it is assumed in theory that a transferee is obliged to take a somewhat more active approach to the assessment of the validity and authenticity of previous indorsements than a debtor is under § 19(2).[63] § 306(2) of the Merchant Shipping Act (and § 14 of the Act on Instruments of Debt) deals with the title to the document as between competing would-be holders and not with the relationship between carrier and holder.

If it were accepted that a holder who extinguishes the objections of competing (previous) holders pursuant to § 306(2) regains legitimation under § 302, it would place a very difficult task on the carrier. It would mean that a carrier who refuses delivery because it discovers that an indorsement in the chain is invalid, *prima facie* removing the legitimation of the person claiming delivery, when faced with an assertion by that person that it has extinguished the rights of previous holders would have to evaluate that assertion, including whether that person was in the requisite good faith when it received the bill of lading. If the carrier wrongly concludes that the person has extinguished previous holders' rights and delivers the goods, the carrier will be exposed to liability for misdelivery because of the lack of passive legitimation. If the carrier wrongly concludes that the person has not extinguished the rights and denies delivery then the carrier will be exposed to a liability for that denial by not complying with the active legitimation of the person claiming delivery.

Based on these very burdensome consequences for the carrier – who has no role in the transfers of the bill of lading and thus in the invalid transfer – and the fact that it seems to contradict the principle of § 302, as supplemented by § 19(2) of the Act on Instruments of Debt, it is submitted that

63 Lyngsø, *Negotiable Dokumenter*, p. 129f. Andersen, Møgelvang-Hansen, and Ørgaard, *Gældsbrevsloven med kommentarer*, p. 151. Gösta Walin and Johnny Herre, *Lagen om skuldebrev m.m. En kommentar*, 3rd ed. (Stockholm: Norstedts Juridik, 2011), p. 175, fn 59, and p. 80.

§§ 306(2) and 302 should not be interpreted to reinstate active legitimation in a holder who extinguishes previous holders' rights pursuant to § 306(2). Admittedly this may lead to situations where the holder, in fact, has a good title to the bill of lading, but is unable to demand delivery of the goods from the carrier. However, that risk, it is submitted, must be placed on the holder who will then have to obtain further evidence that it is, in fact, the rightful holder of the bill of lading.

The question of whether the passive legitimation re-emerges is a somewhat theoretical problem because the carrier will, in fact, be delivering to a person who is entitled to the goods and consequently no loss arises. In some situations, though, a loss may arise on other parties, e.g. an unpaid bank with a security interest in the goods. If the carrier in such situations correctly assesses that the person claiming delivery has extinguished the rights of previous holders there must be passive legitimation. However, if the carrier's assessment is incorrect then it is not discharged even if it would have been had it not initially discovered the invalidity of the indorsement. If the carrier were discharged in such situations, it would run contrary to the principle in § 302. In this regard, the re-emergence of passive legitimation must be considered an "exception to the exception" and not a complete return to the starting point.

4.2 English law

While the main rules under Scandinavian law are set out in the Merchant Shipping Acts supplemented by the general principles applying to negotiable instruments of debt, under English law they are based on common law, including its recognition of the custom of merchants, and to a certain extent supplemented by legislation. It is well-established law that as a general rule the holder of a bill of lading is entitled to demand delivery of the goods and the carrier is entitled to deliver to said holder.[64] This corresponds to the active and passive legitimation function of the bill of lading under Scandinavian law as described in the previous section, but these civil law notions are, of course, not used in English law to describe the principles. Instead, the principles are normally assessed using the document of title terminology with its various meanings described above.[65]

The first question is what steps the carrier must take to obtain a good discharge of its obligation to deliver the goods under the contract of carriage, i.e. what corresponds to the passive legitimation function under Scandinavian law. It is clear that the carrier will obtain a good discharge by delivering the goods upon presentation of the original bill of lading to the

64 See e.g. *Motis Exports Ltd. v. Dampskibsselskabet af 1912 A/S (No. 1)*, [2000] 1 Lloyd's Rep. 211, at p. 216 per Stuart-Smith L.J. (paragraph 19) with reference to the authorities of the past 125 years.

65 *Supra* part 2.2.

person named in the bill, to the person to whom the bill is genuinely indorsed if the bill is an order bill, or to the bearer if the bill is a bearer bill.[66] Surprisingly however, given that it must be a recurring and practical problem, it is not clear to what extent the carrier must check the indorsements of the bill of lading and satisfy itself that they are genuine.[67] The question is therefore what the carrier must do to avoid liability for misdelivery if one or more of the indorsements turn out to be false. The question does not seem to be answered in the authorities. It has been submitted that the answer turns on the construction of the contract of carriage.[68] If the contract is construed as requiring the carrier to deliver against presentation of a bill of lading that appears regular on its face then the carrier will not be liable for delivering to a person (who is named in the bill or) to whom it is indorsed (or to the bearer if indorsed in blank) even though one or more of the indorsements turn out to be false. At least in this respect it is therefore not necessary that the holder is a lawful holder in respect of COGSA 1992.[69] The same is submitted to be the case where the carrier delivers to a party presenting the bill, but to whom it is in fact not made out, if the bill is construed to allow for delivery without requiring the presenter to identify himself.[70] It would seem to be an obvious inference that the carrier cannot obtain a good discharge by delivering to a holder if he has knowledge (or a reasonable suspicion) that one of the indorsements is false. These submissions are said to rely on the rule in *Glynn Mills*. However, while Lord Blackburn in Glynn Mills based the answer on whether the carrier fulfilled his contract and, thus, a construction thereof he stated that "[the carrier] would also [i.e. apart from by delivering to the person named in the bill] fulfil his contract if he delivered to anyone producing the bill of lading with a *genuine* indorsement by [the consignee named in the bill]. He would not fulfil his contract if he delivered them to *anyone else* [...]" (italics added).[71] This would seem to imply that the carrier will only obtain a good discharge if he delivers to a presenter to whom the

66 *Glynn Mills & Co. v. East and West India Dock Co.*, (1882) 7 App. Cas. 591. See the quote at fn 71.

67 Tiberg, "Legal qualities of transport documents", p. 19.

68 Aikens, Lord, and Bools, *Bills of Lading*, para 5.61.

69 See ss. 2(1)(a) and 5(2). Debattista, *Bills of Lading in Export Trade*, p. 35 et seq., submits that a holder should be regarded as lawful under COGSA 1992 based on a narrow understanding of the good faith requirement and that accordingly a carrier should not be obliged to investigate the chain of indorsements even when it is unclear or undated. Such an interpretation of COGSA 1992 seems to presuppose that the term "any indorsement of the bill" in s. 5(2)(b) includes false or unauthorised indorsements. The more general submission that the good faith requirement should be understood narrowly is supported by obiter of Thomas J. in *Aegaen Sea Traders Corp v. Repsol Petroleo SA (The Aegaen Sea)*, [1998] 2 Lloyd's Rep. 39, p. 60.

70 Aikens, Lord, and Bools, *Bills of Lading*, para 5.61.

71 *Glynn Mills & Co. v. East and West India Dock Co.*, (1882) 7 App. Cas. 591, at p. 610 per Lord Blackburn.

bill is properly indorsed and that the risk of an indorsement being false falls on the carrier.[72] Such an interpretation would, however, place a heavy and impractical burden on the carrier to investigate the correctness of the indorsements – something which in practice would in the best case scenario be time consuming and in the worst case scenario be impossible. It has therefore been suggested that bills of lading should, in the absence of a term to the contrary, be interpreted to allow delivery to the holder of a bill which appears to be regular on its face,[73] but there does not seem to be direct judicial authority for this (attractive) suggestion.

With regard to the holder's right to claim delivery, i.e. what under Scandinavian law is termed the active legitimation function, the answer is not completely clear.[74] If the holder is a lawful holder under COGSA 1992 he will have a contractual claim for delivery against the carrier.[75] As with the carrier's right to deliver, it is obviously of importance to establish when a holder is "lawful". Is the holder per se not lawful if an indorsement turns out to be invalid or inauthentic, cf. s. 5(2)(b) and 2(1) e.c. or does it depend upon whether the holder was in the requisite good faith? It is submitted that the interpretation is not necessarily the same when the question is whether the holder can claim delivery as when the question is whether the carrier can obtain a good discharge when delivering to the holder.[76] Thus, whereas it may be reasonable to accept that a carrier who delivers in good faith against presentation of a bill of lading with an unclear string of indorsements will obtain a good discharge it would seem less reasonable to furnish the holder of such a bill with a contractual right to

72 Ibid., p. 614, Lord Blackburn, however, states that "[the master] is justified or excused in delivering according to his contract to the person *appearing to be* the assign of the bill" (italics added). The case did not concern whether the carrier had misdelivered the goods by delivering against the bill as assigned, but rather by delivering against the production of only one bill out of a set of three, see *infra* part 7.2.

73 Bools, *The Bill of Lading – A Document of Title to Goods; An Anglo-American Comparison*, p. 168. Debattista, see fn 69, reaches the same result by suggesting that a holder in such circumstances should be considered a lawful holder under COGSA 1992.

74 Though described as a negotiable bill of lading, under English law the bill of lading only has some characteristics of negotiability, cf. part 2.2, and the rules setting out these characteristics do not regulate the legitimation function. Thus, the holder cannot rely on these rules to support a delivery claim. When termed "negotiable" what is normally meant is "transferable" and it may be asked whether this characteristic can give rise to a delivery claim. This will be discussed below.

75 Even this statement is contested; the question being whether COGSA 1992 deals with the right to delivery or this is a matter of possessory and proprietary rights falling outside of COGSA 1992 which is then seen as limited to questions of privity. See Treitel in both Bridge, *Benjamin's Sale of Goods*, para 18-010, and in Treitel and Reynolds, *Carver on Bills of Lading*, p. 222. See also the discussion in Debattista, *Bills of Lading in Export Trade*, p. 30 et seq.

76 Treitel and Reynolds, *Carver on Bills of Lading*, p. 233, also argues in relation to good faith that this concept should be capable of "bearing different shades of meaning" in relation to different sections of the act.

claim delivery against a carrier who does not feel reassured of the holder's "lawfulness" by the unclear string of indorsements. The question does not seem to have been tried in case law.

Whether the holder of the bill of lading can claim delivery on another basis than contract and thus outside of COGSA 1992 is also the subject of some disagreement in the legal literature.[77] The disagreement turns on whether bailment considerations or the (order) bill's ability to transfer constructive possession by indorsement also in itself gives the indorsee the right to claim delivery. Most authors submit that this is the case whether or not the conditions for the transfer of contractual rights against the carrier are satisfied,[78] but it has been submitted that this is not the case because the mere symbolic possession does not in itself give standing for an action in conversion nor as a matter of law or as a result of a bailment.[79] The question now seems of particular importance in relation to whether a holder can raise a claim for misdelivery against a non-contractual carrier who misdelivers the goods. It may also be of significance when assessing the consequences of a misdelivery.[80]

5 The Hague and Hague-Visby Rules and delivery

The analysis above is based on the national law of the respective countries. However, both England and the Scandinavian countries are parties to the

77 The Contracts (Rights of Third Parties) Act 1999 does not apply to bills of lading, s. 6(5)–(7), and is thus of no avail to the holder.

78 Treitel and Reynolds, *Carver on Bills of Lading*, p. 341f. However, at page 231f it is stated that it is arguable that a transferee who has knowledge of the fact that the transferor has pledged another of a set of bills acquires possession of the bill in good faith and thus becomes a lawful holder. It is then stated that "[c]ertainly [the transferee's] knowledge of the breach should not impair the carrier's right to obtain a good discharge by delivering the goods to [the transferee], and in the case put the carrier's ability to obtain such discharge is based on the assumption of a contractual relationship between himself (the carrier) and [the transferee]". This would seem to imply that the holder would only have a right to claim delivery from the carrier if he has acquired contractual rights against the carrier under COGSA 1992 and thus runs contrary to what is stated at page 341f. Debattista, *Bills of Lading in Export Trade*, p. 29f, states that a holder has such right as a result of a bailment. When at p. 32 Debattista states that "statute [i.e. COGSA 1992], rather than the common law of bailment, now provides the answer" to whether the buyer has the right to claim delivery, he does not seem to mean that bailment can no longer provide a grounds for such a claim, but rather that for practical purposes it is COGSA 1992 on which a buyer will support its claim. Paul Todd, "The bill of lading and delivery: the common law actions", *Lloyd's Maritime and Commercial Law Quarterly*, no. 4 (2006): passim, seems to accept (with regret) that conversion and bailment actions for misdelivery continue to co-exist with contractual claims. Michael Bridge et al., *The Law of Personal Property*, 1st ed. (London: Sweet & Maxwell, 2013), p. 655f, go so far as to say that the bill's "function in embodying this obligation to deliver is not the same as its function in transferring contractual rights against the carrier".

79 Aikens, Lord, and Bools, *Bills of Lading*, para 5.11 et seq.

80 *Infra* part 13.2.

Hague-Visby Rules. A brief survey of the extent to which this convention regulates the issue of delivery therefore seems pertinent. Some of the issues will also be taken up in more detail in other relevant parts.

The Hague and Hague-Visby Rules do not regulate the delivery of the goods directly. The only mention of delivery in both Rules is in connection with the time bar for bringing an action against the carrier under the Rules, article III, rule 6, where the allowed period of time runs from the delivery of the goods.[81] Significantly, the obligations of the carrier are set out in article II and III, rule 2, and do not mention the delivery of the goods. Further, the term "loss or damage" in the liability rule, article IV, rule 2, is often understood as meaning physical loss of or damage to the goods. Also, there is a temporal issue which would normally leave the delivery of the goods outside the scope of application. Therefore, the Rules are generally considered not to cover misdelivery except with regard to the time bar.

This standpoint has, however, been challenged. The liability regimes of the Hague and Hague-Visby Rules apply mandatorily from the time when the goods are loaded on to the time they are discharged from the ship, articles I(e) and II read together, the so-called "tackle-to-tackle" principle. Normally, delivery of the goods occurs after the discharge of the goods from the ship which would leave a potential liability for misdelivery outside the temporal scope of application of the Rules.

However, sometimes delivery takes place at discharge, e.g. when the goods are discharged directly into the receiver's care, which would bring the delivery within the temporal scope of the Rules. A misdelivery could in such an instance be argued to be a breach of the carrier's obligation to "properly and carefully [...] care for [...] the goods carried", article III, rule 2.[82]

Also, it has been suggested that it is a breach of the carrier's obligations under the Rules if it does not ensure that the entity to whom it discharges the goods will only release the goods against the presentation of an original bill of lading.[83] In Scandinavian writings, it has been suggested that a distinction must be made between wilful and negligent misdelivery with the latter being covered by the Rules, but not the former.[84] It seems difficult to

81 Article III, rule 6, also sets out that removal of the goods without giving notice of loss or damage shall be prima facie evidence of the delivery by the carrier of the goods as described in the bill of lading.

82 Simon Baughen, "Misdelivery claims under bills of lading and international conventions for the carriage of goods by sea", in *The Carriage of Goods by Sea under the Rotterdam Rules*, ed. D. Rhidian Thomas (London: Lloyd's List, 2010), p. 168.

83 Ibid., p. 169.

84 Sjur Brækhus, "Bortfrakterens ansvar for utlevering av last til ulegitimert mottager," in *Juridiske arbeider fra Sjø og Land* (Oslo: Universitetsforlaget, 1968), at and in fn 5 (written prior to the Visby amendments and thus relating to the rules implementing the Hague Rules). Tiberg, "Liability for wrongful delivery", *passim*, especially pp. 163 and 68.

accept that the application of these international conventions should rest upon the subjective basis of the carrier for its actions without any part of the wording of the conventions to support this. There is inarguably a difference between an intentional delivery of the goods without presentation of the bill of lading and delivery of the goods against a skilful forgery of the bill of lading, but for the proper consignee holding the bill of lading the goods are not more "lost" in the latter than in the former case bringing the latter within the convention. Instead this situation must be dealt with as a matter of risk allocation.[85]

The consequences of accepting (some instances of) misdelivery claims as being subject to the Rules would seem to be that such a claim for misdelivery would be subject to the exceptions and limitations of the Rules. On the other hand, another important consequence would be that article III, rule 8, sets out that the carrier's liability as regulated in the Rules may not be excluded or relieved by contract. Thus, if liability for misdelivery is subject to the Rules, even an express clause in the clearest terms exempting the carrier from liability would be invalid.

One aspect which is, at least in Scandinavia, generally accepted to be applicable to claims for misdelivery is the time bar of the Hague-Visby Rules. Said time bar applies to "all liability whatsoever in respect of the goods", article III, rule 6, which would prima facie also cover a claim for misdelivery as this must be considered a liability "in respect of the goods". This interpretation is supported by the travaux preparatoires of the Visby amendments.[86] The result, if the application of the Rules' time bar is accepted, is that a claim for misdelivery is subject to a one-year time bar from the date of delivery of the goods. In Denmark and Norway, such one-year time bar is specifically prescribed for misdelivery in the Merchant Shipping Act § 501(1). The corresponding rule in the Swedish and Finnish Merchant Shipping Acts, Chapter 19, 1st §, do not specifically mention claims for misdelivery, but the Supreme Court of Sweden has ruled that such claims are also covered by the time bar.[87]

Outside the question of the application of the time bar there does not seem to be any case law in either England[88] or the Scandinavian countries

85 See also *infra* part 9.

86 Anthony Diamond, "The Hague-Visby Rules", *Lloyd's Maritime and Commercial Law Quarterly* (1978): pp 231 and 56. Also referred to by Baughen, "Misdelivery claims under bills of lading and international conventions for the carriage of goods by sea", p. 172.

87 NJA 1996.483.

88 In the MSC Amsterdam, Aikens J. at first instance stated that misdelivering the goods was a breach of the obligation under article III, rule 2, to "keep and care for" the goods and further that such misdelivery would be subject to limitation of liability under article IV, rule 5 (the package and weight limitation), *Trafigura Beheer BV v. Mediteranean Shipping Co. SA*, [2007] EWHC 944, para 105. The statement was, however, obiter and was not taken up by the Court of Appeal. The case is analysed *infra* Chapter 4, part 5.1.

where the Hague-Visby Rules have been applied directly to a misdelivery claim.[89]

6 Summing up

In the previous sections the main content of the presentation requirement associated with the use of bills of lading and its basis were analysed. As shown, the main content of the presentation requirement is the same under Scandinavian and English law. This is unsurprising as the bill of lading is a transport document that has developed in international trade and thus would not fulfil its purpose and the needs of the international trading community if one of its key features were treated fundamentally different under various legal systems.

The bases of the rules, however, differ largely. Under Scandinavian law, the rules are set out in mandatory legislation in the Merchant Shipping Act supplemented by the Act on Instruments of Debt. Under English law, the rules are mainly based on contract and common law with essential aspects of the transfer of bills of lading regulated in the COGSA 1992. Furthermore, claims in respect of misdelivery may also be based in tort (mainly the tort of conversion) or bailment although this is debated.[90]

In the following parts the focus will be on some specific problems that can arise in the delivery context when using bills of lading. As will be shown, the solutions of English and Scandinavian law also do not differ much with respect to these, but again they rest on different bases. This is of importance when assessing contractual, legislative and technological responses to the problems in practice.

89 In a Swedish verdict reported in ND 1988.30 the Court of Appeal for Skåne and Blekinge did seem to be ready to apply article IV, rule 2, directly to a misdelivery claim. The case did, however, not directly concern a claim for misdelivery but rather the arrest of a vessel in Sweden for a misdelivery claim. The "misdelivery" was also somewhat unusual in that the goods had been delivered in Syria subject to a Syrian court order and under weapon threat. The court in a rather short reasoning stated that the claimant had not substantiated that a claim existed because the carrier would be free of liability subject to the Hague-Visby Rules, article IV, rule 2(g). The court did not make any comments as to the applicability of the Rules to misdelivery claims, neither the temporal issue nor the subject matter issue. Article IV, rule 2(g), is also referred to in a later Swedish Court of Appeal verdict, ND 2001.36. This case also did not directly concern a "normal" misdelivery claim, but rather a claim from the bill of lading holder to have the goods delivered which the carrier refused because of a decision by US authorities under US embargo laws. The court inter alia stated that it also had to consider what would have been the case if the goods had been "lost" and found that article IV, rule 2(g), would have been relevant. As an example of how the goods could be "lost" the court mentioned the situation that the carrier had carried the goods to the USA and handed them over to the US authorities subject to the authorities' decision. This would seem to imply that the court were ready to apply the Rules to a more "normal" case of delivery without presentation of the bill of lading.

90 See further *infra* part 13.2.1.

7 Bills issued in sets

Despite longstanding criticism both in academic writings and by the judiciary, the industry continues the practice of often issuing bills of lading in sets of typically three originals. This gives rise to uncertainty as to how many originals must be presented to obtain delivery and whether the fate of the other originals influences the answer to that question. It also makes it possible that more than one holder of an original bill of lading shows up and demands delivery of the goods.

7.1 Scandinavian law

The issues relating to bills issued in sets are regulated in §§ 302(2), 303 and 306. The former two deal with the relationship between the carrier and the holder while the latter deals with the relationship between different holders of originals.

A consignee may require delivery by presenting just one original bill of lading if the required delivery is at the agreed place of destination whereas all the original bills must be presented if the required delivery is at some other place, § 302(2).[91]

If more than one consignee comes forward and presents separate original bills of lading then the carrier must warehouse the goods at the expense of the rightful party and notify the consignees who have come forward thereof, § 303. It is not specifically set out in the Merchant Shipping Act how it should be determined who is the rightful consignee, but each consignee can apply to the court to have it determined. Although § 303 does not refer to § 272, it is assumed that § 272 applies by analogy to this situation. Accordingly, the carrier can sell the warehoused goods to the extent necessary to cover the carrier's costs.[92]

7.2 English law

Under English law, it is clear that the carrier is also discharged of its delivery obligation if it delivers against the presentation of one original bill of lading out of a set.[93] This is normally based on the case of *Glynn Mills & Co. v. East and West India Dock Co.*[94] However, there is some differences of interpretation as to what the basis of the rule in Glynn Mills is.

91 The travaux preparatoires mention that one original should also suffice outside the place of destination if the consignee has presented the bill of lading at the place of destination but requested an additional transport to another port or if the place of destination cannot be reached and the bill of lading provides for an alternative port in such circumstances, cf. Sølovsudvalget, "Betænkning 1215/1991", p. 85.

92 See *infra* part 10.1 regarding undeliverable goods.

93 If the carrier has knowledge of competing claims the situation is different, *infra* part 8.2.

94 *Glynn Mills & Co. v. East and West India Dock Co.*, (1882) 7 App. Cas. 591.

Carver on Bills of Lading emphasises that the carrier being discharged was a result of the holder of the other original being bound by the term in the bill of lading stating that one part being accomplished, the others to stand void.[95] Aikens, Lord and Bools, however, find this unconvincing as the holder of the other original (the pledgee bank) was not privy to the bill of lading contract. Instead they emphasise the alternative explanation that the bank's claim in conversion failed because the carrier's delivery against just one part of the set was not a wrongful disposal of the goods.[96]

The difference appears if only part of the cargo is delivered, e.g. because the holder of another part of the set becomes aware of the ongoing delivery and presents its part of the set to the carrier claiming to have a better title. In such circumstances no part of the set is in fact accomplished and the others are thus not void pursuant to the contractual term, but the carrier would still not have delivered any part wrongfully and thus not converted the goods already delivered. The editors of *Carver on Bills of Lading*, however, submit that the bill should be considered "accomplished" *pro tanto* and supports this by an alternate reason in *Glynn Mills* given by Lord Blackburn that under the general law pertaining to the assignment of choses in action the carrier would be entitled to perform in favour of its creditor until it received notice of the assignment.[97]

If the carrier is presented with two bills of lading by two different parties the carrier should apply to the court for direction as to whom the carrier should give the goods under the Civil Procedure Rules, Part 86,[98] in order to clarify to whom he may safely deliver the goods.[99] If instead the carrier chooses to deliver to the party whom he believes to be the rightful holder he does so at his own peril.[100] In such circumstances the carrier should be careful not to take steps which might be construed as its recognition of one of the parties' title to the goods as this may create an estoppel.[101]

8 Competing rights

Immediately above, it was described how the carrier must act if more than one person shows up and presents an original bill of lading. Obviously, such persons have competing rights to the goods and it may be asked whether the priority of their rights is solved by maritime law or other areas

95 Treitel and Reynolds, *Carver on Bills of Lading*, p. 391.
96 Aikens, Lord, and Bools, *Bills of Lading*, para 5.53 et seq.
97 Treitel and Reynolds, *Carver on Bills of Lading*, p. 391f.
98 Until 2014, the relevant process was known as interpleader and regulated in RSC Ord. 17. See on this also Stephen Girvin, *Carriage of Goods by Sea*, 2nd ed. (Oxford: Oxford University Press, 2011), p. 143, at and in fn 27.
99 *Glynn Mills & Co. v. East and West India Dock Co.*, (1882) 7 App. Cas. 591, pp. 611 and 13 per Lord Blackburn.
100 Ibid., thus distinguishing the rule of *Fearon v. Bowers*, (1753) 1 H. Bl. 364, 1 Sm. L. C. 8th ed. 782.
101 Aikens, Lord, and Bools, *Bills of Lading*, para 5.60.

of the law. In other situations, the carrier may also have knowledge – or at least a suspicion – of competing rights to the goods of other persons than the person presenting a bill of lading and claiming delivery. The question is whether this affects the carrier's right or obligation to deliver to the person claiming delivery.

8.1 Scandinavian law

Though not an issue relating to the relationship between carrier and shipper or cargo side, the Merchant Shipping Act includes rules regulating the priority of competing rights holders to the bill of lading. § 306, more specifically, regulates the rights of competing holders of original copies of the bill of lading issued in sets. It sets out that the person who has first received in good faith his original copy acquires the right to the goods. If, however, another holder has already in good faith received the goods at the place of destination he shall not be required to give up the goods, thus extinguishing the first holder's right.

Subparagraph 2 sets out that a person who has in good faith acquired an order bill of lading or a bearer bill of lading shall not be obliged to transfer it to the person from whom it was lost. This rule runs counter to the general civil law principle of vindication. A person from whom the bill of lading has been stolen can, thus, not reclaim the bill from a good faith purchaser.

The combined effect of the rules is that the person presenting an original bill of lading duly indorsed will almost always have a right to (delivery of) the goods. The situations most typical in practice are double sale situations, i.e. that the holder has sold the goods (fraudulently) to two different buyers, and pledge situations where the holder has pledged the goods which the bill of lading represents without delivering the full set of bills to the pledgee and also sold them.[102] These situations will be governed by § 306 as between the competing holders of the bill of lading.

As between a holder and the carrier it is, however, a question of legitimation, cf. § 302. Thus, the carrier is entitled and obliged to deliver to the holder who is formally legitimated by the bill of lading. That can be seen as a logical consequence of the rules in § 306 which mean that the formally legitimated person will normally also be materially entitled to the goods.[103]

102 Under Scandinavian law pertaining to pledges of chattels, to perfect the pledge the pledgee must completely deprive the pledgor of control over the pledged goods. If the pledgee has not received the full set of bills of lading it will not have perfected the pledge and cannot enforce it against the pledgor's bankruptcy estate. A pledgee who obtains delivery of the goods by presenting the one part of the bill of lading will, however, probably be protected by § 306 and will also have perfected the pledge by taking delivery.

103 Already in the Danish travaux preparatoires to the 1892 Merchant Shipping Act it is specifically stated that the carrier will not be allowed to deny delivery even if it has doubts that the person presenting the bill of lading is the person with the best material right to the goods, Landstingstidende A 1891, column 2500.

8.2 English law

In English law, the issue of priority between competing holders of bills of lading is not solved in maritime law.

With regard to the delivery obligation of the carrier and its discharge thereof, the carrier must not be aware of competing claims to the goods or have reasonable suspicion that the holder of the bill of lading is not entitled to the goods.[104] The fact that a set of bills of lading has been issued and only one bill of lading is presented to the carrier is, however, not in itself enough to oblige the carrier to interplead and the carrier can safely deliver the goods to a holder presenting an original bill of lading.[105] Thus, the mere possibility of another of the original bills of lading having been pledged to a bank or negotiated to another person should not in itself give rise to suspicion on the part of the carrier. He must have notice of any other claim or title or actual knowledge thereof.[106]

9 Delivery against forged bills of lading

With bills of lading representing potentially very valuable goods, it is no surprise that attempts at fraud occur by forging bills and claiming delivery of the goods.[107] With modern computer and copy technology, it is increasingly easy to produce forgeries which it is very difficult to identify as forgeries (though the same technology also makes it easier to secure documents against copying). The question is who should bear the risk of delivery being made against a forged bill of lading,[108] the carrier or the cargo side. Further, it may be considered whether the carrier in some circumstances should bear the risk completely of forgeries being made such that the carrier is obliged to deliver the goods (or liable to pay damages to) a person holding a forged bill of lading which he has acquired in good faith as to its validity.

9.1 English law

If the carrier is (unwittingly) presented with a forged bill of lading, the party claiming delivery is obviously not a lawful holder. In fact, the party

104 *Kuwait Petroleum Corporation v. I&D Oil Carriers Ltd. (The "Houda")*, [1994] 2 Lloyd's Rep. 541, at p. 553 per Leggatt L.J. and p. 56 per Millet L.J. Aikens, Lord, and Bools, *Bills of Lading*, para 5.60. Girvin, *Carriage of Goods by Sea*, p. 142.

105 *Glyn, Mills & Co. v. East & West India Dock Co.* (1882) 7 App Cas 591, per Lord Blackburn.

106 *Glyn, Mills & Co. v. East & West India Dock Co.* (1882) 7 App Cas 591, per Lord Blackburn. *Motis Exports Ltd. v. Dampskibsselskabet af 1912 A/S (No. 1)*, [1999] 1 Lloyd's Rep. 837, at p. 840 per Rix J.

107 See on the subject generally Paul Todd, *Maritime Fraud and Piracy*, 2nd ed., Maritime and Transport Law Library (London: Lloyd's List, 2010), *passim*.

108 As distinct from the situation where an indorsement on an original bill of lading is forged or unauthorised, see *supra* part 4.

may be said not to be a holder at all as he is not in possession of an original bill of lading. The question is whether the carrier may be discharged of its delivery obligation if it delivers against such forged bill which would leave the risk of forgery on the rightful holder of the original bill. This was the situation in *Motis Exports Ltd. v. Dampskibsselskabet af 1912 A/S (No. 1).*[109] It was firmly stated that the risk of delivering against a forged bill of lading falls on the carrier. At first instance, Rix J. found that a carrier could only have a defence in delivering against a forged bill if a term to that effect was implied and such an implied term would be neither necessary nor reasonable.[110] He added that as a matter of policy he also found this result to be the better one as the alternative would undermine the integrity of the bill as the key to the floating warehouse and, further, it was emphasised that it is the carrier who controls the form, signature and issue of the bill.[111] In the Court of Appeal the question was limited to whether the carrier could rely on an exemption clause. However, the court agreed with Rix J. that delivery against a forged bill was misdelivery; Stuart-Smith L.J. stating that "[a] forged bill of lading is in the eyes of the law a nullity; it is simply a piece of paper with writing on it, which has no effect whatever".[112] It has been criticised that the courts so firmly have placed the risk of forgery on the part of the carrier.[113] The criticism is based on the (assumed) underlying intention of the use of bills of lading in the trading community as expressed as early as 1883 in the famous passage by Lord Justice Bowen that "[t]he object of mercantile usages is to prevent the risk of insolvency, not of fraud".[114] Combined with the assumption that the issue of a document of title, i.e. a negotiable bill of lading, is for the benefit of the cargo side, i.e. the shipper and consignee, and along the reasoning in *Glynn Mills*[115] it was suggested that the risk of forgery should be on the rightful consignee.[116] While it must be acknowledged that there is no conceptual difficulty in placing the risk of forgery on the cargo side and that arguably this is the more reasonable risk allocation it must be stated that the law is clear on this point in that the risk falls on the carrier.

109 [1999] 1 Lloyd's Rep. 837 (QB), [2000] 1 Lloyd's Rep. 211(CA).
110 [1999] 1 Lloyd's Rep. 837, at p. 842.
111 Ibid., at p. 843.
112 [2000] 1 Lloyd's Rep. 211, at p. 216.
113 Paul Todd, "Delivery against forged bill of lading", *Lloyd's Maritime and Commercial Law Quarterly*, no. 4 (1999): p. 453 et seq. Debattista, *Bills of Lading in Export Trade*, p. 37, fn 50, has indorsed the criticism. This criticism was, however, expressly disapproved of by the Court of Appeal in Motis Exports, [2000] 1 Lloyd's Rep. 211, at p. 217 per Mance L.J., which Professor Todd has subsequently acknowledged, cf. Paul Todd, *Maritime Fraud* (London: LLP, 2003), p. 68, fn 58.
114 *Sanders v. Maclean*, (1883) 11 Q.B.D. 327, at p. 343.
115 *Glynn Mills & Co. v. East and West India Dock Co.*, (1882) 7 App. Cas. 591.
116 Fn 113.

There do not seem to be any cases where an acquirer of a forged bill of lading has made a claim against the carrier for failing to deliver against the forged bill. Based on the statements in the *Motis Exports* case[117] it seems likely that such a claim would not fare well. Thus, Stuart-Smith L.J.'s characterisation of a forged bill of lading as "simply a piece of paper with writing on it" does not seem to leave much chance for a claim of any kind against the carrier on the basis of the document. Further, Rix J. in his judgment rhetorically asked whether a shipowner could be obliged to deliver against a forged bill and answered "It seems impossible to think that he can."[118]

9.2 Scandinavian law

Under Scandinavian law, there are no reported cases where the carrier has delivered the goods against a forged bill of lading. Nor are there cases where a good faith holder of a forged bill has filed a claim against a carrier for denying delivery against the bill which it recognised to be forged.

With respect to the former situation, it is submitted, that the carrier cannot obtain a good discharge of its delivery obligation by delivering (in good faith) to a holder of a forged bill of lading.[119] Pursuant to § 302 of the Merchant Shipping Act passive legitimation in relation to a person claiming delivery arises when said person presents a bill of lading and from its text or a chain of indorsements or an indorsement in blank *appears* to be the person entitled to the bill of lading.[120] The word "appears" in this context only refers to the indorsements and not to the bill of lading itself. This is also reasonable seeing as the indorsements are made by the cargo side while the bill of lading is outside the carrier's sphere and the carrier therefore has no influence on their appearance and clarity, whereas the form and appearance of the bill of lading itself is something that the carrier decides. It should therefore at least in theory be easier for the carrier when presented with a bill of lading to ascertain whether the bill of lading itself is genuine than whether the indorsements are. As the passive legitimation function does not arise, the carrier does not obtain a good discharge by delivering to the holder of a forged bill of lading.

With passive legitimation not arising, it seems a natural inference that active legitimation does not arise either. A good faith holder of a forged bill of lading can thus not demand delivery and such holder cannot claim damages from the carrier denying delivery either. This is supported by the principle in § 17 of the Act on Instruments of Debt which sets out the so-called "strong" objections, i.e. objections that are not extinguished even by

117 Fn 109.
118 [1999] 1 Lloyd's Rep. 837, at p. 842.
119 Per Vestergaard Pedersen, *Transportret* (Copenhagen: Thomson, 2008), p. 481.
120 *Supra* part 4.1.

a good faith acquirer of the negotiable instrument, and which includes that the instrument is forged.

§ 17 must be read in conjunction with § 15 which sets out the so-called "weak" objections, i.e. objections which are extinguished by a good faith acquirer of the instrument of debt. Under subsection 3 of that rule a debtor can secure its interests by having the objection which could otherwise be extinguished added to the instrument of debt itself, most commonly a notification that an extraordinary payment has been effected, thus taking away a future acquirer's good faith. Subsection 3, however, contains a modification that the notification must not be made in such a manner that it is easily removed. It has been submitted that this modification could also apply to bills of lading such that the carrier's objection that the bill of lading is a forgery or at least has been falsified could be lost if the carrier's handling of the document or other conduct has made it easy to forge the bill.[121] It is, however, difficult to see what type of objections added to a bill of lading would be subject to the rule. "Payment" in this respect would be delivery of the goods and the lawfulness of such delivery would rely on the ordinary rules pertaining to delivery and not a notification added on the bill. Further, it is difficult to imagine circumstances where the carrier acted in a manner which would lead to its being held liable under this rule. Certainly, no requirement exists that the carrier must include security measurements in its paper bills of lading.

The rules thus firmly place the risk of delivering against a forged bill of lading on the carrier, but the risk of acquiring a forged bill not giving a right to delivery on such acquirer.

10 Undeliverable goods

When no original bill of lading, duly indorsed if necessary, is presented to the carrier at the place of destination, the main principles regarding the use of bills of lading dictate that the (bonus pater) carrier should not deliver the goods to anyone, but instead keep them in its custody.[122] This may cause grave practical problems for the carrier who may have to keep the goods loaded on board and thus be delayed in its next assignment. It is therefore necessary that the carrier can in such circumstances take other steps with regard to the goods. This question may often be subject to laws or customs of the port which may apply irrespective of the proper law of the contract of carriage.

121 Pedersen, *Transportret*, p. 481.

122 As is well known, in some trades it is standard practice to deliver the goods without presentation of the bill, but rather against a letter of indemnity, see Chapter 1.

10.1 Scandinavian law

If no consignee comes forward and claims delivery within the period stipulated by the carrier,[123] then the carrier may store the goods under safe-keeping at the expense of the consignee, Merchant Shipping Acts § 271. If no time limit for taking delivery is stipulated then the rule applies if the goods are not claimed within a reasonable time. The carrier must in such event give notification that the goods have been put into storage and stipulate a reasonable time limit for the collection of the goods, subsection 2. The notification must be given to the notify party and if this is not possible then to the cargo owner if said owner can be identified and otherwise to the shipper, § 262(3). § 271 is written in permissive language and it is thus for the carrier to decide whether to avail itself of the possibility.[124] However, the general duty to mitigate loss would suggest that if suitable storage is available, the carrier should avail itself of this option and may otherwise run the risk of not being able to recover its loss in full.

Once the stipulated time limit has passed, the carrier is entitled to sell the goods to the extent necessary to cover its costs and any other claim that the carrier would have against the consignee if the consignee had taken delivery.[125] The goods may be sold either at public auction or by private sale.[126] The only requirement is that the carrier must act with due diligence, § 272.

Probably the most interesting aspect for the carrier in this regard is that the carrier by placing the goods in storage can unilaterally end the period of responsibility, § 274(3), no. 2.[127] It is, however, a prerequisite that the carrier has given proper notice[128] and that he has ensured that the goods are stored in a manner that they can be considered as having been stored under safe-keeping. This assessment must be made on a case-by-case basis of the individual facts.

123 § 268 sets out that the consignee must receive the goods at the place and within the period of time stipulated by the carrier.

124 It should also be noted that §§ 271 and 272 are not mandatory and may thus be derogated from by contract, cf. § 254(2). See on delivery clauses and the presentation rule *infra* Chapter 4, part 7.

125 Namely freight and other claims stipulated in the bill of lading as well as claims secured by a maritime lien in the cargo (e.g. reward for salvage). § 273(2) clarifies that the carrier is not obliged to sell the goods to recover the claims that the consignee would be liable for and that if the proceeds of a sale do not cover the carrier's claims in full then the shipper is liable for the remainder.

126 Sølovsudvalget, "Betænkning 1215/1991," p. 62.

127 Based on the Hamburg Rules, article 4(2)(b)(ii).

128 Cf. U 1977.999 where the Maritime and Commercial Court of Copenhagen found that the carrier had not given proper notice and was thus held liable as carrier.

10.2 English law

The problems related to undeliverable goods are no longer regulated by statute under English law. Previously, the Merchant Shipping Act 1894[129] did regulate the matter. Under section 493, if the owner of the goods did not take delivery at the agreed time or in the absence of such agreement within 72 hours (Sundays and holidays excluded) of the master's report in accordance with customs laws then the shipowner would be allowed to land the goods and place them on a wharf or in a warehouse. This part of the Merchant Shipping Act 1894 was repealed in 1993[130] and no similar provisions were included in the Merchant Shipping Act 1995. Instead, the issue was left to common law and to a very large extent contractual regulation by the parties.[131]

Under common law, the consignee must be allowed a reasonable time to receive the goods. If the consignee does not so take delivery within reasonable time, the carrier may discharge the goods and put them into storage at the expense of the cargo owner.[132] If the cargo side's failure to take delivery results in detention of the ship, it may become liable for demurrage and if the situation does not fall within the relevant demurrage provision, it may become liable for unliquidated damages.[133]

11 Delivery according to law or custom at the port of discharge

In various ports around the world local laws, customs or practices dictate that the carrier hands over the goods without presentation of an original bill of lading. Often such handing over is to be made to customs or other authorities or to a stevedoring company or terminal with a monopoly in that port. Thus, the carrier may find itself in a position with seemingly no choice but to hand over the goods without presentation of a bill of lading. The question is whether the carrier will obtain a good discharge by following such laws, customs or practices.

11.1 English law

Under English law it seems clear that a carrier who delivers without presentation of a bill of lading pursuant to law or to custom in its strict sense will obtain a good discharge of its delivery obligation.[134] However, this only

129 57 & 58 Vict. Ch. 60.
130 Statute Law (Repeals) Act 1993, 1993 c. 50, Section 1(1), Schedule 1, Part XV, group 6.
131 See *infra* Chapter 4, part 7, on such clauses.
132 Girvin, *Carriage of Goods by Sea*, p. 159.
133 Aikens, Lord, and Bools, *Bills of Lading*, para 13.30.
134 *Sucre Export SA v. Northern River Shipping Ltd. (The Sormovskiy 3068)*, [1994] 2 Lloyd's Rep. 266, p. 275.

applies to customs in the strict sense, i.e. one that is reasonable, certain, consistent with the contract, universally acquiesced in and not contrary to law.[135]

Consequently, it is not enough that a practice at the port of discharge exists if it does not amount to a custom. A carrier who hands over the goods to e.g. customs authorities without being obliged to do so must thus ensure that the customs authorities will only deliver the goods against presentation of a bill of lading in order to avoid liability for misdelivery.[136]

11.2 Scandinavian law

Under the Merchant Shipping Act § 274(1), cf. subparagraph (3), the carrier's period of responsibility for the goods ends, inter alia, when the carrier has handed over the goods to an authority or other third party to whom, pursuant to law or regulations applicable at the port of discharge, the goods must be handed. This is based on the Hamburg Rules, article 4, but the wording is not exactly the same. Pursuant to article 4(b)(iii), the carrier is in charge of the goods "until the time he has *delivered* the goods [...] by handing over the goods to an authority [...]" (italics added).

The wording of the Hamburg Rules, thus, indicates that the handing over of the goods to an authority or other third party constitutes delivery whereas the wording of the Merchant Shipping Act states that such handing over ends the period of responsibility and, in fact, § 274 mentions as another way in which the period of responsibility is ended that the carrier "has *delivered* the goods to the consignee" (italics added), cf. subparagraph (3)(1). It could be argued that ending the period of responsibility for the goods is something distinct from discharging the carrier of its obligation to only deliver against a bill of lading. It should be remembered that the Scandinavian countries are not parties to the Hamburg Rules and Scandinavian courts are therefore not bound to interpret § 274 in conformity with that convention. The travaux preparatoires do not, however, indicate that the change in wording was intended to change the content of the rule, but rather supports that § 274 is fully based on article 4.

It could be noted that § 274 is in a different sub-part of part 13 headed "liability of the carrier" than the rules on delivery of the goods which are in the sub-part headed "bills of lading and sea waybills". Accordingly it could be argued that § 274 does not end the carrier's obligation to deliver only against an original bill of lading. On the other hand, it would seem a rather inconsistent regulation if the carrier were free from liability if the goods were damaged or lost while in the custody of the customs authorities, but were liable for misdelivery if the goods were handed over to a receiver without presentation of the bill of lading. This would de facto mean that

135 Ibid.
136 *East West Corp. v. DKBS 1912*, [2003] Q.B. 1509, para 61 and 68.

the carrier were vicariously liable for the actions and omissions of the customs authorities with regard to the delivery of the goods, but not for the customs authorities' handling of the goods. Such a difference does not seem warranted.

As noted by Clarke J. in The Sormovskiy 3068, if the carrier were not discharged of its delivery obligations under the contract of carriage by delivering to an authority which it was obliged by law to deliver to, then "that contract could not be lawfully performed, which could not have been intended by the parties".[137] Unsurprisingly, it is also a principle of Scandinavian law that a contract which runs contrary to the law will not be upheld; in Denmark set out in the (still-valid) Danish Act of 1683, rule 5-1-2.

The above supports the conclusion that a carrier will be discharged of its delivery obligations if it hands over the goods to customs or other authorities without presentation of a bill of lading because the carrier is obliged to do so by the law or regulations applicable at the port.

This conclusion is also supported by a Swedish Court of Appeal verdict from 2001 with a similar problem.[138] The case concerned a transport of water tanks from Canada to Libya via Germany. The problem was not that laws at the port of discharge obliged the owner to deliver to local authorities without presentation of the bill of lading, but rather that the goods, which were produced in the United States, were subject to the United States' sanctions against Libya and United States' authorities therefore ordered the carrier not to deliver the goods to the bill of lading holder (even though the holder claimed delivery in Germany where the goods were situated). The city court, with whom the Court of Appeal agreed in full, found that the carrier was allowed to deny delivery to the bill of lading holder. The court stated that the obligation to deliver could not be seen as isolated from the carrier's liability in case of loss of the goods and pointed to the rule in the Hague-Visby Rules, article IV, rule 2(g), as incorporated in Swedish law. On this basis combined with the serious consequences for the carrier of not complying with the order of the United States' authorities the court found that it would be unreasonable to oblige the carrier to deliver to the bill of lading holder.[139]

137 *Sucre Export SA v. Northern River Shipping Ltd. (The Sormovskiy 3068)*, [1994] 2 Lloyd's Rep. 266, p. 275.

138 ND 2001.36 (Court of Appeal for Western Sweden), ND 2000.24 (City Court of Gothenburg).

139 Another Swedish court of appeal verdict from 1988, ND 1988.30 (Court of Appeal for Skåne and Blekinge), also relied on the exception in the Hague-Visby Rules, article IV, rule 2(g). The case concerned a rather extreme example of the "law" of the port of discharge, Tarthous, Syria. Under weapon threat the master was forced to deliver the goods to a state-owned company on the basis of a Syrian court order and without presentation of a bill of lading. The unpaid seller of the goods arrested the vessel in a Swedish port, but the arrest was lifted because the court found that the carrier was excepted of liability pursuant to article IV, rule 2(g). The direct application of article IV, rule 2(g) to a misdelivery claim seems highly questionable, Hannu Honka, "New

12 Lost bills of lading and delivery against letters of indemnity

As stated in Chapter 1, the key problem challenging the use of bills of lading, especially in some trades, is that the bill of lading is not available at the place of destination. This may be due to the physical delivery of the bill being slower than the actual transit time for the goods, that the bill is held up in the documentary credit transaction, or simply that the bill is lost somewhere in the process. As set out in the previous sections, the main rule in such situations is that the carrier cannot deliver the goods and thus be discharged of its delivery obligation under the contract of carriage. It may be asked, though, if there are any particularly qualified situations in which the bill is unavailable that give rise to exceptions to the main rule.

12.1 Scandinavian law

The Merchant Shipping Acts contain one section dealing with the situation where the bill of lading has been lost, although only in a limited manner. Pursuant to § 305 a lost bill of lading may be cancelled in accordance with the rules in the legislation on cancellation ("mortification") of securities[140] which in practice means that a court must declare the bill of lading null and void (a direct translation of the Danish term is "dead and powerless") after a specific procedure. § 305 contains an additional specific rule for bills of lading setting out that once a public announcement has been made pursuant to said procedure or if the court so decides, delivery of the goods may be demanded against provision of security for claims which the holder of the lost bill of lading may invoke against the carrier. Thus, the Merchant Shipping Act provides a right to demand delivery without presentation of the bill of lading, but it requires the cumbersome procedure for cancellation ("mortification") of securities to be applied.[141] It should be noted that

Carriage of Goods by Sea – The Nordic Approach", in *New Carriage of Goods by Sea*, ed. Hannu Honka (Åbo: Institute of Maritime and Commercial Law, Åbo Akademi University, 1997), p. 141, fn 376. See further Erling Selvig, *Fra kjøpsrettens og transportrettens grenseland* (Oslo: Universitetsforlaget, 1975), p. 71 at and in fn 14. See also *supra* fn 88.

140 In Denmark Consolidated Act no 639/1986 with later amendments; In Norway Act of 18 December 1959 no. 1 with later amendments; In Sweden Act 2011:900; In Finland Act 14.8.1901/34a with later amendments.

141 The procedures of the four countries are similar. In short the Danish procedure is as follows; The person who is assumed to have lost the bill of lading and have title to it must apply to the court at the place of destination to have it cancelled, §§ 1 and 3(2). The applicant must apply to the court to issue a public summons to anyone with an objection to the cancellation, § 4. The court will then hold a hearing in which the applicant must prove that it is likely that the conditions for cancellation are fulfilled, §§ 5(1) and 4(2). If the court is satisfied then it will issue summons to a public hearing which must be published in the first issue in a quarter of the official Danish Gazette, §§ 5(2) and 6(1)–(3). The public hearing must be at a time at least three months later than the publication of the summons, §6(5). At the hearing, the claimant must prove that the conditions for cancellation are fulfilled and the court will then by verdict declare the document "dead and powerless", § 7(1)–(2).

the rule does not relieve the carrier of liability for misdelivery towards a rightful holder of the bill of lading but simply obliges the carrier to deliver the goods against a security being provided for that liability.[142]

With the carrier not being discharged of its delivery obligation towards the rightful holder of a bill of lading even where the carrier is obliged by § 305 to deliver against a security being provided it seems obvious that a carrier will not be discharged in other situations either where the carrier chooses to deliver against a letter of indemnity or other security without being obliged to by law.[143]

Aside from the special rule in § 305 and the cancellation procedure there are no exceptions to the general principle that the carrier is only discharged of its delivery obligation when it delivers against presentation of the bill of lading. The fact that there is a good explanation for what has happened to the bill or that a letter of indemnity is provided does not change that fact.

12.2 English law

The widespread practice of delivering the goods without presentation of a bill of lading if a letter of indemnity is provided to the carrier has especially raised two questions, namely whether the carrier is free from liability when delivering against a letter of indemnity and whether the carrier is free from liability if the person demanding delivery can provide a reasonable explanation of what has happened with the bill of lading; a letter of indemnity being provided or not.

In the situation where a letter of indemnity is provided, said indemnity is precisely aimed at setting off the liability which the carrier may incur by delivering the goods without the bill of lading. It is not aimed at and in fact cannot be set up as a defence for the carrier. In *The Houda*, in which the dispute was as to the lawfulness of a time charterer's order to the master to deliver against an indemnity, Leggatt L.J. stated: "In default of production of the bill of lading an indemnity is afforded to the shipowner not on account of the lawfulness of the order to deliver but so as to protect him if he does what he is *not* contractually obliged to do."[144] Thus, it is the carrier's choice if it decides to accept to deliver against an indemnity,[145] but it has no bearing on its potential liability for misdelivery.

It has been submitted that the carrier may deliver the goods without presentation of the bill of lading if it is reasonably satisfied that the person

142 For a critique of this fact see Brækhus, "Bortfrakterens ansvar for utlevering av last til ulegitimert mottager", p. 338.

143 Grönfors and Gorton, *Sjölagens bestämmelser om godsbefordran*, p. 279. Lyngsø, *Negotiable Dokumenter*, p. 293f.

144 *Kuwait Petroleum Corporation v. I&D Oil Carriers Ltd. (The "Houda")*, [1994] 2 Lloyd's Rep. 541, p. 553.

145 Ibid., at p. 552 per Neill L.J.

demanding delivery is entitled to possession of the goods and there is a reasonable explanation as to what has happened with the bill of lading.[146] This seems mainly to be based on statements made by Clarke J. in *The Sormovskiy 3068*.[147] The starting point must, however be – and in fact also was for Clarke J. – the "simple working rule"[148] stated by Lord Denning in *Sze Hai Tong Bank Ltd. v. Rambler Cycle Co. Ltd.* that "[...] a shipowner who delivers without production of the bill of lading does so at his peril".[149] Clarke J. stated that

> In order to cater for that problem [i.e. that the bill of lading might have been lost or stolen] it is no doubt necessary to imply a term that the master must deliver cargo without production of an original bill of lading in circumstances where it is proved to his reasonable satisfaction both that the person seeking delivery of the goods is entitled to possession and what has become of the bill of lading.[150]

That proposition has however been severely doubted.[151]

In the *Motis Exports* case, Rix J. found that a carrier could not be obliged to deliver the goods even to the true owner without the presentation of the bill of lading and that it would not be necessary to imply a term that the carrier would be entitled to deliver the goods without presentation of the bill.[152] This issue was not taken up in the Court of Appeal which was only faced with the applicability of an exemption clause. In *The Houda,* reference to *The Sormowskiy 3068* was not made, but there the "simple working rule" was stated without qualification.[153] In *East West Corp. v. DKBS 1912,* Mance L.J., with whom Laws and Brooke LL.J. agreed, also questioned whether there would be any justification for delivering without presentation of the bill of lading in the circumstances contemplated in *The*

146 Girvin, *Carriage of Goods by Sea*, p. 142. The author does, however, express that this view has been doubted and the section has been softened since the first edition of the book. Paul Todd has argued that given the extent to which letters of indemnity are used in practice, particularly on short voyages where the bill will rarely be able to get to the place of destination in time, a claim should not be able to be made based on the bill after delivery against an indemnity, cf. Todd, "The bill of lading and delivery: the common law actions", p. 567. The argument seems, however, to be a policy statement rather than a statement of the law.

147 *Sucre Export SA v. Northern River Shipping Ltd. (The Sormovskiy 3068)*, [1994] 2 Lloyd's Rep. 266.

148 So called by Neill L.J. in *Kuwait Petroleum Corporation v. I&D Oil Carriers Ltd. (The "Houda")*, [1994] 2 Lloyd's Rep. 541, at p. 552.

149 [1959] 2 Lloyd's Rep. 114, at p. 120.

150 *Sucre Export SA v. Northern River Shipping Ltd. (The Sormovskiy 3068)*, [1994] 2 Lloyd's Rep. 266, at p. 274.

151 Treitel and Reynolds, *Carver on Bills of Lading*, p. 330.

152 [1999] 1 Lloyd's Rep. 837 (QB), at p. 841f.

153 Fn 148.

Sormovskiy 3068.[154] In *The Erin Schulte* Teare J. reiterated the doubts but did not take an own stance as he found that the carrier had not proven that it could rely on the exception even if it existed.[155]

In conclusion, it seems highly unlikely that a claim would succeed that a term should be implied into the bill of lading allowing the carrier to deliver or, even more, the claimant to demand delivery without presentation of the bill of lading if a reasonable explanation of what has become of the bill is given.

13 Consequences of breach of the obligation to deliver against bill of lading

If the carrier delivers other than in accordance with the rules and principles described above, it breaches one of its fundamental obligations under the contract of carriage. A number of questions as to the consequences of that fact arise. Can the aggrieved party claim damages and what is the basis of a potential liability? From whom can the aggrieved party claim damages, only the contractual carrier or also from a non-contractual carrier? Can the carrier limit its liability under the statutory rules on limitation of liability[156] and what is the time bar for claims for misdelivery? Also, how should damages for misdelivery be calculated?

This part is intended to provide an overview and analyse some of these issues in more detail. It is, however, not intended to provide an exhaustive analysis of these rather comprehensive issues which to some extent rely on general rules and principles of contract and tort law.

13.1 Scandinavian law

13.1.1 Basis of liability

If the carrier delivers the goods other than in accordance with the rules and principles set out above it both breaches the contract of carriage and the obligations set out in the Merchant Shipping Act. The Merchant Shipping Act does not, however, contain rules on liability ensuing from such breach. Instead the liability has been developed in case law as a supplement to the rules. In a "classical" misdelivery context where the carrier agrees to deliver the goods without presentation of a bill of lading the carrier deliberately breaches its obligations under the contract of carriage and the Merchant Shipping Act and is thus liable in damages.

154 *East West Corp. v. DKBS 1912*, [2003] Q.B. 1509, para 47.
155 *Standard Chartered Bank v. Dorchester LNG (2) Ltd.*, [2013] EWHC 808, para 77.
156 Whether the carrier can rely on contractual clauses exempting or limiting liability is dealt with in Chapter 4.

The liability in damages is a sanction for delivering the goods to a person lacking legitimation. It is thus separate from the carrier's liability for breaches of its obligation to care for the goods.[157] When the breach is deliberate there is no difficulty in establishing a liability.

Where the misdelivery is not a result of the carrier's deliberate delivery of the goods without presentation of a bill of lading, but rather inadvertent misdelivery, e.g. delivery against a forged bill of lading or an original bill of lading with an invalid indorsement, the question of liability is a bit more uncertain. Only very little has been written on this issue. It has been suggested both that such types of undeliberate misdelivery should be treated as a case of "loss" of the goods under the convention-based rules,[158] i.e. equal to a theft of the goods, and that it should be subject to liability "pursuant to ordinary rules on negligence with a reversed burden of proof and on unlimited liability".[159] Other authors describe the liability as one for delivering the goods to a person lacking legitimation in a manner which seems to imply that the qualification of the liability does not rely on the subjective intent of the carrier.[160]

It is submitted that the latter view is preferable. Above, it was analysed what the carrier's obligations are and whether the carrier obtains a good discharge when it delivers against a bill of lading with an invalid indorsement, without properly checking the identity of the receiver, or against a forged bill of lading. The answers largely derive from the Merchant Shipping Act supplemented by analogous application of the Act on Instruments of Debt. Under an instrument of debt if the debtor does not obtain a good discharge because he has failed to live up to his obligations or because the Act places a risk on him then the consequence is that the debtor must pay the amount again to the correct creditor (an instrument of debt is by definition for payment of an amount of money). Under a bill of lading the situation is different. The carrier (the debtor) cannot simply be obliged to perform the obligation to deliver the goods again as these have already been given to someone else. To obtain the same effect the

157 Grönfors and Gorton, *Sjölagens bestämmelser om godsbefordran*, pp 278 and 97. Selvig, *Fra kjøpsrettens og transportrettens grenseland*, pp 71 and 79. Brækhus, "Bortfrakterens ansvar for utlevering av last til ulegitimert mottager", *passim*, discusses whether the liability should be considered a liability for "loss of or damage to the goods" ("transportansvar"), but concludes that it should not.

158 "Bortfrakterens ansvar for utlevering av last til ulegitimert mottager", p. 341, fn 5. The issue is not developed further in the article as it deals with intentional delivery without presentation of the bill of lading. Tiberg, "Liability for wrongful delivery," p. 168. The statement is made in relation to insufficient checking of the indorsements or unnecessary compliance with directions to deliver.

159 Pedersen, *Transportret*, p. 585f. The statement is made in relation to two situations, viz. that the receiver is not the consignee (incl. by indorsement) and that the receiver incorrectly pretends to be the consignee.

160 Grönfors and Gorton, *Sjölagens bestämmelser om godsbefordran*, p. 297. Selvig, *Fra kjøpsrettens og transportrettens grenseland*, pp 71 and 85. Also Selvig in ND 2003 p. xiii.

obligation must instead be converted into an obligation to pay the damages the rightful holder of the bill of lading (the creditor) has suffered.[161] The rules set out the standards that the carrier must live up to in order to obtain a good discharge (e.g. perform a reasonable check of the indorsements and the identity of the person presenting the bill of lading). Adding an extra condition that the carrier must have acted negligently in order to be liable to pay the damages suffered would seem to be an unfounded addition.[162] Rather, the liability is a natural result of the placing of obligations and risks on the carrier and the cargo side respectively. For some of the obligations, e.g. in the case of delivery against a bill of lading with (an) invalid indorsement(s), the assessment of the carrier's conduct, i.e. whether it has performed an acceptable check of the indorsements, would seem to be fundamentally the same as if the assessment was of whether the carrier had acted negligently. For other situations, e.g. delivery against a forged bill of lading, that will not be the case. The quality of the forgery may be so high that the carrier cannot be said to be negligent in assuming that it is original and yet be held liable for misdelivery.

13.1.2 Limitation of liability

A related question is whether the carrier can limit its liability for misdelivery under the rules on package/weight limitation.[163] It is the generally accepted view that liability for intentional misdelivery is not subject to limitation.[164] Thus the package/weight limitation in § 280 implementing the

161 Folke Schmidt et al., *Huvudlinjer i svensk frakträtt*, 2nd ed. (Stockholm: P. A. Nordstedt & Söners Förlag, 1962), p. 142, also state that the protection of the rightful holder of the bill of lading can only be obtained through liability in damages.

162 In U 2004.1142 (Maritime and Commercial Court of Copenhagen) the goods were delivered to a company who presented an original order bill of lading where the consignee was a named person (a guarantor) with the addition of the company as "c/o" address, but without an indorsement to the company. The court stated that there was no indorsement to the company, nor could the company be seen as an agent for the named consignee. Accordingly, the carrier was held liable for misdelivery towards the named consignee. In finding so the court made no assessment of whether the carrier had acted negligently.

163 This term is used here for convenience and the omission of the word "unit" which appears in the Hague and Hague-Visby Rules is thus not intended to have an independent meaning.

164 Brækhus, "Bortfrakterens ansvar for utlevering av last til ulegitimert mottager", p. 340 et seq. Selvig, *Fra kjøpsrettens og transportrettens grenseland*, p. 79f. Kjeld Rosenmeyer, *Transportret* (Copenhagen: Juristforbundets Forlag, 1982), p. 221ff. Honka, "New Carriage of Goods by Sea – The Nordic Approach", p. 139. The fact that carriers when releasing goods against a letter of indemnity are advised by the P&I Clubs to demand that the indemnity or guarantee is for an amount equal to 200 per cent of the c.i.f. value of the cargo also clearly suggests that it is the accepted view of the trade that the liability is unlimited, cf. Hazelwood and Semark, *P & I Clubs Law and Practice*, para 10.143.

Hague-Visby Rules will not apply to claims for intentional misdelivery. Some writers seem to rely on the deliberate nature of the breach, i.e. in the "classical" misdelivery situation where the carrier delivers the goods without presentation of the bill of lading at all, to be the reason for the consequence that the carrier cannot rely on contractual defences[165] or those of the Merchant Shipping Act, i.e. the package/weight limitation.[166] The basis for this assumption is, however, not very well developed and will be discussed below.

Emphasising that it is the deliberate nature of the carrier's action which carries the consequence that the carrier cannot limit its liability under the Merchant Shipping Act is based either on an assumption that the categorisation of the misdelivery as a "loss" of the goods (potentially bringing the misdelivery within the ambit of the limitation rules) is dependent on the misdelivery not being intentional or that the right to limit is subject to an "overriding obligation" not to cause intentional harm.[167] Both assumptions are closely connected to how the basis of liability is viewed. Thus the liability rule in the Merchant Shipping Act for loss of or damage to cargo is closely interlinked with the rule prescribing the right to package/weight limitation of the liability. The latter assumption, however, presupposes that liability for misdelivery is as a starting point a claim subject to limitation. If that is accepted then stating that the deliberateness of the carrier's action leads to the loss of such right of limitation presupposes that the misdelivery is in fact the act of the carrier itself or someone who is identified with the carrier. Thus, to lose the right of limitation the requirements of the Merchant Shipping Act § 283, based on the Hague-Visby Rules article IV, rule 5(e), have to be fulfilled. This means that if it is the master of the ship or a terminal operator who without the knowledge or authority of someone who can be identified with the carrier wilfully delivers the goods without presentation of the bill of lading the right to limit the liability will not be lost. Obviously, another consequence is that the carrier can limit liability for negligent misdelivery.

As stated above, it is submitted that the better view is that the liability is separate from the cargo damage liability and is a liability for delivering to the wrong person by breaching the rules that give the bill of lading its negotiable nature. This liability does not fall within the ambit of the package/weight limitation rules. Consequently liability for delivery of the goods to a person not legitimated by the bill of lading cannot be limited

165 This is dealt with in Chapter 4.

166 Brækhus, "Bortfrakterens ansvar for utlevering av last til ulegitimert mottager", pp. 340–42, 46, and 48–49. Brækhus argues that the liability for intentional misdelivery falls wholly outside the ambit of the limitation rules while negligent misdelivery should be treated as loss of cargo. Tiberg, "Liability for wrongful delivery", p. 172ff.

167 "Liability for wrongful delivery", p. 172f.

under the package/weight limitation rules and that is irrespective of whether such delivery is intentional or unintentional.[168]

13.1.3 Tort or contract? Claims against sub-carriers

Another issue is whether the liability is one in contract or in tort. This is mainly of interest in relation to two issues, namely whether the claimant can sue someone other than the contractual carrier and whether the claimant by claiming in tort can avoid a potential limitation of liability. The former issue is particularly relevant where the delivery is performed by a sub-carrier, i.e. someone other than the contractual carrier. The possibility of claiming against a sub-carrier is, of course, not unique to misdelivery claims, but is a well-known issue in relation to many other types of claims in maritime transport law. Since 1973, the Scandinavian Merchant Shipping Acts have had a general rule on this issue.

Pursuant to § 286 a sub-carrier shall be liable for that part of the carriage it performs pursuant to the same provisions as the contractual carrier. It further sets out that § 282 shall apply correspondingly. § 282 contains the important rule that the carrier's defences and limits of liability shall apply even if the claim is not based on the contract of carriage, i.e. is a claim in tort. § 286 does not in fact state towards whom the sub-carrier shall be liable but the rule has been interpreted to include liability towards the shipper/cargo side (as opposed to towards the contractual carrier).[169] In academic writings, the relationship between shipper and sub-carrier has been termed a "contract-like" relationship, but the problem is that this term does not help much in determining which contract terms apply between the two parties.[170] Especially the question is whether the sub-carrier can only be held to the mandatory statutory rules or also to the individual contract terms agreed between the contractual carrier and the shipper. This should be dealt with on a term-by-term basis determining whether the individual term has such a particular connection with the contracting parties that it should not apply as between the shipper and sub-carrier.[171]

With respect to delivery of the goods, the obligation to deliver only to the person legitimated by presenting the bill of lading – duly indorsed if

168 Erling Selvig, *Unit Limitation of Carrier's Liability* (Oslo: Oslo University Press, 1961), §4.21, §4.34, and §4.53. The analysis there is made of the Hague Rules, but the amendments made to the Scandinavian Merchant Shipping Acts as a result of implementing the Visby Protocol has not changed the situation, cf. *Fra kjøpsrettens og transportrettens grenseland*, p. 79, fn 32. Schmidt et al., *Huvudlinjer i svensk frakträtt*, p. 142, fn 38.

169 Vibe Ulfbeck, *Kontrakters relativitet* (Copenhagen: Thomson, 2000), p. 370 (with further references).

170 Ibid., p. 371 et seq.

171 Ibid., p. 372.

necessary – is an inherent part of any contract of carriage where a bill of lading is issued and prescribed in the Merchant Shipping Act as supplemented by the Act on Instruments of Debt. There is therefore no doubt that the obligation to deliver only against presentation of the bill of lading applies also to a sub-carrier and if it breaches that obligation it will be liable in the same way as the carrier. Above it was submitted that liability for misdelivery, whether this be intentional or unintentional, is not subject to package/weight limitation. If it is accepted, however, that such claims are subject to limitation then that right would also extend to the sub-carrier pursuant to § 286 and § 282 and that is irrespective of whether the claim is made in contract or in tort. With the Act setting out the obligations of the carrier and extending these to the sub-carrier as well as making any defences and limitations available to both carrier and sub-carrier independent of whether the claim be founded in contract or tort and with the applicability of bill of lading terms having to be assessed on an individual basis it serves no independent purpose to seek to categorise the nature of the claim as one in contract or tort.

13.1.4 Time bar

The time bar for bringing a claim for misdelivery is one year from the date when the goods should have been delivered or in fact were delivered, whichever is later. This is clearly prescribed in the Norwegian and Danish Merchant Shipping Acts and is established in Supreme Court Practice in Sweden.[172]

3.1.5 Damages

The calculation of the damages cannot be put into one formula, but must instead be assessed on an individual basis in each case. It will also depend on whether the aggrieved party is the seller of the goods, the buyer of the goods or someone holding a security interest in the goods. Below, some general and non-exhaustive observations are set out.

The starting point will normally be (especially if the claimant is the seller of the goods) the invoice price of the cargo.[173]

172 *Supra* part 5.

173 Tiberg, "Liability for wrongful delivery", p. 169. If the aggrieved party is instead someone with a security interest in the goods, that party will only have lost the amount that he could have obtained by a substitute sale of the goods at the place of destination. The value of the goods at that place and time must therefore be the starting point of the calculation of damages for such a party. In U 1972.849 (Maritime and Commercial Court of Copenhagen) it was, however, stated without any reservation as to the capacity of the claimant that the starting point should be the value of the goods at the port of destination as set out in the Merchant Shipping Act § 120 (now § 279)(based on the Hague-Visby Rules article IV, rule 5(b)), p. 862, which sets out that the value must be

There is no obligation on the aggrieved party to first attempt to get the goods back from the party who has obtained delivery without presentation of the bill of lading. Further, if it is a buyer of the goods who has obtained delivery without first paying for the bill of lading and thus for the goods, the seller is not obliged to first try to obtain the purchase price from the buyer.[174] If the seller does obtain payment or partial payment, such payment must be deducted from the claim as the seller's loss will have been mitigated by that amount.[175]

The general value of the goods at the destination may be much lower than the invoice price because there are no other buyers in the area or the seller would have to exercise considerable time and costs in order to find another buyer. As a starting point this is however also not relevant when assessing the damages.[176]

If the buyer rejects the goods due to defects after having obtained delivery – or been given access to inspect them – without presentation of the bill of lading and thus without having paid the purchase price, the seller may be considered not to have suffered a loss as a consequence of the wrongful delivery if the buyer would in fact be entitled to reject the goods under the sales contract. However, the issue of liability for misdelivery and the right to reject goods as between buyer and seller under the sales contract are two separate issues. It will therefore presumably be difficult for the carrier in a

established on the basis of the goods exchange price, the market price or in the absence of such notations, the current value of goods of the same kind and quality. In that case, the information available could not support a conclusion that the value was lower than the invoice value and the claimant was also awarded a commission which he had a contractual right to, ibid. The stated starting point thus had no bearing on the actual damages awarded in the case.

174 Selvig, *Fra kjøpsrettens og transportrettens grenseland*, p. 73. Johs. Jantzen and Nils Dybwad, *Godsbefordring til Sjøs*, 2nd ed. (Oslo: Fabritius & Sønners Forlag, 1952), p. 447.

175 In ND 1995.109 (Maritime and Commercial Court of Copenhagen), 20 containers containing milk powder were delivered to the consignee without presentation of the bills of lading and the seller/shipper therefore sued the carrier for the unpaid part of the invoice price of the goods. During the course of the litigation, the buyer made several partial payments. The carrier was held liable for the remainder of the invoice price and for procedural interest of the full amount initially claimed until the time of each partial payment. The carrier could, however, not be held liable for interest pursuant to an agreement made between buyer and seller at a time long after the carriage and the time when delivery was initially to have taken place. The awarding of procedural interest shows that the seller was right to sue for the entire amount even though negotiations to obtain payment from the buyer were also taking place.

176 The circumstances of FED 2000.1572 (Maritime and Commercial Court of Copenhagen) were somewhat unusual. The claimant had sold five containers of frozen shrimp to a Chinese buyer. Due to an alleged mistake, six containers were picked up and shipped to China by the defendant carriers. The sixth container was released without presentation of the bill of lading. The court awarded damages in an amount equal to the price that shrimp of the same quality and quantity had previously been sold to the same buyer for and in doing so disapproved of a submission that because the shrimp had already been shipped, the buyer would have been able to negotiate a better price, p. 1581.

case regarding its liability for misdelivery to prove that the claimant did not suffer a loss (or at least only the value of the goods at the destination if the goods have not been placed at its disposal upon the rejection) because the party who obtained delivery was entitled to reject the goods.[177,178] If the issue of the rejection of the goods has been settled separately it may, of course, prove easier for the carrier.

13.2 English law

13.2.1 Basis of liability – contract, tort or bailment

Under English law, a carrier who delivers the goods other than in accordance with the rules described above can be in breach of contract and bailment and be liable in the tort of conversion. The three are not mutually exclusive and the carrier can be found to be liable on all three bases for the same misdelivery.[179]

Breach of contract obviously requires that the claimant has a right of suit in contract against the carrier. When the claimant is a rightful holder of a bill of lading this will be the case either by way of being an original party to the contract or pursuant to COGSA 1992, s. 2(1). Where the claimant is the original shipper, however, he may have divested himself of his rights of suit on the bill of lading by transferring the bill of lading to someone else, s. 2(5). In such cases the shipper may instead be able to raise a claim in

177 Selvig, *Fra kjøpsrettens og transportrettens grenseland*, p. 73f and 76f, seems to take as the starting point that the carrier is free from liability because no loss has been suffered if the faulty goods are placed at the disposal of the seller but he acknowledges that the carrier has a heavy burden of proof to lift in such case.

178 This was stated quite clearly in the somewhat old verdict U 1965.829 (Maritime and Commercial Court of Copenhagen). A Portuguese company had sold 5,000 kilos of yarn to a Danish company. A part shipment of 3,000 kilos was delivered to the Danish company without presentation of the bill of lading and without the purchase price being paid. The company then rejected the yarn under the sales contract claiming that it was faulty. The Portuguese seller sued the carrier for wrongful delivery. The court set out by stating that the issue under scrutiny was not whether the goods were faulty, but whether the carrier was liable for misdelivery. The court found that it was and awarded the Portuguese seller damages in an amount equal to the invoice price. In doing so it also rejected a claim that the damages should be lower because the rejected goods were said to have been placed at the disposal of the seller. In the more recent case FED 2000.1572, referred above, the claimant had undisputedly paid an amount of US$ 8,000 to the buyers which were stated to be compensation for defects. However, because the claimant did not know at the time of payment that the container had been released without presentation of the bill of lading, the court found that the claimant could not be blamed for not having set the amount off against the claim for the purchase price and thus mitigate its loss.

179 A recent example can be found in *Glencore International AG v. MSC Mediterranean Shipping Company SA*, [2015] EWHC 1989, where the carrier was held liable in contract and bailment and Andrew Smith J. was ready to hear further arguments as to whether the misdelivery was also a conversion.

bailment.[180] It is debated, with widely differing opinions being strongly held by different authors, whether the transferee of a bill of lading also becomes (successor in title to the) bailor by virtue of becoming the bill of lading holder.[181] This question does not seem to be answered authoritatively in case law.

Conversion is one of the torts concerning wrongful interference with goods. The three basic features of the tort of conversion were set out by Lord Nicholls of Birkenhead in *Kuwait Airways Corp v. IAC (No. 6)* (his lordship set out "features" rather than a definition because "[c]onversion of goods can occur in so many different circumstances that framing a precise definition of universal application is well nigh impossible"):

> First, the defendant's conduct was inconsistent with the rights of the owner (or other person entitled to possession). Second, the conduct was deliberate, not accidental. Third, the conduct was so extensive an encroachment on the rights of the owner as to exclude him from use and possession of the goods. The contrast is with lesser acts of interference. If these cause damage they may give rise to claims for trespass or in negligence, but they do not constitute conversion.[182]

As can be seen, the claimant must either be the owner of the goods or have a right of possession. In a misdelivery context, the second feature must also be noted. It is the delivery of the goods to a receiver that must be made deliberately by the carrier. The carrier does not need to know that the receiver is not the true owner of the goods or that the carrier is delivering against a forged bill of lading.[183] In that way the deliberateness can be said to go to delivery, not misdelivery. It should also be noted that a conversion will occur both when the carrier delivers the goods to the wrong person and when a rightful holder of a bill of lading (subsequently) demands delivery of the goods which the carrier cannot honour.[184] Even a holder who did not have an immediate right of possession at the time the goods were delivered by the carrier to the wrong person can thus avail himself of the possibility of claiming in conversion by making a fresh demand for delivery from the carrier.[185]

180 This was the situation in *East West Corp. v. DKBS 1912*, [2003] Q.B. 1509.

181 The question turns on the normal requirement for an attornment which the carrier, of course, does not give in the ordinary sense on each transfer of the bill of lading. See *supra* fn 78 and 79.

182 *Kuwait Airways Corp. v. Iraqi Airways Co.*, [2002] UKHL 19, para 39.

183 *Motis Exports Ltd. v. Dampskibsselskabet af 1912 A/S*, [1999] 1 Lloyd's Rep. 837, at 845.

184 Aikens J. held this to be the case in *Trafigura Beheer BV v. Mediteranean Shipping Co. SA*, [2007] EWHC 944, 69. Baughen, "Misdelivery claims under bills of lading and international conventions for the carriage of goods by sea", p. 165f.

185 Todd, "The bill of lading and delivery: the common law actions," inter alia p. 540f.

Whether the claimant can base his claim in contract, in bailment or in conversion will depend on the circumstances of the individual case and especially on whether the claimant is the shipper, the holder of a bill of lading, the owner of the goods or a bank with a security interest in the goods. As stated, the claimant will often be able to claim under more than one of these options. While it is obviously of great importance for a claimant to be able to claim based on one of the other bases if all the avenues are not open to the claimant the difference between claiming on the different bases are not as great as one might immediately think. One important aspect making the differences less far-reaching is that a claimant cannot avoid contractual exclusions or limitations of liability by suing in tort when he could sue in contract.[186]

The liability in contract and in conversion can be described as strict.[187] In bailment the liability is fault-based, but with a presumption of liability.[188] The other – rather subtle – differences lie mainly in the calculation of losses, including perhaps a difference in the test for remoteness, and in the burden of proof.

13.2.2 Limitation of liability

With regard to limitation of liability, the Hague-Visby Rules have been implemented in English law by the Carriage of Goods by Sea Act 1971. The Act gives the Hague-Visby Rules the force of law. Unlike in the Scandinavian countries the Rules have not been transformed into English rules and the temporal ambit of the Rules has not been extended. It is thus a direct application of the Hague-Visby Rules article IV, rule 5, that could be relevant to a misdelivery claim. As mentioned in part 5 there is some judicial support that this rule could be interpreted to cover claims for misdelivery. However, a misdelivery occurs outside the temporal ambit of the Rules unless the delivery occurs simultaneously with the discharge such that the two can be equated[189] which will rarely be the case. There does not

186 Treitel and Reynolds, *Carver on Bills of Lading*, p. 755ff. Todd, "The bill of lading and delivery: the common law actions", p. 564f. "Excluding and Limiting Liability for Misdelivery", *Journal of Business Law*, no. 3 (2010): p. 251 et seq., states that the carrier's delivery of the goods to someone not presenting the bill of lading is a repudiatory breach and that the bill of lading holder may repudiate the contract of carriage and then make a fresh claim for delivery on the basis of the bill of lading whereby the carrier and then be guilty of a new conversion when it cannot honour the claim. Todd discusses whether the bill of lading holder by claiming on the new conversion can avoid exclusions in the contract of carriage which may not have survived the repudiation.

187 Baughen, "Misdelivery claims under bills of lading and international conventions for the carriage of goods by sea", pp. 164 and 66.

188 "Bailment or conversion? Misdelivery claims against non-contractual carriers," *Lloyd's Maritime and Commercial Law Quarterly* (2010): p. 420.

189 Treitel and Reynolds, *Carver on Bills of Lading*, p. 732.

seem to be any reported case where article IV, rule 5, has been applied as a result of the misdelivery being within the temporal ambit of the Rules.[190] For article IV, rule 5, to be applied to a claim for post-discharge misdelivery it is therefore probably necessary that the application of the Rules has been extended by contract to the period after discharge of the goods. This issue is therefore analysed in Chapter 4 on contract terms and misdelivery.

13.2.3 Liability of non-contractual carriers

The question of to what extent a non-contractual carrier can be held liable for misdelivery has surprisingly received very little judicial and academic attention. Unlike in the Scandinavian countries the issue is not dealt with in statute. With no contract between the claimant and the non-contractual carrier, the claimant will have to rely on conversion or bailment (or both) to found its claim. Several difficult questions arise in this context. First and foremost it must be considered what delivery obligation the actual carrier is subjected to, especially in situations where the contractual carrier (e.g. a time charterer) has issued a bill of lading and the actual carrier has issued a bill of lading to the contractual carrier. Second, it may be asked whether the non-contractual carrier is liable for misdelivery if it has handed over the goods to an independent contractor (e.g. a terminal operator) who delivers the goods to the wrong person which includes questions of whether the delivery is within the non-contractual carriers duties and if so whether the obligation is non-delegable. Third, it is uncertain on what terms a bailment will be, including whether the non-contractual carrier can rely on exceptions and limitations in the bill of lading or the terms of the head bailment (if they differ from those of the bill of lading). It falls outside the scope of this part, which seeks to provide an overview of the consequences of breaching the obligations to deliver only against a bill of lading, to analyse these issues further.[191]

13.2.4 Time bar

Under the Limitation Act 1980 the general time bar for bringing an action is six years.[192] The question is whether the short time bar of one year in the Hague-Visby Rules, article III, rule 6, may be applicable to a misdelivery

190 In *Sucre Export SA v. Northern River Shipping Ltd. (The Sormovskiy 3068)*, [1994] 2 Lloyd's Rep. 266, the misdelivery occurred on discharge. The bills of lading contained a clause paramount, but the carrier does not seem to have argued that the Hague-Visby Rules' limitation should apply to the claim.

191 See instead Baughen, "Bailment or conversion? Misdelivery claims against non-contractual carriers". See also the analysis of bailment and conversion claims more generally in Paul Todd, "The bill of lading and delivery: the common law actions", *Lloyd's Maritime and Commercial Law Quarterly*, no. 4 (2006).

192 Ss. 2, 3 and 5.

claim. This question includes two sub-questions,[193] viz. whether the time bar covers claims for misdelivery as a type and a temporal issue, i.e. whether it covers post-discharge delivery. With regard to the former, the wording of article III, rule 6, is wider than that of the rules imposing liability and allowing limitation of the liability in that it is "all liability whatsoever in respect of the goods" that the carrier is discharged of if suit is not brought within the time limit. The travaux preparatoires to the Visby Protocol supports that this extension of the wording contained in the Hague Rules was exactly aimed at including claims for misdelivery.[194] That misdelivery is covered by the wording of article III, rule 6, is also seemingly supported by the views of Bingham L.J. in *The Captain Gregos* which, however, did not concern a true misdelivery, but rather a conversion of part of the cargo by the carrier while en route.[195]

With regard to the temporal issue the problem is, once again, that the Hague-Visby Rules apply mandatorily, as it is normally said, from tackle to tackle, i.e. from the loading of the goods onto the ship until discharge. As misdelivery will most often occur after discharge of the goods from the ship it may be questioned whether the time bar in article III, rule 6, applies to such a misdelivery. The question is thus whether the time-bar rule differs from e.g. the rules imposing liability and applies also to post-discharge events. With the travaux preparatoires to the Visby Protocol showing that the intention behind changing the wording of the article was to include misdelivery there seems to be good reason in extending the application of the time bar to misdelivery occurring after discharge.[196]

Neither of the two questions has been decided authoritatively by the courts.[197] Apart from the question of whether the Hague-Visby Rules are apt to time bar a claim for misdelivery it is, of course, a prerequisite that the misdelivery occurs under a relationship to which the Hague-Visby Rules apply either by mandatory application or by way of a Paramount Clause. As the Hague-Visby Rules apply to contracts, the time bar would not apply to a

193 The questions are similar to those raised in part 5 regarding the applicability of the liability and limitation of liability rules of the Hague Visby Rules, i.e. one of the material scope and one of the temporal scope.

194 Treitel and Reynolds, *Carver on Bills of Lading*, p. 689. Diamond, "The Hague-Visby Rules", p. 256, especially fn 88.

195 *Compania Portorafti Commerciale S.A. v. Ultramar Panama Inc. and others (The Captain Gregos)*, [1990] 1 Lloyd's Law Reports 310, at 315.

196 Aikens, Lord, and Bools, *Bills of Lading*, para 10.94. Treitel and Reynolds, *Carver on Bills of Lading*, p. 689f. Todd, "Excluding and Limiting Liability for Misdelivery", p. 248f. Diamond, "The Hague-Visby Rules", p. 256 ("albeit with considerable doubt").

197 William Leung, "Misdelivery of Cargo without Production of Original Bill of Lading: Applicability of the Mandatory Legal Regime of Hague-Visby and the One Year Time Bar", *Journal of Maritime Law & Commerce* 39, no. 2 (2008), discusses the case law from England, Hong Kong and Australia on this issue without drawing any conclusions on the applicability.

non-party to the contract of carriage basing its claim in tort.[198] Further, it is possible that the parties in their Paramount Clause have decided on both the temporal and the material application of the Hague-Visby Rules as such or of the time bar therein, e.g. by extending the application to also cover the period after discharge.[199] Deciding the application of the time bar can thus entail difficult issues of construction of both the Hague-Visby Rules themselves and the bill of lading. It is somewhat surprising that this important issue in relation to the Hague-Visby Rules has not been more clearly decided.

13.2.5 Damages

As under Scandinavian law, the calculation of damages cannot be put into one formula but must be assessed on the facts of each case.[200] The theoretical criteria for the recovery of damages in contract and in tort differ but the practical consequence for the direct loss is very limited.[201] The normal measure of damages both in contract and in conversion will be the market value of the misdelivered goods at the place where they should have been delivered. In contract the relevant time is the time when they should have been delivered whereas in conversion it is as a starting point the time when the carrier converted the goods.[202]

It can be difficult to assess the market value if there is in reality no market in place at the place where delivery should have been made. However, this is a question of evidence and recourse may be had e.g. to the price at a different time or place.[203]

The damages must, of course, fulfil the requirements of causation and remoteness. With regard to remoteness the test is different in contract and in tort. In tort the damage must be of a kind that was a reasonably foreseeable consequence of the tortious act whereas in contract the damage must be of a kind that the defaulting party should reasonably have contemplated would flow from the breach.[204] However, it has been submitted that this

198 *Compania Portorafti Commerciale S.A. v. Ultramar Panama Inc. and others (The Captain Gregos)*, [1990] 1 Lloyd's Law Reports 310, 318. Aikens, Lord, and Bools, *Bills of Lading*, para 10.184, fn 379, and 10.367.

199 In his note to The MSC Amsterdam, Todd points to the pitfall for bill of lading drafters that inserting a clause seeking to relieve the carrier of liability altogether outside the tackle-to-tackle period (which will rarely protect the carrier against a misdelivery claim) may support a conclusion that the application of the Hague-Visby Rules has not been extended to apply outside the mandatory period, Paul Todd, "Liability for misdelivery: Trafigura v MSC", *Journal of International Maritime Law* 13 (2007): pp. 362 and 65.

200 For a detailed analysis of the issue of damages see Harvey McGregor, *McGregor on Damages*, 19th ed., The Common Law Library (London: Sweet & Maxwell, 2014), with regard to misdelivery especially Chapters 30 and 36.

201 Aikens, Lord, and Bools, *Bills of Lading*, para 13.5.

202 McGregor, *McGregor on Damages*, para 30-010 and 36-11 et seq.

203 Ibid., para 30-011.

204 Aikens, Lord, and Bools, *Bills of Lading*, para 13.4.

difference will hardly play a role in bill of lading cases because courts will take a pragmatic approach inferring on the carrier when necessary knowledge or presumed knowledge of the practices of the relevant trade which in turn infers knowledge of the possible consequences of a breach of contract.[205]

The difference may play a larger role when it comes to consequential loss.[206] The reason for this being that the remoteness test for consequential loss in conversion, where the liability is strict, seems to depend on whether the converter acted innocently or dishonestly, a factor which is of obvious relevance in connection with misdelivery. Thus, Lord Nicholls of Birkenhead in *Kuwait Airways Corp v. IAC (No. 6)* found that where the conversion is innocent the test should be one of reasonable foreseeability whereas in the case of dishonest conversion a wider test of whether the loss arose directly and naturally from the conversion should be applied.[207] In a misdelivery context this difference is very relevant as both delivery of the goods against a forged bill of lading which the carrier believes to be genuine and delivery without presentation of a bill of lading at all may constitute conversion of the goods but the remoteness test may thus differ making it easier to recover consequential loss in the latter case.[208]

14 P&I Club cover

The P&I Clubs all exclude cover for liabilities the carrier may incur by delivering goods without presentation of bills of lading, although some clubs reserve discretion to cover such liability in appropriate cases.[209] After the House of Lords' decision in the *Rafaela S*[210] most clubs changed their rules to also exclude cover when delivery is made without presentation of a straight bill of lading.[211] Carriers thus have no insurance cover of their liability for wrongful delivery.

205 Ibid.

206 The qualification of a loss as direct or consequential can sometimes be difficult. In the MSC Amsterdam, *Trafigura Beheer BV v Mediterranean Shipping Co SA*, [2007] 2 C.L.C. 379, Aikens J. had decided that the relevant value was the value of the goods at the time of judgement. In the Court of Appeal Longmore L.J. pointed out that the judge could also have chosen to award the rise in value of the goods between the time of conversion and the time of judgment as consequential damages for loss of use, para 41.

207 *Kuwait Airways Corp. v. Iraqi Airways Co.*, [2002] UKHL 19, para 99-104. McGregor, *McGregor on Damages*, para 36-070.

208 In the MSC Amsterdam, fn 206, delivery was made against a skillful forgery and Aikens J. applied the test of foreseeability, see Baughen, "Misdelivery claims under bills of lading and international conventions for the carriage of goods by sea", p. 177f.

209 Hazelwood and Semark, *P & I Clubs Law and Practice*, para 10.94.

210 *J.I. MacWilliam Co. Inc. v Mediteranean Shipping Co. S.A. (Rafaela S.)*, [2005] 1 Lloyd's Rep. 346.

211 *P & I Clubs Law and Practice*, para 10.108.

As described above, it is, especially in some trades, a widespread practice to deliver the goods without the presentation of the bill of lading but against a letter of indemnity for the liability the carrier exposes itself to by delivering without presentation of the bill of lading. Though the P&I clubs discourage the practice of delivering without presentation of the bill, to aid its members the International Group of P&I Clubs has produced a recommended wording for letters of indemnity in six versions for three different situations.[212]

15 Summing up

Unsurprisingly, the main principles pertaining to delivery of goods under bills of lading are the same under Scandinavian and English law. It is a necessity for bills of lading to play the important role in global trade that they do, that the main principles regarding their use are the same in most jurisdictions. As always, the Devil is in the detail and this is where differences occur.

Whereas the main principles are the same under English and Scandinavian law, their foundation is not. When assessing possible alternatives to the bill of lading, especially the use of electronic alternatives, which must work better in practice but still fulfil the functions of the bill of lading in global trade, it is necessary to know what the foundation of the legal effects of the use of bills of lading are.

Under English law, the main principles are based in common law, including its recognition of the customs of merchants, and legislation regarding the transfer of contractual rights and obligations as well as rules of tort and bailment. Many of the rules are based in contract (law) which gives parties to bill of lading contracts a wide margin for setting out solutions to problems that the bill of lading system creates in relation to delivery of the goods. On the other hand, the fact that the core features of bills of lading to a large extent rely on the bill of lading being recognised as a document of title at common law as a result of a custom of merchants creates challenges to the parties to find solutions because this effect will not extend to alternatives to bills of lading even if they are intended to fulfil the same functions. Thus, the parties cannot simply decide that another document or electronic alternative should be regarded as a document of title and it is unrealistic that a custom should evolve in today's complicated business world that would be recognised by the common law.

Under Scandinavian law, the main principles, although originally arising out of the same practices which have been recognised as customs under English law, are to a large extent founded on the rules of the Merchant

212 The standard forms can be downloaded from the websites of most members of the International Group, e.g. from www.skuld.com – enter search term "letter of indemnity."

Shipping Act and heavily supplemented by the rules and principles of the law pertaining to negotiable (in the strict sense) instruments. The rules of general tort law also play a role. The statutory rules are for the most part mandatory and there is thus very little room for the parties to create solutions by way of contract to the problems that exist. On the other hand, bearing in mind the Scandinavian tradition for making fairly detailed legislation and basing it to a large degree on the practices and needs of the shipping industry, such statutory rules and principles can be seen to be more easily extended to alternatives to the bill of lading and, in fact, the travaux preparatoires to the Danish Merchant Shipping Act indicate that the rules are intended to also cover electronic bills of lading.[213]

With the global nature of shipping and international trade involving the use of bills of lading any solutions sought to the problems in relation to delivery of goods must be able to function in both of these prima facie opposing systems (as well as other systems not dealt with in this book).

213 See *infra* Chapter 6, part 3.1.

4 Exemption clauses and delivery of goods

1 Introduction

The use of clauses excluding or limiting the liability of the carrier is very widespread in contracts for the carriage of goods by sea. Indeed, it was the widespread exclusion of liability of the carriers in the late nineteenth and early twentieth centuries which led to the adoption of rules at the international level regulating contracts for the carriage of goods by sea, i.e. the Hague Rules. These Rules, and subsequent international conventions in this area, also include both exclusions and limitations of the carrier's liability.

Both contractual and statutory rules excluding and limiting liability have led to difficult questions of construction over the years. Issues of construction of limitation and exclusion clauses are, of course, not unique to maritime transport and the construction of clauses in contracts for the carriage of goods by sea has evolved on the backdrop of the principles of construction of limitation and exclusion clauses in general. However, due to the widespread use of and the length of time in which such clauses have been used in contracts for maritime transport, the construction of clauses in contracts for the carriage of goods by sea has had a significant impact on the general principles of construction of such clauses, particularly in English law, but also in Scandinavian law.

As a potentially substantial liability, it would be an obvious possibility for carriers to attempt to limit or exclude the liability for misdelivery. The desirability (for carriers) of such clauses is exacerbated by the problems with bills of lading not being available at the port of destination in time which often, at least in some trades, puts carriers under substantial commercial pressure to deliver the goods without presentation of an original bill of lading.

Regulating the liability for misdelivery can take many shapes. One may attempt to contractually extend the liability regime, or more likely the limitation of liability, of the applicable international convention to also cover the delivery of the goods.[1] Another possibility is to regulate the delivery

1 Cf. Chapter 3, part 5, regarding the direct applicability of the conventions to claims for misdelivery.

procedure allowing, in certain circumstances, for delivery of the goods without presentation of a bill of lading. Instead, one might include a clause in specific terms exempting the carrier from liability or limiting said liability for misdelivery. A more common approach has, however, been to, once confronted with a claim for wrongful delivery, submit that such liability is covered by an exemption or limitation clause in general terms.

In this chapter, first a short examination of the general treatment of exemption and limitation clauses will be made. Then a more detailed analysis of the treatment of such clauses in relation to their use in bills of lading and particularly in relation to misdelivery will be performed following which an example of some specific clauses currently used in practice will be assessed. This will be followed by an assessment of the effect of clauses regulating undeliverable goods on the presentation requirement. Issues pertaining to charteparty terms obliging the owner to deliver goods without presentation of the bill of lading fall outside the scope of this book and will not be dealt with here. Further, much of the regulation of exemption clauses in general has been made in relation to consumer contracts. As consumer contracts hardly play any role in connection with bills of lading, this will not be dealt with here.

2 Construction of exemption clauses

The construction (in a broad sense) of exemption clauses is often said to be "strict" both under English and Scandinavian law. The precise content of the "strictness" is, however, more elusive,[2] but the process can draw on all parts of the "construction toolbox", i.e. principles of incorporation of terms, interpretation of the wording, implication of terms, and legislation-based "censoring".

Under Scandinavian law,[3] it is generally recognised that the distinction between interpretation of the contract and implication of terms, and even the issue of incorporation, is not very strictly adhered to by the courts who are not always very clear in stating whether the construction (in a broad

2 Kurt Grönfors, *Tolkning av fraktavtal* (Gothenburg: Sjörättsföreningen, 1989), p. 82 et seq., contains an interesting and slightly provoking analysis of the principle concluding (at p. 86) that it is mainly a justification for the judge to intervene to the benefit of the party to whose detriment the clause works ("a psychological support for the judge" (my translation)).

3 The Scandinavian countries have virtually identical contracts acts based on a collaboration over a century ago. Also the introduction in the 1980s of § 36 which gave the courts the possibility to set aside or amend unreasonable contract terms was a result of a joint Scandinavian effort, see further in part 3. Still the treatment of exemption clauses has mainly developed in case law and differences do exist between the countries. However, the similarities are so extensive that for this short introduction of the construction of exemption clauses in general, Scandinavian law will be dealt with as one.

sense) of a contract or a clause is a result of interpretation or implication,[4] and if the former, which factors have been decisive.[5] This is, at least on the theoretical level, in contrast to construction of contracts under English law where there is a stronger focus on the distinction between the interpretation of the contract within its wording and implication of terms which is subject to different conditions.

To serve as a foundation for the following parts on the application of exemption clauses to misdelivery this part provides a brief introduction to some of the general approaches of the courts to construction of exemption clauses in general.[6]

2.1 Interpretation contra proferentem

When interpreting the wording of exemption clauses, it is often said almost as self-evident that exemption clauses must be construed "contra proferentem". The principle of contra proferentem construction is recognised both as a canon of construction in English law and an interpretation "rule" in Scandinavian law (in the Scandinavian languages called "koncipistreglen", literally "the draughtsman rule"). To a large extent, they function in the same way and it is under both Scandinavian and English law that a key area of application has been exemption clauses.

This prima facie very basic principle sets out that a clause which is unclear should be interpreted disfavourably to the party who drafted it and is now relying on it. The principle thus requires that the clause is ambiguous, but in the words of David Yates "the courts are not reluctant to discover such ambiguity where to do so would permit them to remove the shield of an exclusion".[7] "Drafted" must be understood broadly and includes clauses drafted by the party's lawyer or, more relevant, introduction of a set of

4 A literal translation of the Scandinavian terms is "interpretation" and "filling-in". "Filling-in" is perhaps a better description as the process is often one of adjusting the contract to resemble the solution of the non-mandatory rules in the area in question rather than implying individual terms that the parties are assumed to have wanted to include in their contract.

5 Carsten Munk-Hansen, *Ansvarsregulering i overdragelsesaftaler* (Copenhagen: Jurist- og Økonomforbundets Forlag, 2007), p. 25. Lennart Lynge Andersen and Palle Bo Madsen, *Aftaler og mellemmænd*, 6th ed. (Copenhagen: Karnov Group, 2012), p. 225, emphasises the fact that the courts' reasoning is also limited to a certain extent by the arguments put forward by the parties as the interpretation of contracts is within the party autonomy under Danish procedural law.

6 The literature on exemption clauses and construction thereof is vast both for English and Scandinavian law. As this part is meant as a brief introduction only, no attempt is made at providing exhaustive references to this body of literature.

7 David Yates, *Exclusion Clauses in Contracts*, 2nd ed. (London: Sweet & Maxwell, 1982), p. 138.

standard terms whether drafted by the party itself or not.[8] The principle is, however, not relevant if the clause has been the subject of real negotiations and therefore cannot be seen as having been "drafted" by one party or must be seen as part of the bargain struck by the parties. Furthermore, its relevance is greatly diminished if the clause is typical in the trade in question or if the other party is aware of their common use.

2.2 The influence of negligence or intent

When construing exemption and limitation of liability clauses a classical question is whether the clause also exempts or limits liability for negligent or even intentional acts.

In Scandinavia, exemption clauses were in the middle of the twentieth century generally not accepted as applying to cases where the party seeking to rely on the clause had acted negligently.[9] That starting point has since developed so that today there is probably no assumption against an exemption clause covering acts of simple negligence.[10] The situation is different when it comes to acts done with intent or gross negligence. Thus, exemption clauses will normally not be accepted to cover such acts whether such result is obtained by interpretation of the clause or by setting it aside.[11]

The starting point that an exemption clause does not cover gross negligence may, however, not hold sway if other factors support that the clause should be accepted as comprising gross negligence. This could for instance be that the commercial relationship is in a business where exemption clauses are very common and therefore are assumed to be known by the actors in that business or if there are factors supporting that the exemption clause is part of a bargain,[12] inter alia if a set of standard terms is considered

8 The contra proferentem rule in Scandinavian law is often used in an interplay with the so-called minimum rule which sets out that if a clause which places a particular duty or obligation on one party is unclear it should be given the meaning which places the least burden on that party.

9 J. Günther Petersen, *Ansvarsfraskrivelse* (Copenhagen: Ejnar Munksgaards Forlag, 1957), p. 139 et seq., especially p. 45. This was at least the starting point in Denmark. In Norway, the starting point may in fact have been the opposite based on a Supreme Court verdict from 1948, Rt. 1948.370, on the basis of which it was claimed that any liability could be contractually exempted except liability for acts done intentionally or with gross negligence by the proferens himself, see Viggo Hagstrøm, *Obligasjonsrett*, 2nd ed. (Oslo: Universitetsforlaget, 2011), p. 644 et seq. The approach of the two countries now seem to have neared each other.

10 Vibe Ulfbeck, "Fortolkning af ansvarsfraskrivelser", in *Avtalslagen 90 år*, ed. Boel Flodgren *et al.* (Stockholm: Norstedts Juridik AB, 2005), pp 486ff and 92, states that this is at least probably so within maritime law whereas clearer wording may be required in other types of contracts.

11 Andersen and Madsen, *Aftaler og mellemmænd*, p. 344. Ulfbeck, "Fortolkning af ansvarsfraskrivelser", pp 483f., 88f, and 92f. Hagstrøm, *Obligasjonsrett*, pp. 652ff and 68ff.

12 Andersen and Madsen, *Aftaler og mellemmænd*, p. 360.

to be an "agreed document". Thus, the Danish Supreme Court in UfR 2005.2438 ruled that the limitation of liability clause found in the General Conditions of the Nordic Association of Freight Forwarders (NSAB)[13] § 5 was to be understood literally so that the benefit of limitation would only be lost if the carrier had acted with intent; not if the carrier had only acted with gross negligence. In UfR 2006.632, the Supreme Court further ruled that the same clause should not be modified or set aside as unreasonable under § 36 of the Contracts Act.[14] In the latter case, the Supreme Court placed emphasis on the fact that the NSAB was considered to be an agreed document and that the limitation of liability clause was part of the bargain struck therein.[15] Still today, it must be assumed that an exemption clause to cover acts done with intent must be extremely clear in its wording to that effect and it would, it is submitted, be very likely to be set aside under § 36 of the Contracts Act.[16]

Under English law, it has also been a recurrent question whether an exemption clause excludes liability for negligence and deliberate acts. With respect to negligence it seems well-established that clear words are required[17] and this may even be the case where the exemption clause is individually drafted.[18] The landmark case in this respect is the *Canada Steamship* case.[19] In that case, Lord Henry of Morton set up three principles for construing exemption clauses in relation to negligence; 1. If the clause expressly exempts the proferens from the consequences of negligence, effect must be given to that wording; 2. If there is no express reference to negligence then the court must examine whether the words in their ordinary meaning are wide enough to cover negligence and any doubts in this respect must be construed contra proferentem; and 3. If the words are wide enough to cover negligence then the court must examine whether "the head of damage may be based on some ground other than that of negligence", and if so, then the clause should be construed as not to cover negligence.[20]

13 An English translation of the NSAB can be found at http://dasp.dk/sites/dasp.dk/files/pictures/nsab2000.uk1_.pdf.

14 *Infra* part 3.

15 In Rt. 1994.626, the Norwegian Supreme Court also upheld the NSAB limitation of liability in a case of gross negligence. Here, however, the fact that the NSAB is an agreed document did not seem to play a particularly important role, see Hagstrøm, *Obligasjonsrett*, p. 669.

16 See also *infra* at fn 64 regarding ND 1989.225. Under the Montreal Convention regarding air carriage, it is however the situation that the carrier's right to limit its liability cannot be lost even if the cargo damage is caused with intent, cf. article 22(3), cf. (5) e.c.

17 Hugh Beale, *Chitty on Contracts*, 31st ed., vol. I, The Common Law Library (London: Sweet & Maxwell, 2012), para 14-010. Edwin Peel, *Treitel's The Law of Contract*, 13th ed. (London: Sweet & Maxwell, 2011), para 7-034.

18 Gerard McMeel, *The Construction of Contracts – Interpretation, Implication, and Rectification*, 2nd ed. (Oxford: Oxford University Press, 2011), para 21.30.

19 *Canada Steamship Lines Ltd v. The King*, [1952] A.C. 192.

20 Ibid., 208.

As can be seen, the third principle only comes into play if the first principle turns out in the negative and the second principle turns out in the positive. The third principle is also the one that has been questioned the most since the Canada Steamship case while principle one and two seem generally accepted.[21] The uncertainty is that the third principle prima facie seems like an objective test which must be applied in a "mechanical" way and will give a certain answer. However, that is not so. Lord Henry of Morton himself added that the other ground for the damage "must not be so fanciful or remote that the proferens cannot be supposed to have desired protection against it"[22] and it has since been discussed how "mechanistic" the test should be applied and whether the House of Lords in *Investors' Compensation Scheme v. West Bromwich Building Society*[23] discarded with the principles as "intellectual baggage". In *HIH Casualty and General Insurance Ltd v. Chase Manhattan Bank*,[24] the House of Lords, however, cited the principles while at the same time stressing that the principles are guidelines and not a code and that the clause must be construed in its context including the commercial context of the contract. The conclusion seems to be that the third principle of Lord Henry of Morton should be seen as a helpful guideline, but must not be applied in a mechanistic way, particularly not to commercial contracts between professional parties.[25]

The need for clarity of wording is the more present if an exemption clause is to be construed so as to cover deliberate breach of the contract or personal wrongdoing.[26] In *Internet Broadcasting Corporation Ltd (t/a Nettv) v. Mar LLC (t/a Marhedge)*, the deputy High Court judge, Mr Gabriel Moss QC, stated that for an exemption clause to cover a case of deliberate, repudiatory breach involving personal wrongdoing would require "'clear' language in the sense of 'strong' language, for example, '*including deliberate repudiatory acts by [the parties to the contracts] themselves…*'."[27] Still, sufficiently clear words can exempt a party from liability for deliberate and negligent wrongdoing, and the requirement for strong words is probably less hard when it is the deliberate or negligent wrongdoing of employees or agents.[28]

21 *The Construction of Contracts – Interpretation, Implication, and Rectification*, para 21.40.

22 *Canada Steamship Lines Ltd v. The King*, [1952] A.C. 192, 208.

23 *Investors Compensation Scheme v. West Bromwich Building Society*, [1998] 1 W.L.R. 896.

24 *HIH Casualty and General Insurance Ltd v. Chase Manhattan Bank*, [2003] UKHL 6.

25 *The Construction of Contracts – Interpretation, Implication, and Rectification*, para 21.47.

26 Peel, *Treitel's The Law of Contract*, para 7-029. When it comes to gross negligence, Peel, ibid., para 7-038, points out that the concept of gross negligence has never been accepted as a concept in English law, but that it has been stated that the issue in respect of exemption clauses applying that expression is to find out the meaning of the term in the relevant clause.

27 *Internet Broadcasting Corporation Ltd (t/a Nettv) v. Mar LLC (t/a Marhedge)*, [2009] EWHC 844, para 32 and 33.

28 *Photo Productions Ltd v. Securicor Transport Ltd*, [1980] A.C. 827. McMeel, *The Construction of Contracts – Interpretation, Implication, and Rectification*, para 21.22.

2.3 Nature and basis of obligation exempted from

Two further factors increasing the need for clarity is the importance and basis of the obligation the breach of which exemption is sought for.

The interplay between and lack of clear distinction between interpretation and implication of terms in Scandinavian law is perhaps most clearly seen through the fact that the interpretation will be contrasted with the non-mandatory solution that would otherwise apply to the context in which the contract is operational. Thus, it is generally assumed that the farther the interpretation of a clause or contract argued for lies from the "normal" solution, the clearer the wording or other relevant factors to support such interpretation must be.[29]

A similar basic presumption is present in English law when it comes to the construction of exemption clauses. The presumption is that the parties by entering into a contract have intended to accept the implied obligations of that particular type of contractual relationship. Therefore an exemption clause must be construed strictly and "the degree of strictness appropriate to be applied to their construction may properly depend upon the extent to which they involve departure from the implied obligations".[30] This construction is, however, not a censorship as such by the courts of the reasonableness of the exclusion clause. In the words of Lord Diplock; "But this does not entitle the court to reject the exclusion clause, however unreasonable the court itself may think it is, if the words are clear and fairly susceptible of one meaning only."[31]

While fundamental breach as a substantive doctrine was rejected several decades ago the fundamental nature of the breach plays an important role in the construction of exemption clauses. Thus, it is a principle, normally attributed to *Glynn v. Margetson*, that a clause will not be construed in a manner which runs counter to the main object and intent of the contract.[32] This principle is of considerable importance in relation to claims for misdelivery as the obligation to deliver only against an original bill of lading is one of the most central obligations under the bill of lading contract.

The central importance of the obligation breached is also a factor in the construction of exemption clauses under Scandinavian law.[33] Thus, in U 2010.3113 the Danish Supreme Court as a seemingly decisive factor

29 Andersen and Madsen, *Aftaler og mellemmænd*, p. 343f (with further references). Munk-Hansen, *Ansvarsregulering i overdragelsesaftaler*, p. 25.

30 *Photo Productions Ltd v. Securicor Transport Ltd*, [1980] A.C. 827, 850-1 per Lord Diplock. McMeel, *The Construction of Contracts – Interpretation, Implication, and Rectification*, para 21.03. Peel, *Treitel's The Law of Contract*, para 7-026 et seq.

31 *Photo Productions Ltd v. Securicor Transport Ltd*, [1980] A.C. 827, 850-1.

32 *Glynn v Margetson & Co*, [1893] A.C. 351. Todd, "Excluding and Limiting Liability for Misdelivery", p. 250. McMeel, *The Construction of Contracts – Interpretation, Implication, and Rectification*, para 21.12 et seq.

33 Hagstrøm, *Obligasjonsrett*, p. 654 et seq. Pedersen, *Transportret*, p. 688.

amongst others placed emphasis on the fact that it was a "central contractual obligation"[34] that the security company in question had breached. The importance of this factor is assessed in an interplay with other factors such as the clarity of the wording of the clause and the degree of negligence on the breaching party.

It should be noted that under English law there is authority stating that limitation clauses should be treated with more leniency in the construction than exclusion clauses.[35] Limitation clauses must still be clearly expressed and will be interpreted contra proferentem, but not by the same exacting standards[36] and probably leaving more room for a commercial evaluation of the balance between the limitation clause and the obligation to be performed by the party and the remuneration therefore.[37] Still, this distinction cannot be applied mechanistically, for instance if the limitation amount is so low that it is tantamount to an exclusion clause.[38]

2.4 Summing up

As can be seen, many of the considerations underlying the approach taken by courts towards exemption clauses are the same in English and Scandinavian law and some of the construction "techniques" are the same while others differ. The basic approach is that exemption clauses are something which alters the division of obligations and risk which the law would otherwise subscribe and that they must therefore be construed in a limiting manner. However, the starting point differs. In English law, the starting point is that if sufficiently clearly drafted the liability for any breach of contract can be excluded through an exemption clause.[39] The only real limitation to this starting point is that the agreement must retain the

34 At p. 3122 (my translation).

35 *Photo Productions Ltd v. Securicor Transport Ltd*, [1980] A.C. 827. *Ailsa Craig Fishing Co. Ltd v. Malvern Fishing Ltd*, [1983] 1 W.L.R. 964. Referring to Ailsa Craig, Simon J. in *Bikam OOD v. Adria Cable Sarl*, [2012] EWHC 621, para 36, went so far as to say that "[n]or does any residual hostility apply to clauses which attempt to limit the liability of parties to a fixed financial amount".

36 *Ailsa Craig Fishing Co. Ltd. v. Malvern Fishing Ltd*, [1983] 1 W.L.R. 964, p. 970, per Lord Fraser of Tullybelton. Kim Lewison, *The Interpretation of Contracts*, 5th ed. (London: Sweet & Maxwell, 2011), p. 617 et seq.

37 *Ailsa Craig Fishing Co. Ltd. v. Malvern Fishing Ltd*, [1983] 1 W.L.R. 964, p. 966, per Lord Wilberforce.

38 *HIH Casualty and General Insurance Ltd v. Chase Manhattan Bank*, [2003] UKHL 6, para 63, per Lord Hoffmann. McMeel, *The Construction of Contracts – Interpretation, Implication, and Rectification*, para 21.28. Conversely, Todd, "Excluding and Limiting Liability for Misdelivery", p. 250, states that limitation clauses "could never fall foul of [the Glynn v. Margetson principle]" which suggests that they should never be treated in the same way as exclusion clauses. This seems doubtful; see the discussion *infra* part 5.1 re MSC Amsterdam.

39 Provided that the situation is outside the scope of the Unfair Contract Terms Act 1977.

characteristics of a contract, i.e. in the context of a contract of carriage that the carrier must still be obliged to do something.[40] In Scandinavian law, the starting point is that there are limits as to what can be excluded. The essence of this notion is encompassed in the Contracts Acts § 36 which give the courts the possibility to amend or set aside clauses which the courts deem unreasonable.

3 Legislation on exemption clauses

In the previous part, some of the fundamental principles of construction of exemption clauses were described. However, the validity of exemption clauses has also been heavily regulated in statute law in both Scandinavia and England.

For close to four decades, under English law, exemption clauses (in whatever shape they may come) have been regulated by the Unfair Contract Terms Act 1977.[41]

The Act applies to both commercial and consumer contracts, but the restrictions in relation to consumer contracts are more extensive.[42] For all intents and purposes the Act does not, however, apply to commercial contracts for maritime transport of goods. Thus, Schedule 1, § 2, excludes charterparties and contracts for the carriage of goods by ship or hovercraft (except for consumer contracts which play hardly any role in maritime transport). The exception is the rule in section 2(1) whereby a person cannot exclude its liability for negligence resulting in death or personal injury. The Act may still have some impact outside of its direct scope of application[43] and the content of the Act will therefore be briefly explained.

The gist of the Act is twofold; one cannot exclude or restrict liability for death or personal injury resulting from negligence;[44] and for other loss or damage the exclusion or restriction of liability is dependent upon the exemption clause[45] satisfying the "requirement of reasonableness", section 2(1) and (2).

The requirement of reasonableness in relation to contract terms is set out as "that the term shall have been a fair and reasonable one to be included having regard to the circumstances which were, or ought reasonably to have

40 Todd, "Excluding and Limiting Liability for Misdelivery", p. 249f.

41 1977 Chapter 50.

42 S. 1(3)(a) more specifically states that the act applies to "business liability, that is liability for breach of obligations or duties arising from things done or to be done by a person in the course of a business".

43 *Infra* at fn 46.

44 Negligence is defined in the Act as inter alia "breach of any obligation, arising from the express or implied terms of a contract, to take reasonable care or exercise reasonable skill in the performance of the contract; [or] of any common law duty to take reasonable care or exercise reasonable skill (but not any stricter duty)", section 1(1)(a) and (b).

45 Termed the "term or notice" in the Act.

been, known to or in the contemplation of the parties when the contract was made", section 11(1). This is further developed in Schedule 2 which sets out five factors which when relevant should be given regard in the application of the reasonableness test. These include the bargaining strength of the parties; whether the customer has received something in return for the inclusion of the exemption clause; whether the customer ought to have known of the existence and extent of the clause, including whether such clauses are a custom of the trade, Schedule 2(a)–(c).

Outside of its direct scope of application, the Act may be expected to also have an impact in two respects. First, having a means (i.e. in the shape of the Act) of openly setting aside unfair exemption clauses, courts may be less inclined to set aside or limit the application of exemption and limitation clauses in commercial contracts through a strained construction. This can be said to have led to a more realistic construction of exemption clauses in commercial contracts probably giving an effect to such clauses more resembling the intentions of the business community.[46] Second, one might expect that the factors included in the "Guidelines" in Schedule 2 of the Act may have a "spill-over" effect onto the construction of clauses not directly covered by the Act. It may be questioned, though, whether that also applies in respect of contracts of carriage by sea. The reason for excluding such contracts from the scope of the Act was that they are worldwide to a large extent entered into using standard contracts based on English law and for competition reasons it was therefore found desirable not to have different rules from the rest of the World.[47] It would seem surprising if the same principles were then introduced onto such contracts "via the back door". Accordingly, exemption clauses in bills of lading would seem to be subject to freedom of contract limited by the construction of such terms developed in the common law.

In the Scandinavian countries, there is no legislation specifically regulating contract clauses limiting or excluding liability. However, the Contracts Act § 36, which was introduced in 1975, contains a general rule whereby contract clauses may be modified or set aside on the basis of their unfairness and which has been seen as having exemption clauses as one of its main scopes of application. § 36 sets out that a contract "may be modified or set aside wholly or partly if it would be unfair or contrary to honest dealing to enforce it" (my translation). The assessment of whether the contract should be modified or set aside must "take into consideration the circumstances at the time of the contract formation, the content of the contract, and subsequent circumstances", subsection 2 (again my translation).

46 McMeel, *The Construction of Contracts – Interpretation, Implication, and Rectification*, para 21.01.

47 W.V.H. Rogers and M.G. Clarke, *The Unfair Contract Terms Act 1977* (London: Sweet & Maxwell, 1978), Annotation to Schedule 1, referring to the proceedings in the House of Lords.

The main scope of application of § 36 is consumer contracts, but it also applies to commercial contracts and it has in fact been so applied to commercial contracts, especially in Danish case law. However, there is no published case law where § 36 has been applied to a contract of carriage of goods by sea or a charterparty.[48]

Apart from its direct scope of application, the introduction of § 36 seems to have had an important impact on the construction of contracts in two ways in particular. First, the introduction legitimated what has been called the "holistic" approach to contract construction. This means that it is the effects of the contract as a whole which must be assessed, i.e. the overall allocation of rights, risks and obligations, both as they could be foreseen at the conclusion of the contract and as subsequent circumstances have turned out.[49] This latter point differs from the reasonableness test under the Unfair Contract Terms Act where it is an assessment of the reasonableness of including the clause in the contract.

Second, as with the introduction of the Unfair Contract Terms Act in England, the possibility of performing an "open" fairness censoring of contracts has diminished the need for courts to exercise a "hidden" censoring through strained constructions, including setting high bars for accepting that the parties have, in fact, agreed to include the clause in question.[50] Whether that effect can actually be documented can probably be called into doubt.

The assessment under § 36 of whether a clause or an entire contract is unfair is free and will depend entirely on the facts of the concrete case. However, the courts seem to have identified some typical factors which can trigger the application of § 36. These factors do not differ much from those comprised in the guidelines in Schedule 2 of the Unfair Contract Terms Act, and include whether the contract differs from the usual business practices of the trade, the bargaining strength of the parties, and whether there is a substantial imbalance between the parties' obligations, rights, and

48 § 36 has been argued in several cases. For instance in U 1999.1161 where the Danish Supreme Court refused to set aside a "freight prepaid and non-refundable"-clause pursuant to § 36 despite the carrier having made serious faults leading to the total loss of ship and cargo.

49 Anders Møllmann, *Certepartifortolkning – i nordisk og engelsk ret* (Copenhagen: Jurist- og Økonomforbundets Forlag, 2007), p. 90. Another sense of "the holistic approach" is also used, viz. that § 36's authority for the courts to perform an open censoring of the fairness of the contract complements the traditional means of construction by which courts have limited exemption clauses, i.e. the rules on formation of the contract, interpretation, implication of terms, rules on invalidity, and the duty of good faith in contract which is accepted as existing in Scandinavian contract law. As the courts' assessment of the contract will be performed in "one go", the court can take a holistic approach to the contract including all these aspects which can be said to concern the entire "life cycle" of the contract, ibid., p. 89 et seq.

50 Ibid., p. 89. Joseph Lookofsky, *Consequential Damages in Comparative Perspective* (Copenhagen: Jurist- og Økonomforbundets Forlag, 1989), p. 206 et seq.

risks.[51] In relation to commercial contracts, it will especially be in situations where there is a noteworthy imbalance in the parties' bargaining strength that § 36 will come into play.[52]

The two main differences between censoring of exemption clauses under the Unfair Contract Terms Act and § 36 of the Scandinavian Countries' Contracts Acts respectively are that the standard of reasonableness under the former relates to the reasonableness of including the clause based on the circumstances at the time of formation of the contract whilst the latter relate to the fairness resulting from the clause or contract as a whole including circumstances arisen after the formation of the contract and, thus, also includes how the parties seek to rely on the clause; and that the former does not apply directly to contracts of carriage of goods by sea while the latter do.

4 Exemption clauses in bills of lading

How do these principles of construction then apply to the characteristics of bills of lading and particularly in relation to clauses exempting the carrier of liability for misdelivery? In this part, some observations will be made regarding exemption clauses in general in bills of lading followed in the next parts by more detailed analyses of exemption clauses in relation to misdelivery.

Several characteristics of the bill of lading contract relationship point in opposite directions when it comes to construing exemption clauses in bills of lading.

The bill of lading is a standard form contract and is only signed by the carrier. Furthermore, it is often only the evidence of the contract of carriage rather than the contract itself and is issued after the goods have been delivered for carriage. A subsequent lawful holder of the bill will also under varying conditions become bound by the bill of lading terms without actually signing the bill.

The exemption clause itself is most often on the back of the bill of lading in small print although most carriers nowadays have the bill of lading terms and conditions readily available on their websites in easily legible format. As will be shown below, some carriers have also inserted aspects relating to the delivery obligation in the attestation clause on the front of the bill of lading.

On the other hand, exemption clauses have in some form or other been part of virtually every bill of lading form for well over a century and it must be known to anyone involved in the carriage of goods by sea that a bill of lading is bound to include some sort of exemption clause. These have,

51 Møllmann, *Certepartifortolkning – i nordisk og engelsk ret*, p. 193 et seq. (with further references).

52 Ibid., p. 194, at and in fn 13.

however, tended to be very wide in their wording and the question is therefore whether the wording is clear enough to cover e.g. liability for negligence or even deliberate acts. Over the years, the wording of such clauses have in many cases become more and more elaborate and specific – often building on case law where the wording has not been found sufficiently clear to cover the situation.

With these counterweighting factors in mind, it would seem no surprise if exemption clauses are relatively easily accepted as having been incorporated in the bill of lading contract, but with a contra proferentem construction limiting the scope of clauses drafted in wide terms. In relation to liability for misdelivery, the fundamental nature of the obligation to deliver only against an original bill of lading furthermore makes it likely that the *Glynn v. Margetson* principle[53] and the corresponding tendency in Scandinavian law[54] may be applied in the construction of clauses which are attempted set up as a defence against liability for misdelivery.

4.1 Scandinavian law

Contracts for the carriage of goods are regulated in the Merchant Shipping Acts Chapter 13.[55] The carrier's period of responsibility is based on the Hamburg Rules, article 4, and thus extends to the entire period while the goods are in the carrier's charge.[56] The rules of Chapter 13 are with few exceptions mandatory.[57] This leaves little room for exemption clauses to apply. Accordingly, in Scandinavian case law it is obvious that the mandatory nature and extent of the regulation of carriage of goods by sea in the Merchant Shipping Acts, Chapter 13, plays a crucial part in establishing the effectiveness of exemption clauses in bills of lading.[58] Cases really dealing with the construction of the exemption clause in ocean bills of lading are quite rare.[59] Instead, some cases on exemption clauses in multimodal bills

53 *Supra* fn 32.

54 *Supra* fn 33.

55 *Supra* Chapter 3, part 3.1.

56 § 274.

57 § 254.

58 Recent Supreme Court cases from Denmark regarding inter alia exemption clauses have, thus, not turned on a construction of the clauses, but on an interpretation of whether the incident happened inside or outside the mandatory period of responsibility, see U 2011.271. In that case a bill of lading had, in fact, not been issued and the exemption clause was in a framework agreement between the parties. However, the same rules are directly applicable if a bill of lading is issued.

59 Prior to the Merchant Shipping Acts of 1994, the mandatory period of responsibility was limited to the "tackle-to-tackle"-principle. The case law relating to this legislation, however, also to a very large extent turned on whether the damage occurred inside or outside the mandatory period of responsibility rather than on construction of the exemption clause itself. There are a few more cases regarding through bills of lading. With some reservations regarding the special nature of multimodal transports, the principles of those cases can be applied to ocean bills of lading.

of lading can serve as indications of how the courts construe exemption clauses in bills of lading.

One example of the restrictive approach towards exemption clauses can be seen in the judgment of the Maritime and Commercial Court of Copenhagen in U 1981.216. Here, a carrier had issued a through bill of lading on a "CONLINETHRUBILL". Damage occurred during the on-carriage by truck and the carrier sought to rely on a clause relieving the carrier of liability for damage occurring after the discharge from the vessel. The Maritime and Commercial Court simply stated that "No clause in the bill of lading concerned is deemed to be able to lead to exemption from liability or limitation of [the carrier's] liability".[60]

In U 1996.895, the Danish Supreme Court considered a cargo claim regarding a deck cargo of timber.[61] The bills of lading contained both a typed exemption clause for deck cargo next to the description of the cargo on the front and standard clauses excluding liability for deck cargo on the back. A majority of three judges found in favour of the carrier on the grounds that they considered that the carrier had proved that it had not acted negligently and, thus, did not consider the exemption clauses. A minority of two judges, without mentioning the question of negligence, found that the exemption clauses were applicable and would protect the carrier. The two judges first stated that the carrier had "sufficiently clearly and unambiguously" excluded its liability for deck cargo.[62] They then went on to say that nothing in the proven facts regarding the loading, stowing or transport showed "circumstances that could warrant that the exemption clause could not apply".[63] They did not elaborate on what such circumstances could have been.

It is likely that the circumstances, which could have been relevant, are the same as were more elaborately discussed in a published Norwegian arbitration award that also concerned an exemption clause for deck cargo.[64] The case concerned a contract of carriage where the carrier had undertaken to carry two port cranes on the carrier's own "seagoing pontoon" which was to be towed by a named tugboat owned and operated by an independent contractor. The tug and tow were lost in rough weather

60 At p. 290 (my translation). For a more lenient approach by the same court, see U 1983.576, where the court accepted a similar clause in a through bill of lading because the parties had had prior dealings on the same terms and the merchant therefore was bound by the terms even though they only were part of a bill of lading to which the contract of affreightment referred.

61 Under the pre-1994 Merchant Shipping Act, it was possible to exclude liability for deck cargo. This is not possible under the current Merchant Shipping Act. It was the pre-1994 Act which was applicable in the case.

62 At p. 906 (my translation).

63 Ibid. (my translation).

64 ND 1989.225. The tribunal consisted of professor Sjur Brækhus, Norwegian Supreme Court judge Jan F. Halvorsen and attorney Ole Lund.

and the cause was found to be insufficient power in the tugboat. The tribunal first stated that the exemption clause was "clear and absolute" and refused to interpret it narrowly, i.e. to only cover damage which resulted from the cargo being carried on deck.[65] Any "censoring" of the clause should be made openly.[66] The tribunal then stated that it was a firm Norwegian rule that a contract party could not exclude liability for its own breach of contract done with intent or gross negligence.[67] When the contract party is a company, this also applies to the actions of high-level employees and directors, but the question was whether this rule also applies to the high-level employees and directors of independent contractors. The tribunal found that it did – at least when the contractor is contracted to perform central parts of the contract. Finally, the tribunal analysed whether the clause should be set aside as unreasonable pursuant to the Contracts Act § 36 which the tribunal rejected.[68] In this connection, the tribunal stressed that the contract was between professional parties of equal bargaining strength and that the exclusion of liability was for a risk which could be insured by either party. The carrier had in its offer immediately after the exemption clause noted that the cargo was to be insured by the shipper.

4.2 English law

Under English law, the case law on construction of exemption clauses in bills of lading is much more extensive. A couple of quite recent cases may be mentioned.

In the *Tasman Discoverer*,[69] the Privy Council had to construe a limitation clause in a bill of lading. The Hague Rules were contractually incorporated into the bill of lading. The incorporation clause contained a further part which stated that "for the purpose of this sub-paragraph the limitation of liability under the Hague Rules shall be deemed to be" £100 sterling in paper money per package.[70] Lord Bingham of Cornhill, delivering the advice of the Privy Council, first reiterated the "general rule" that if a party wishes "to exclude or limit his liability or to rely on an exemption, he must do so in clear words; unclear words do not suffice; any ambiguity or lack of clarity must be resolved against that party".[71] His Lordship went on to say "[t]here may reasonably be attributed to the parties to a contract such as this such general commercial knowledge as a party to such a transaction

65 At para 5.22.
66 Ibid.
67 At para 5.23.
68 At para 5.24.
69 *Dairy Containers Ltd v. Tasman Orient Line CV*, [2005] 1 W.L.R. 215.
70 Clause 6(B)(b)(i) as referred ibid., para 7.
71 Ibid., para 12.

would ordinarily be expected to have, but with a printed form of contract, negotiable by one holder to another, no inference may be drawn as to the knowledge or intention of any particular party".[72] The Privy Council found that the purpose of the clause was clear and that it could only be given one meaning, namely to alter the limit of liability in the Hague Rules. It was thus upheld.

In *The Irbenskiy Proliv*,[73] the extent and interplay of contra proferentem construction and the *Glynn v. Margetson* principle[74] were at issue. The case concerned a cargo damage claim and the carrier sought to rely on a very wide and somewhat repetitious exemption clause. The claimants submitted that the exemption clause was so wide as to leave the holder of the bill of lading with no remedy for any breach of contract by the carrier and that it was therefore repugnant to the main object of the contract. Ian Glick QC, sitting as deputy High Court judge, applied the *Glynn v. Margetson* principle stating that "[i]f to give words in a contract, 'their full and complete meaning', would produce a result at odds with the main object of the contract then [...] the court will put upon those words a restricted meaning".[75] Furthermore, the contra proferentem principle should not be extended to construing a clause as wide as possible so as to be able to find that it is repugnant to the main object of the contract.[76] HHJ Glick found that the clause shifted most risks to the holder of the bill, but not all, e.g. not for loss as a result of the carrier's dishonesty, and that this was not inconsistent with the purpose of a commercial contract because the bearer of risks can insure against them.[77]

4.3 Summing up

As can be seen, there is considerable resemblance in the methods applied and factors deemed relevant in the construction of exemption clauses in England and Scandinavia and yet there are considerable differences. One major difference is the mandatory legislation which is much wider both in terms of the issues regulated and of scope of application. This leaves much less room for contractual exclusion and limitation of liability under Scandinavian law. A derivative effect of this fact, combined with the fact that the Scandinavian countries do not enjoy the same popularity as forum of choice as England, is that there is much less case law on the construction of exemption clauses in bills of lading.

72 Ibid.
73 *Mitsubishi Corporation v. Eastwind Transport Ltd (The Irbenskiy Proliv)*, [2004] EWHC 2924.
74 *Supra* at fn 32.
75 *Mitsubishi Corporation v. Eastwind Transport Ltd (The Irbenskiy Proliv)*, [2004] EWHC 2924, para 28–29.
76 Ibid., para 33.
77 Ibid., para 31.

An interesting observation is also that despite the different approach normally taken under English law to the construction of limitation and exclusion clauses respectively, the distinction does not seem to play a particularly big role in the construction of such clauses in bills of lading despite the fact that it is an area where both exclusions and limitations are widely used both in legislation and contractually.

5 Generally worded exemption and limitation clauses in cases of misdelivery

With any bill of lading almost inevitably containing some variation of a clause limiting liability for the carrier or exempting the carrier of liability the question arises whether such clause also applies to liability for misdelivery. The answer will, of course, depend on the nature and content of the individual clause. Often the exemption clause is set out in one of the following ways. One way is to limit the carrier's liability temporally from tackle-to-tackle. Another is to extend the Hague (Visby) Rules' limits of liability to all claims. A third is to exempt the carrier from any liability as wide as possible. They share the characteristic that they are general in their terms and, thus, not specifically aimed at liability for misdelivery. Yet such clauses have been claimed by carriers as a defence against claims for misdelivery.[78] That situation is analysed in this part. In the following part, the situation where more specifically worded clauses have been set up as a defence will be examined.

5.1 English law

The leading case on this issue is the decision of the Privy Council in *Sze Hai Tong Bank Ltd. v Rambler Cycling Co. Ltd.*[79] There, the carrier's agent delivered the goods intentionally without presentation of an original bill of lading, but rather against a letter of indemnity.[80] The nature of the agency

78 Todd, *Maritime Fraud and Piracy*, p. 172, like here states that carriers have normally relied on wide but unspecific wording.

79 [1959] AC 576.

80 Mention should also be made of *Chartered Bank of India, Australia, and China v. British India Steam Navigation Company Ltd.*, [1909] AC 369. There the Privy Council accepted that a Cesser of Liability Clause which purported to exempt the carrier of all liability after the goods were free of the ship's tackle applied to a situation where the goods were delivered without presentation of the bill of lading. This case was distinguished by the Privy Council in the Sze Hai Tong Bank case on the grounds that the misdelivery was performed by a fraudulent servant whose actions could not be imputed to the carrier, [1959] AC 576, at p. 588. It has been suggested that today a generally worded exemption clause would not be accepted as comprising a deliberate breach performed by a servant or employee, see Beale, *Chitty on Contracts*, I, para 14-016, fn 113. See also Rix J's comment in the *Motis Exports case*, [1999] 1 Lloyd's Rep. 837, at p. 846, that "Chartered Bank has not appeared to have been influential".

and the delivery was such that the delivery was to be treated as if performed by the carrier itself and not as a matter of vicarious liability.[81] The clause in the bill of lading on which the carrier sought to rely had the following content;

> "During the period before the goods are loaded on or after they are discharged from the ship on which they are carried by sea, the following terms and conditions shall apply to the exclusion of any other provisions in this bill of lading that may be inconsistent therewith, viz., (a) so long as the goods remain in the actual custody of the carrier or his servants" (here follows a specified exception); "(b) whilst the goods are being transported to or from the ship" (here follows another specified exemption); "(c) in all other cases the responsibility of the carrier, whether as carrier or as custodian or bailee of the goods, shall be deemed to commence only when the goods are loaded on the ship and to cease absolutely after they are discharged therefrom."[82]

Lord Denning in his famous speech started by stating that the wording of the clause could hardly be more comprehensive and could cover a situation as the one at hand, i.e. delivery of the goods to someone whom the carrier knew was not entitled to them. He immediately went on to say that if that was the proper construction of the clause, it would seem it should also cover situations where the carrier gave the goods away to some passer-by, burnt them or threw them into the sea.[83] Such an effect could not have been the intention of the parties and there was therefore an implied limitation on the clause. Lord Denning went on to support such limitation on the principle in *Glynn v Margetson*[84] stating that the clause must be "limited and modified to the extent necessary to enable effect to be given to the main object and intent of the contract" one of which were the proper delivery of the goods by the shipping company.[85] Asking the rhetorical question how far the clause had to be limited or modified, Lord Denning answered that it should "at least be modified so as not to permit the shipping company *deliberately* to disregard its obligations as to delivery" (italics added).[86] Consequently the shipping company's contention was rejected.

In a more recent case, the *Motis Exports* case,[87] the carrier had misdelivered the goods unintentionally against presentation of forged bills of

81 [1959] AC 576, at p. 588.
82 [1959] AC 576, at p. 586.
83 [1959] AC 576, at p. 586f.
84 *Supra* at fn 32.
85 [1959] AC 576, at p. 587.
86 Ibid.
87 *Motis Exports Ltd. v Dampskibsselskabet af 1912 A/S (No. 1)*, [1999] 1 Lloyd's Rep 837 (QB), [2000] 1 Lloyd's Rep. 211 (CA), discussed *supra* Chapter 3, part 9.1, in relation to the risk of delivering against forged bills of lading.

lading. The carrier again sought to rely on a clause which purported to limit the carrier's potential liability temporally by excluding liability outside the period while the goods were on board the vessel (i.e. tackle-to-tackle);

> 5. CARRIER'S RESPONSIBILITY
> …3. Carriage to and from Countries other than USA…
> (b) Where the carriage called for commences at the port of loading and/or finishes at the port of discharge, the carrier shall have no liability whatsoever for any loss or damage to the goods while in its actual or constructive possession before loading or after discharge over ship's rail, or if applicable, on the ship's ramp, however caused.

That contention was not successful. The language was wide enough to be apt to include liability for misdelivery, but a natural reading of it would not include such liability. In establishing the natural meaning of the clause it was relevant that the meaning contended for would go against the main object and intent of the contract, cf. *Glynn v Margetson.*[88] Furthermore, the clause would have adequate content even if it was not accepted that it covered misdelivery.[89] Thus, Lord Justice Stuart-Smith considered that the clause would cover loss or damage caused by fire, flood or other perils, and also would cover theft of the goods without the consent of the bailee,[90] and Lord Justice Mance also considered that the clause was concerned with responsibility for physical perils.[91] Consequently, the carrier could not rely on the exemption clause to cover the misdelivery. The fact that the carrier did not misdeliver the goods with intention to do so, but was deceived to do so, did not bring the misdelivery within the ambit of the clause.

In the *MSC Amsterdam*,[92] the situation was also that the carrier had been deceived to deliver the goods against forged bills of lading. The carrier conceded that two clauses which in quite detailed terms, but without mention of misdelivery, sought to limit the carrier's liability to the tackle-to-tackle period did not relieve the carrier of liability for misdelivery. Lord Justice Longmore noted that the concession was based on the long line of authority saying that "very clear words are required to exclude such a serious breach of duty".[93] Instead, the carrier sought to rely on a clause which

88 *Supra* at fn 32.

89 Stuart-Smith L.J. at para 20.

90 At para 13.

91 At para 6.

92 *Trafigura Beheer BV v. Mediterranean Shipping Co. SA*, [2007] EWCA Civ 794, [2007] 2 C.L.C. 379, [2007] 2 Lloyd's Rep. 622.

93 His lordship referred to Glynn, *Mills Currie & Co. v. East and West India Dock Co.*, *The Stettin*, *Sze Hai Tong Bank Ltd v. Rambler Cycle Co. Ltd.*, and the Motis Exports case, [2007] 2 C.L.C. 379, at para 29 et seq.

on its face extended the limitation of liability in the Hague or Hague-Visby Rules to all claims against the carrier. The relevant part, however, was found in a long clause regulating several different subjects;

> 22. CLAIMS VALUATION, PACKAGE LIMITATION TIME-BAR. The indemnity payable by the Carrier for non-delivery of the cargo in whole or in part is calculated at the option of the Carrier on the basis of the invoice value or on the basis of market values at destination, less duties and expenses saved due to the shortage, except in USA jurisdiction where the sound market value at destination shall be considered. In any event the Carrier's liability shall not exceed the usual sound market value of the goods at the time and place of shipment. However, should the invoice value of the goods be lower than the usual sound market value at the time and place of shipment, the Carrier will only pay the invoice value. For lack of any usual sound market value or invoice value, this provision shall apply to the common value accordingly. *Neither the Carrier nor the ship shall in any event be or become liable for any loss or damage to or in connection with goods in an amount exceeding the limitation allowed under the Hague Rules or the Hague-Visby Rules /SDR limitation or the COGSA limitation, depending on which of these is contractually or compulsorily applicable, per package or unit, unless the nature and the value of such goods have been declared by the Merchant before shipment and inserted in the Bill of Lading.* However, declaration of value for the purpose of calculation of freight shall not be considered a declaration in the above sense. *This limitation of liability shall apply to all contractual claims as well as to any claims arising from other causes.* In so far as goods are shipped to or from the United States, the Carrier's liability shall be limited to $500 per package or customary freight unless excess value is inserted on the face hereof and extra charge paid. The words 'customary freight unit' shall mean (under COGSA) the unit of weight or measurement customarily used to calculate freight. Where the goods have been packed into sealed containers by or on behalf of the Merchant, it is expressly agreed that each container shall constitute one package for the purpose of application of limitation of the Carrier's liability, since the Carrier cannot verify its contents. If the Merchant has a shortage in goods or numbers shipped under a Bill of Lading, the Carrier shall have the option to deliver as substitute any surplus goods of similar kind or quality. Notice in writing of loss or damage must be given to the Carrier's Agent at the Port of Discharge or Final Destination, promptly after delivery of the goods, and in any case within 3 running days from the date of delivery as defined in Clause 7, and the Carrier to be invited to participate, at his option, in a joint survey. The cargo is otherwise prima facie considered delivered by the Carrier in the same condition as described in the B/L. Claims are to be addressed to the MSC Agent supported by, at least, the following documents: claim narrative

> identifying clearly the claimant and providing evidence on his title to sue, Original B/L Commercial Invoice of damaged goods, Letter of Subrogation, if any, survey reports. In any event, the Carrier shall be discharged from all liability if suit is not commenced within one year after delivery of the goods or the date that the goods should have been delivered, for claim related to loss or damage during the carriage by sea and nine months for claims related to loss or damage during non-water inland port [sic: probably 'non-water transport' is intended]. Agreed claims will be settled by the carrier only once with one of the parties that is entitled to sue, i.e. with the Shippers POL or with the Consignees at the POD, but not with both. Settlement of an agreed claim by the Carrier with either of the above discharges the Carrier from all and any liability for the same loss or damage under this B/L. (not in italics in original)[94]

It was the two sentences set out in italics which the carrier sought to rely on. Thus, it was not an exclusion clause, but rather a clause making the limitation rules of the Hague Rules applicable. Lord Justice Longmore, with whom Lords Justices Tuckey and Lloyd agreed, found it "so unlikely as not to be the case" that it was "the intention of the parties that liability for the failure to perform obligations of such importance as the obligation to deliver the goods against presentation of a properly indorsed original bill of lading should be limited by sentences buried within a clause of such length and complexity".[95] As in the *Motis Exports* case, Lord Justice Longmore went on to say that the clause could be given another meaning and, quoting Lord Justice Mance in that case, that the carrier's construction of the clause "appear to undervalue the importance which both parties must be taken to have attached to the ship's obligation to deliver against presentation of original bills of lading".[96]

The three cases thus deal with three different types of clauses; one temporal limitation of the period of responsibility, one general exclusion of liability and one numerical limitation of liability. However, all of them were set out in general terms and did not mention liability for misdelivery. Furthermore, the situations differ on the subjective intent of the carrier. In the *Sze Hai Tong Bank* case, the carrier intentionally delivered the goods without the presentation of the bill of lading as so often happens in practice, whereas the carriers in both the *Motis Exports* case and the *MSC Amsterdam* case were deceived by fraudsters who presented forged bills of lading. Thus, the carriers in those cases did not intend to deliver without presentation of the bill of lading.

94 Set out in extenso in the judgment of Lord Justice Longmore, para 33.

95 Para 35 and 34.

96 Para 37.

These authorities all show that very clear words are needed to relieve the carrier of all or part of its liability for misdelivery. This is irrespective of whether it is a total exemption of liability, a temporal limitation of the carrier's period of responsibility (i.e. excluding the post-discharge delivery of the goods), or an amount limitation of that liability. In the two former cases, this has been further supported by the authority of *Glynn v. Margetson*[97] whereas that authority has not been directly cited in the latter case. In fact, it has been stated that the *Glynn v. Margetson* principle is not applicable to clauses which merely limit liability.[98] However, in the *MSC Amsterdam*, very similar arguments were used in relation to the limitation clause stressing that it was a limitation of liability "for the essential obligation to deliver against original bills of lading"[99] and citing Lord Justice Mance in the *Motis Exports* case where he stated that the construction contended for would "appear to undervalue the importance which both parties must be taken to have attached to the ship's obligation to deliver against presentation of original bills of lading".[100] Thus, it seems that much emphasis is also placed on the delivery obligation's importance as a main obligation of the contract in relation to clauses limiting liability rather than excluding it.

Further, the requirement of very clear words applies both to situations where the clause in question is set up as a defence against a deliberate delivery without presentation of an original bill of lading and where the delivery without presentation is not made deliberately, e.g. where the carrier is deceived by fraudsters. Based on the courts' general approach to construction of exemption clauses in respect to negligent and deliberate acts one might still expect that the requirement for clarity will be even more exacting for a clause to comprise deliberate acts.

It is noteworthy that the dispensing of the various generally worded clauses as defences to misdelivery claims only to a limited extent is made using the "ordinary tools" used for limiting the effect of exemption and limitation clauses.[101] Thus, common canons of construction such as the contra proferentem and "individual clauses before standard clauses" as well as requirements of notification play only a very limited role in these cases. Instead, the main emphasis has been placed on the centrality of the delivery obligation and the consequent need for clear words to avoid liability for breach thereof, as described above. An attempt to explain this fact must be speculative, but it may be due to the fact that exemption and limitation of liability clauses are so common in bills of lading that requiring clear notification of a generally worded exemption clause seems unnecessary. Instead

97 *Supra* at fn 32.
98 Todd, "Excluding and Limiting Liability for Misdelivery", p. 250.
99 [2007] 2 C.L.C. 379, at para 37.
100 Ibid.
101 *Supra* part 2.

a limiting construction of the clause seems more natural and the effect of such a construction is the same as an application of the contra proferentem canon of construction would have even if this canon is not specifically mentioned in the construction.

5.2 Scandinavian law

In Scandinavia, there does not seem to be any relatively recent reported cases where a generally worded exemption or limitation clause has been attempted relied upon as defence against a claim for misdelivery. This question has, however, been at issue in some older Norwegian cases. These cases are from before the current Merchant Shipping Acts, but the principles are still of interest.[102]

In ND 1923.641, the Norwegian Supreme Court had to decide whether a generally worded limitation clause applied to a case of misdelivery. The clause sought to be relied on had the following wording;

> The carriers' liability in case of loss or detention or damage to goods for which they might be responsible shall be calculated on the basis of and in no case exceed the invoice's net price...
>
> (my translation from Norwegian)

The case concerned a consignment of coffee from Java to Stavanger, Norway, with transhipment in Oslo, Norway. The correct number of bags (125) were transhipped and arrived in Stavanger, but only four of these had the correct marks and the consignee refused the other bags and claimed damages for the market price of the coffee which was higher than the invoice price. The most likely reason for the fault was that the Stavanger-consignment had inadvertently been delivered to receivers of coffee in Oslo. The carrier accepted liability, but only up to the amount of the invoice's net price in accordance with the limitation clause set out above. The Maritime Court stated that as between the owner of the cargo and the ship, the cargo must be considered lost and the applicability of the clause did not seem to depend upon how that loss occurred. The Supreme Court upheld the judgment of the Maritime Court but reasoned this by saying that the clause was applicable in a case such as this where it was an inadvertent misdelivery and there were no questions of deceit being committed. The generally worded limitation clause was thus applied to the loss due to misdelivery.

102 This section will deal with the construction of generally worded clauses. Whether clauses exempting or limiting liability for misdelivery even in the clearest words can in fact be upheld or are contrary to mandatory legislation will be dealt with below in part 6.2.

In a lower court case from 1930, ND 1930.291, the City Court of Bergen had to decide on the applicability of a clause which, like the one in the above-mentioned case, limited liability to the invoice value of the goods in a case where the goods had deliberately been delivered without presentation of the bill of lading, but rather against a bank guarantee. The court stated that the misdelivery was a deliberate breach of contract and that exemption clauses as well as limitation clauses could not be set up against deliberate breaches. The court's reasoning is quite unclear and has been criticised, while the result has been found to be correct.[103] The judgment is in line with a lower court case from 1925.[104]

In a more recent case, the Maritime and Commercial Court of Copenhagen made a statement on the necessity of clarity in exemption clauses. The case, ND 1995.109, concerned a clause which purported to regulate the situation where goods are not claimed in time by the consignee.[105] It is important to note that the regulation in the Merchant Shipping Acts of the situation where goods are not claimed is specifically non-mandatory and can thus be derogated from by agreement. The carrier warehoused the goods, but failed in two ways. The carrier did not notify the consignee of the warehousing, which it would be obligated to do under the Merchant Shipping Act, and the goods were later released from the warehouse without presentation of the bill of lading. The Maritime and Commercial Court stated that the invoked clauses were far-reaching derogations from the Merchant Shipping Act's rules on bills of lading and then stressed that "[i]n the interest of secure performance of maritime transports it must be required that such derogations are clear and unequivocal" (my translation).[106]

103 Brækhus, "Bortfrakterens ansvar for utlevering av last til ulegitimert mottager", p. 345f.

104 In that case, ND 1925.484, the City Court of Oslo decided on the applicability of an exemption clause to a deliberate misdelivery. The consignment of almonds had been delivered without presentation of the bill of lading, but against a bank guarantee. The bill of lading was not taken up by the consignee and the shipper therefore claimed damages from the carrier. The carrier sought to rely on a clause which purported to exclude liability for any damage as a result of fault or neglect by the ship's captain. The court found that the clause was only aimed at liability for damage to goods and thus not applicable to the situation at hand. Another case from the time which can be mentioned is ND 1927.364 City Court of Oslo. The consignment was not carried under a bill of lading, but rather a type of waybill used in the coastal trade of Norway. The consignment had been delivered contrary to the delivery instructions and against a guarantee. The carrier sought to rely on a notification requirement in the waybill. The court found that despite the clause being unclear, it had to be understood to apply to cases where the goods were damaged or lost and this was not the case in a situation like the one at hand where the carrier had purposely disregarded the instruction. The decision was upheld by the Supreme Court, but on different grounds, ND 1930.1.

105 It is therefore analysed in further detail *infra* part 7.2.

106 ND 1995.109, p. 114.

The Maritime and Commercial Court thus stressed the need for clarity when attempting to exempt or limit liability for misdelivery. As the case concerned a case where the goods were undeliverable, it cannot necessarily be concluded e contrario that sufficiently clear wording can relieve the carrier of liability for other misdelivery.

In summing up, the older verdicts seem to place heavy emphasis in the construction of the generally worded exemption or limitation clauses on whether the misdelivery of the goods was made deliberately or not. It is interesting that the Norwegian Supreme Court was willing in 1923 to apply a generally worded limitation clause to a case of misdelivery as long as the misdelivery was made unintentionally. This is in stark contrast to the rulings in the *Motis Exports* and the *MSC Amsterdam* cases[107] where the fact that the carriers were deceived by fraudsters did not have any impact on the construction of the generally worded exemption and limitation clauses. It seems more in line with the contemporary *Chartered Bank of India* case.[108] It must be noted that it is from the time before the Hague Rules were adopted and thus from a time when freedom of contract ruled much more than today in Scandinavia. Further, the limitation clause did not limit liability to an unreasonably low amount, but rather to the amount the claimant had in fact paid for misdelivered goods.

By contrast, the other above-mentioned older cases show that generally worded exemption or limitation clauses would not be construed so as to apply to deliberate misdelivery and this seems to still hold true based on the 1995 judgment of the Maritime and Commercial Court of Copenhagen where it was specifically stated that clear and unequivocal clauses would be required. Whether clear and unequivocal language is enough to absolve the carrier of liability will be discussed in the following part.

6 Specifically worded clauses

In the previous part, it was shown that generally worded exemption and limitation clauses have (with very few exceptions) not been accepted by the judiciary as applying to cases of misdelivery; the courts often stating that exempting of or limiting liability in such circumstances would require a clause in very clear terms. In this part, analyses will be made of some situations where clear words are used. This will include analyses of the limited case law and some currently used bill of lading terms. The latter is meant to serve as an example showing the difficulties in drafting and construing such clauses.

107 *Supra* part 5.1.
108 *Supra* fn 80.

6.1 Case law

There are very few cases where clauses specifically mentioning misdelivery have been under scrutiny. One case often referred to is the *New York Star*.[109] In that case, however, it is not completely clear which of several clauses in the bill of lading that kept the stevedoring company who had misdelivered the goods from being held liable.

A consignment of 37 cartons of razor blades had been carried on the *New York Star* from St John, New Brunswick, to Sydney. At Sydney the goods were discharged by stevedores employed by the carrier's agent and put into storage from which they were later released by carrier's employees to thieves without presentation of the bill of lading. The bill of lading included a Himalaya clause which also included "every independent contractor from time to time employed by the carrier".

The bill of lading contained three clauses that could relieve the stevedore of liability if it could rely on the defences in the bill of lading as a result of the Himalaya clause. First, clause 17 contained a time-bar requiring suit to be brought within one year after the delivery of the goods or the date when the goods should have been delivered and the case was not brought within that time limit. Second, clause 5 contained a combined tackle-to-tackle and exemption clause. Third, clause 8 contained a delivery clause obliging the consignee to take delivery of the goods from the vessel's rail immediately the ship was ready to discharge and giving the carrier various rights of action if the consignee did not fulfil its obligations as well as relieving the carrier of liability in such circumstances. Further, clause 14 contained an exemption for liability due to fire. This was not directly applicable to the situation at hand, but the clause is set out in extenso by Lord Wilberforce as an aid in the interpretation of the interrelationship between the clauses. In this context, the interesting part is that clause 5 in addition to the more generally worded exemption included the following sentence;

> The carrier shall not be liable in any capacity whatsoever for any nondelivery or misdelivery, or loss of or damage to the goods occurring while the goods are not in the actual custody of the carrier."[110]

The question which was at issue before the Privy Council was an argument put forward by the consignee, termed by the Privy Council the "capacity" argument, namely that the loss occurred at a time when the goods had been discharged and were no longer in the custody of the carrier and that

109 *Port Jacksom Stevedoring Pty. Ltd. v. Salmond and Spraggon (Australia) Pty. Ltd.*, [1981] 1 W.L.R. 138. For instance, Longmore L.J. in the MSC Amsterdam notes that the clause in the New York Star referred to "misdelivery", *Trafigura Beheer BV v. Mediterranean Shipping Co. SA*, [2007] 2 C.L.C. 379, p. 397.

110 Set out in extenso by Lord Wilberforce, *Port Jacksom Stevedoring Pty. Ltd. v Salmond and Spraggon (Australia) Pty. Ltd.*, [1981] 1 W.L.R. 138, p. 146.

the stevedore was therefore not acting as an independent contractor performing the carrier's duties under the bill of lading but rather was acting as a bailee.[111] This question was answered on the basis of an analysis of the clauses referred above and their interrelationship. Lord Wilberforce initially stated that the construction had to be made in the light of the practice that consignees rarely take delivery at the ship's rail but will take delivery some time later from the storage where the goods have been placed. From this starting point, Lord Wilberforce went on to explain that the application of the various parts of clauses 5 and 8 would depend upon whether or not the carrier demanded that the consignee take delivery of the goods directly from the ship's rail. Lord Wilberforce concluded that had the carrier itself performed the storage of the goods, it would have done so under the contract contained in the bill of lading and thus could have relied on the defences therein. Consequently, the same applied for a stevedore employed by the carrier to perform such storage. The stevedore could therefore make use of the defences contained in the bill of lading but it seems that it was in fact the time-bar and not the exemption of liability contained in clause 5 that relieved the stevedore of liability in the concrete case. For this reason, one should probably be careful in concluding that the case shows an example of an exemption clause which has the sufficient clarity to be applicable to a case of misdelivery.[112]

With the case law showing clearly that general terms will not be enough to avoid liability for misdelivery one might expect that carriers by now would have adjusted their general terms and conditions to reflect that (if the carrier indeed wishes to exempt itself for liability for misdelivery). It is therefore interesting to look at an example of current terms and conditions.

6.2 Maersk Line's terms and conditions – an example

In the *Motis Exports* case,[113] it was Maersk Line's bill of lading terms that were under scrutiny. Maersk Line have since changed several aspects of their terms and conditions – some changes seemingly as a direct result of that case. Other shipping lines have made similar changes, including making explicit reference to misdelivery.[114] As an example of terms and conditions currently in use, an analysis of Maersk Line's terms and conditions will be made as regards liability for misdelivery. The intention is to show the many difficulties in contractually regulating the liability for misdelivery. Particular emphasis will be put on the differences under English and

111 Ibid., p. 145.

112 See also Todd, "Excluding and Limiting Liability for Misdelivery", p. 260, at fn 107.

113 *Motis Exports Ltd. v Dampskibsselskabet af 1912 A/S*, [2000] 1 Lloyd's Rep. 211. *Supra* part 5.1.

114 E.g. MSC and ZIM.

Scandinavian law as a result of the delivery obligation being regulated in mandatory statute law in Scandinavia while it is basically subject to contract law under English law. While the analysis is of Maersk Line's bill of lading terms it should thus be seen as an example of contract clauses of this type.

6.2.1 The clauses

Of importance to the delivery obligation, Maersk Line has made the following changes. First, the "attestation clause" (the preprinted text on the front just above the signature) now includes the following;

> [...] Where the bill of lading is non-negotiable the Carrier may give delivery of the goods to the named consignee upon reasonable proof of identity and without requiring surrender of an original bill of lading. Where the bill of lading is negotiable, the Merchant is obliged to surrender one original, duly endorsed, in exchange for the goods. The Carrier accepts a duty of reasonable care to check that any such document which the Merchant surrenders as a bill of lading is genuine and original. If the Carrier complies with this duty, it will be entitled to deliver the Goods against what it reasonably believes to be a genuine and original bill of lading, such delivery discharging the Carrier's delivery obligations. [...] .

Second, the general clause on the carrier's responsibility is found in clause 5. Clause 5.1 makes the Hague Rules, art. 1–8, applicable as a matter of contract for loss of or damage to the goods occurring between the time of acceptance by the carrier of custody of the goods at the port of loading and the time of the carrier tendering the goods for delivery at the port of discharge. Clause 5.2 then states;

> The carrier shall have no liability whatsoever for loss or damage to the Goods, howsoever caused, if such damage arises before acceptance by the Carrier of custody of the Goods or after the Carrier tendering the cargo for delivery. Notwithstanding the above, to the extent any applicable compulsory law provides to the contrary, the Carrier shall have the benefit of any right, defence, limitation and liberty in the Hague Rules as applied by clause 5.1 during such additional compulsory period of responsibility, notwithstanding that the loss or damage did not occur at sea.

Third, clause 10 bears the heading "Application of terms and conditions" and states;

> These Terms and Conditions shall apply in any action against the Carrier for any loss or damage whatsoever and howsoever occurring

> (and, without restricting the generality of the foregoing, including delay, late delivery and/or delivery without surrender of this bill of lading) and whether the action be founded in contract, bailment or in tort and even if the loss, damage or delay arose as a result of unseaworthiness, negligence or fundamental breach of contract.

Fourth, clause 22 obliges the Merchant to take delivery within the time specified in the Carrier's applicable tariff and gives the Carrier various rights of action if the Merchant does not do so.

The three clauses set out in extenso on their face seem to purport to influence the carrier's liability for misdelivery in four ways, namely by removing the requirement of presentation for straight bills of lading, by changing the nature of the risk of forged bills of lading being presented, by exempting the carrier of liability for misdelivery, and by making the Hague Rules' limitation of liability applicable to misdelivery. These four issues must be analysed in turn.

6.2.2 Presentation of straight bill of lading

As set out in Chapter 3, part 3, it is highly likely that under English law a straight bill of lading must be presented to obtain delivery of the goods and under Scandinavian law it certainly must. The question is whether this can be derogated from by contract and whether the attestation clause in this case is sufficiently clear to do so.

As for the latter question, it must be said that the wording very clearly dispenses with the requirement of surrender of non-negotiable bills. However, the sentence is part of a longer passage in small print. That passage, though, concerns issues which are almost always dealt with in a passage of this kind above the signature (the "attestation clause") on the front of the bill of lading. It is therefore hardly a surprise that this passage concerns important information regarding inter alia the presentation of the bill of lading.[115] Also the very placing of the text on the front of the bill of lading right above the signature must be considered as giving significance to the term. It therefore seems unlikely under both English and Scandinavian law that an interpretation of the clause in itself would take away the meaning clearly stated by the wording. What effect, if any, such a term will have on the document's status as a bill of lading will not be pursued further here.

115 While Lord Steyn and Lord Bingham in the *Rafaela S* were ready to hold that presentation of a straight bill were necessary without an express clause requiring this they did place emphasis on the fact that the attestation clause did require surrender of the bill, *J.I. MacWilliam Co. Inc. v. Mediteranean Shipping Co. S.A. (Rafaela S.)*, [2005] 1 Lloyd's Rep. 346, p. 354, para 20, per Lord Bingham and p. 59, para 45, per Lord Steyn.

As for the former question, it seems likely that the answer will differ under English and Scandinavian law. In the *Rafaela S*,[116] the straight bill of lading in question contained in the attestation clause above the signature an express requirement that the bill of lading be surrendered in exchange for the goods. However, both Lord Bingham and Lord Steyn expressed as obiter dicta that they would hold that production of the bill of lading was a necessary precondition for requiring delivery of the goods even if there were no express provision to that effect.[117] There is no mandatory legislation on the matter and there is no definitive authority either. Instead, the matter is one of contract and it therefor seems safe to conclude that a sufficiently clear clause dispensing with the requirement to produce the bill may be given effect.[118]

Under Scandinavian law, the requirement of presentation of the straight bill of lading to obtain delivery flows directly from the Merchant Shipping Acts §§ 302 and 304. These sections are mandatory pursuant to § 254(1) and contractual clauses derogating from these rules are therefore null and void. Thus, under Scandinavian law, the carrier cannot be relieved of liability for misdelivery if it has delivered the goods without presentation of a straight bill pursuant to the attestation clause set out above.[119]

6.2.3 Delivery against forged bills of lading

The attempt to change the nature of the risk of delivering against forged bills of lading can be seen as the most direct result of the *Motis Exports* case[120] and the situation which was the cause of that case. The *Motis Exports* case firmly placed the risk of delivering against forged bills on the carrier and the same would be the result under Scandinavian law.[121] The prima facie effect of this part of the attestation clause is to change the strict liability for delivering against forged bills of lading to a duty of reasonable care for the carrier to check that the bill of lading is genuine and original.[122]

The first obstacle that this attempt may meet is one of pure construction. The wording of the attestation clause requires that it is "the Merchant" who surrenders the alleged bill of lading. "Merchant" is defined in clause 1 as

116 Ibid.

117 *Supra* Chapter 3, part 3.2.

118 Girvin, "Bills of Lading and Straight Bills of Lading: Principles and Practice", p. 113, states clearly that such a clause would be contractually binding. Also in *Carriage of Goods by Sea*, p. 153f, where Girvin also raises the question whether such a clause would affect the bill of lading's status as a document of title.

119 Tiberg, "Legal qualities of transport documents", pp. 10 and 32.

120 *Motis Exports Ltd. v Dampskibsselskabet af 1912 A/S*, [2000] 1 Lloyd's Rep. 211.

121 *Supra* Chapter 3, part 9.2.

122 In the important case *Photo Productions Ltd v. Securicor Transport Ltd*, [1980] A.C. 827, the clause in question also substituted a strict liability (in casu a vicarious liability for employees' torts or wrongdoing) for a due diligence obligation. This was accepted by the House of Lords.

including "the Shipper, Holder, Consignee, Receiver of the Goods, any Person owning or entitled to the possession of the Goods or of this bill of lading and anyone acting on behalf of such Person". The person presenting a forged bill of lading could be the consignee or a person owning or entitled to the possession of the goods (or even be the shipper), but this is unlikely. It is much more likely to be fraudsters attempting to obtain delivery for criminal purposes. The question is therefore whether such person is included in the term "Receiver of the Goods". That term is not defined in the bill of lading. Nor is it a term of art. With the definition of "Merchant" including both the holder, the consignee, any person owning or entitled to possession of the goods or the bill of lading and persons acting on their behalf it must be logically inferred that a "Receiver of the goods" means someone else. It is difficult to imagine someone other than those comprised by the former categories of persons having a rightful claim to delivery of the goods. It therefore seems a natural understanding of the term "Receiver of the goods" to mean anyone claiming delivery of the goods and obtaining such delivery despite not having a right to require such delivery. A different interpretation would exclude the application of this part of the attestation clause to what must be presumed to be the core situations which the clause was intended to apply to, namely the presentation of forged bills of lading by fraudsters. It is, thus, submitted that the term "Merchant" should in this respect be interpreted so as not to exclude the application of the attestation clause to situations where someone not entitled to delivery of the goods presents a non-genuine or unoriginal bill of lading.

The next question is whether the carrier can in fact so change the risk of delivering unwittingly against forged bills of lading by a clause in the bill. In the Motis Exports case, Mr Justice Rix at first instance considered whether the carrier was in fact guilty of misdelivery when delivering against false bills of lading, i.e. whether the carrier would be discharged of its delivery obligation as a result of such delivery. He stated that if that were so it could only be by reason of an implied term. He found that such a term should not be implied as it was not necessary to do so.[123] This particular point was not taken up by the Court of Appeal, but the Court agreed that the delivery constituted a misdelivery; Lord Justice Stuart-Smith making the famous statement that a forged bill of lading is "simply a piece of paper with writing on it".[124] Here, on the other hand, there is an express term discharging the carrier of its delivery obligation when it delivers against what it with reasonable care has thought to be an original bill of lading even if it turns out to be forged. The requirements of necessity and reasonableness for implying a term to that effect, thus, do not apply.

123 [1999] 1 Lloyd's Rep. 837, p. 842.

124 *Motis Exports Ltd. v. Dampskibsselskabet af 1912 A/S*, [2000] 1 Lloyd's Rep. 211, para 20.

When construing the clause, it should first be noted that it is given a prominent place in the attestation clause on the front of the bill of lading and in direct continuation of the express requirement that an original bill of lading must be surrendered to obtain delivery of the goods.[125] While the clause changes the nature of the delivery obligation, an obligation so central to the bill of lading contract, it does not give the carrier a general discretion to deliver without presentation of the bill of lading. Nor does it generally exclude liability for misdelivery or limit such liability in general. Rather it changes the risk of the carrier not detecting that the bill of lading being presented to it is forged. It is difficult to see that such a clause runs counter to the main object and intent of the contract to such an extent that using the principle of *Glynn v. Margetson*[126] it should be given some sort of narrower interpretation. Further, the clause cannot be said to change the obligations of the carrier to such an extent that the bill of lading contract does not retain the characteristics of a contract.[127] Still clear words must be required. It is submitted that this clause lives up to that requirement. It clearly states that the carrier must only show reasonable care in checking the genuineness and originality of the bill of lading and sets out the consequence if the carrier fulfils that obligation, namely that the carrier will be discharged of its delivery obligation. Furthermore, its placement in direct continuation of the express requirement that one original bill of lading must be surrendered in exchange for the goods makes it clear, it is submitted, that it is a modification to the main rule.

It still remains to be established what the standard of reasonable care entails in this situation. This is for the courts to decide in the specific circumstances. However, taking into account the emphasis placed by Rix J. in the High Court in the Motis Exports case on the fact that it is the carrier who controls the form and substance of the bill, it seems likely that the courts will require quite a high degree of diligence on the part of the carrier.[128] This is of course speculative.

Under Scandinavian law, it is a bit more difficult to answer whether the risk of delivering against a forged bill of lading can be changed by a clause in the bill of lading. The rights and liabilities of a carrier in relation to delivery flow from the Merchant Shipping Act §§ 302–305 supplemented by an analogous application of the rules in the Act on Instruments of

125 In the MSC Amsterdam, Longmore L.J. seemed to place quite a lot of emphasis on the fact that the attestation clause expressly required surrender of an original bill of lading *Trafigura Beheer BV v. Mediterranean Shipping Co. SA*, [2007] 2 C.L.C. 379, p. 394.

126 *Glynn v. Margetson & Co.*, [1893] A.C. 351. See *supra* at fn 32.

127 Todd, "Excluding and Limiting Liability for Misdelivery", p. 249, where Todd mentions this as one of two caveats to the starting point that it is possible to exclude or limit liability for the most serious breaches of contract – the other caveat being the *Glynn v. Margetson* principle.

128 [1999] 1 Lloyd's Rep. 837, at p. 843.

debt.[129] Thus, the Merchant Shipping Act § 302 sets out that a person who presents a bill of lading and appears to be the rightful holder of it is legitimated as consignee of the goods. What this legitimation entails must, however, be established on the basis of the general principles applying to negotiable instruments and specifically the rules in the Act on Instruments of debt. With regard to whether the carrier will obtain a good discharge, it is what is referred to as the "passive" legitimation function which is relevant, i.e. whether the real debtor is discharged by performing in good faith to the person legitimated by the document.[130] While the precise content of the legitimation function must be derived from an interplay between the rules, it may, however, safely be stated that the basic requirement that the bill of lading must be presented for legitimation in any form to arise is set out in § 302 and this paragraph refers to a genuine bill of lading even if the indorsements may in some instances objectively be false without this fact removing the legitimation function. As stated above, § 302 is mandatory and thus cannot be derogated from by agreement. It may be objected that the wording of § 302 seems mainly directed at the "active" legitimation function, i.e. the holder's right to claim delivery, but it is a necessary inference from this that the carrier cannot obtain a good discharge by delivering against a forged bill of lading as this would in effect circumvent the functioning of § 302.[131] In conclusion, it is the (passive) legitimation function which gives the carrier a good discharge and such legitimation arises from the presentation of the bill of lading as a result of § 302 which must be interpreted to only refer to genuine bills of lading. The part of the attestation clause which purports to change the risk of delivering against forged bills of lading would in effect extend the passive legitimation function to such forged bills, as long as the carrier fulfils its duty of reasonable care, and would thus derogate from the risk allocation set out in § 302. It would therefore be invalid pursuant to § 254.

6.2.4 Exemption or limitation of liability for misdelivery

The third issue is the possible exemption of the carrier for liability for misdelivery as a result of the "before and after clause". This clause is contained in the first sentence of clause 5.2 which exempts the carrier of all liability for loss or damage arising before the carrier's acceptance of custody of the goods and after the carrier tendering the cargo for delivery. This must be read in conjunction with clause 10 which clarifies that the terms and conditions shall apply to any loss or damage including as a result of delivery without surrender of the bill of lading.[132] It is thus a temporal

129 *Supra* Chapter 3, part 2.1 and 4.1.
130 Ibid.
131 See also Pedersen, *Transportret*, p. 481.
132 See the wording of the clauses, *supra* part 6.2.1.

limitation of the period in which the carrier can become liable as a carrier for its actions and an exclusion of all liability outside that period.

As stated above, in Scandinavia the obligation to deliver only against presentation of a bill of lading stems from the mandatory provision in the Merchant Shipping Act § 302 while the liability for breaching this obligation has been developed in case law. The mandatory nature of § 302 is not as such linked to the carrier's mandatory period of responsibility although that period will normally only end with the carrier's delivery of the goods to the consignee, § 274(1) cf. (3)(1). The wording of § 254 setting out the mandatory nature of part 13 of the Act provides that any provision "shall be void to the extent it derogates from the provisions of this part as well as the part regarding the limitation of actions". With the liability for breach of the delivery obligation not being specifically regulated in this part it could be submitted that an exemption of liability for misdelivery or an application of the Hague Rules' limitation of liability to such liability is not a derogation from part 13 of the Merchant Shipping Act and thus not void pursuant to § 254. However, it would be an obvious circumvention of the mandatory obligation in § 302, if the exemption of liability for misdelivery was accepted. The first sentence of clause 5.2 will therefore be invalid under Scandinavian law and would not offer a defence against liability for misdelivery whether or not the misdelivery occurred inside or outside the period prescribed in clause 5.2.

Under English law, clause 5.2 and clause 10 are not faced with such mandatory legislation beyond what the Hague-Visby Rules, as implemented in COGSA 1971, dictate. The effect of the clauses is thus a matter of construction.

One initial question will be to establish whether the misdelivery, in fact, occurred inside or outside the period established by clause 5.2. The terms and conditions do not define the term "tendering the cargo for delivery". One issue would seem to be to whom such delivery must be tendered, i.e. whether it must be to the notify party, to the bill of lading holder, or to someone who claims delivery, but does not hold the bill of lading. Another issue is at what point the misdelivery occurs. It will depend on an interpretation of the above-mentioned term and on the individual facts whether the misdelivery is found to be inside or outside the prescribed period.

In construing the effects of the clauses one might note that the clauses differ from that in the *New York Star*.[133] There, the clause specifically relieved the carrier of liability for misdelivery. Here, clause 10 seeks to clarify that the terms and conditions, even if worded in general terms, apply also to misdelivery and fundamental breaches of contract while the actual exemption is contained in clause 5. One must also remember that *The New York*

133 *Port Jacksom Stevedoring Pty. Ltd. v. Salmond and Spraggon (Australia) Pty. Ltd.*, [1981] 1 W.L.R. 138. *Supra* part 6.1.

Star shall not necessarily be seen as an acceptance that the exemption clause sufficed to relieve the carrier of liability for the misdelivery.[134] The interplay between clause 10 and clause 5 raises various questions of interpretation.

Clause 5 regulates several different situations. Clause 5.1 makes the Hague Rules applicable to loss of or damage to the goods occurring during the period from the carrier accepts custody of the goods until they are tendered for delivery while the first sentence of clause 5.2 exempts the carrier of liability for any loss or damage arising outside that period. The second sentence of clause 5.2 extends the application of the benefits for the carrier of the Hague Rules to any liability the carrier nevertheless incurs for loss or damage arising in the period mentioned in the first sentence as a result of mandatory law. Clause 5.3 regulates certain aspects where the US COGSA is mandatorily applicable and clause 5.4 deals with certain aspects of pre- and on-carriage by an inland carrier. The question is how clause 10 applies to this interplay in clause 5.

One possibility is to say that clause 10 is a clarification of all parts of clause 5 which in essence would make both the first and second sentence of clause 5.2 applicable to misdelivery. This is the widest possible interpretation of clause 10. Another and more limited interpretation is to say that clause 10 only clarifies the second sentence of clause 5.2 which would extend the application of the benefits of the Hague Rules, most relevant the limitation of liability, also to misdelivery.

The wording of clause 10 does not seem to warrant a distinction between the first and second sentence of clause 5.2 stressing as it does that it is the application of the terms and conditions onto "loss or damage whatsoever and howsoever occurring" with which it deals. On the other hand it must be remembered that the obligation to deliver only against an original bill of lading is one of the most fundamental obligations of the carrier under the bill of lading contract and this is stressed by the attestation clause. In that respect it is worth noting that the first sentence of clause 5.2 despite a change in the period in question is in essence the same as the clause sought to be relied on by Maersk Line in the *Motis Exports* case,[135] i.e. a temporal limitation of the liability of the carrier as an ocean carrier. In the *Motis Exports* case the Court of Appeal found that the wording was apt to cover liability for misdelivery, but that a natural reading of it would not include such liability and in establishing the meaning of the clause it was relevant that the meaning contended for by the carrier would go against the main intent and object of the contract, cf. the *Glynn v. Margetson* principle. The question is whether clause 10 is sufficiently clear to change this interpretation of the first sentence of clause 5.1.

134 *Supra* part 6.1 in fine.
135 See *supra* at fn 87.

Interpreting clause 10 to also make the first sentence of clause 5.2 applicable to liability for misdelivery would create an inconsistency between the attestation clause specifically requiring surrender of an original bill of lading and clause 5.2 exempting the carrier of any liability for delivering without such surrender. Further, such an interpretation would still (as in the *Motis Exports* case) go against the main intent and object of the contract. It is therefore relevant to see whether the clauses can be given a different interpretation which would still give content to the clauses.

As noted above, it is a possibility to say that clause 10 must be understood to only extend the second sentence of clause 5.2, i.e. the Hague Rules' limitation of liability, to cases of misdelivery. Such an interpretation would not cause a conflict with the attestation clause; nor would it, in principle give rise to a direct application of the *Glynn v. Margetson* principle.[136] Such an interpretation would not render the first sentence of clause 5.2 without content as this would still apply to inter alia physical perils to the goods after they have been tendered for delivery in accordance with the interpretation of the Court of Appeals of the clause in the *Motis Exports* case. Clause 10 and the second sentence of clause 5.2 would, obviously, be given an independent content through this interpretation with clause 10 clarifying that the generally worded second sentence of clause 5.2 also applies to cases of misdelivery – an interpretation which would not be made without clause 10.

It is difficult to predict with certainty how the courts will interpret the clauses. However, it seems likely that the courts will not find it plausible that the parties have intended for an interpretation which will create a conflict between the attestation clause and the other standard clauses, particularly not when such an interpretation will fundamentally change one of the main obligations of the carrier and one of the main characteristics of a bill of lading contract.

As for the fourth issue, the attempt at extending the benefits for the carrier of the Hague Rules also to misdelivery, the above analysis shows that it is likely that clause 10 will be interpreted to be a clarification of the second sentence of clause 5.2. Clause 10 specifically mentions delivery without surrender of the bill of lading and that the liability may stem from a fundamental breach of contract. This wording, it is submitted, must be considered clear enough to establish that it is the intention to apply the second sentence of clause 5.2 to cases of misdelivery. The fact that one has to combine the two clauses to ascertain the full meaning does not, it is submitted, make the meaning unclear to an extent so as to warrant a

136 Todd, "Excluding and Limiting Liability for Misdelivery", p. 250. See however the observation *supra* at fn 99.

different interpretation.[137] A submission that the second sentence of clause 5.2 should apply to a case of liability for misdelivery would thus seem to have a fair chance if it came before an English court.[138]

Under Scandinavian law, again the situation seems to differ. As set out above, the liability for breach of the delivery obligation is not specifically regulated in part 13 of the Merchant Shipping Acts, yet a clause exempting the carrier of liability for delivering without production of a bill of lading will be invalid. The rules of part 13 on limitation of liability also do not apply to liability for misdelivery.[139] It could therefore be submitted that an application of the Hague Rules' limitation of liability to such liability is not a derogation from part 13 of the Merchant Shipping Act and thus not void pursuant to § 254. However, as with a complete exclusion of liability it is likely that a court would find that a limitation of liability derogates from the obligations of part 13. Thus, even if the unlimited liability for breach of the obligation only to deliver against an original bill of lading does not stem directly from the Merchant Shipping Act, but rather from the fact that the rules on limitation in the Merchant Shipping Act do not apply to liability for misdelivery, a contractual limitation of that liability must be seen as a derogation from the Merchant Shipping Act. In that regard, the rules of part 13 on limitation of liability must be regarded as exhaustive (apart from the rules on global limitation of liability in part 9).

6.2.5 Summing up

It is interesting that several carriers have changed their bill of lading terms and conditions so that the exemption clauses therein specifically mention misdelivery or even expressly mention delivery without production of an original bill of lading. This may be seen as part of the industry's attempt at overcoming some of the perceived problems inherent in the bill of lading system.

137 In the Australian case The Antwerpen, *Glebe Island Terminal PTY Ltd v. Continental Seagram PTY Ltd and another*, [1994] 1 Lloyd's Rep 213 (CA NSW), a generally worded exemption clause was applied to a misdelivery, which was in reality a form of theft, because another clause stated that the exemptions, etc. in the bill of lading should apply even if the loss was a result of "actions constituting fundamental breach of contract", p. 247. Gaskell has questioned whether an English court would also hold that such a general clause should excuse a deliberate decision to deliver without a bill, Nicholas Gaskell, *Bills of Lading: Law and Contracts* (London: LLP, 2000), p. 452. It should be noted that Maersk Line's clause 10, contrary to the clause in *The Antwerpen*, specifically mentions "delivery without surrender of this bill of lading".

138 In the MSC Amsterdam, *Trafigura Beheer BV v. Mediterranean Shipping Co. SA*, [2007] 2 C.L.C. 379, the Court of Appeal refused to apply the Hague Rules' limitation to a case of misdelivery, but there the relevant sentences were "buried within a clause of such length and complexity", para 34.

139 *Supra* Chapter 3, part 13.1.2.

As shown, the different bases of the presentation rule in English and Scandinavian law have a fundamental impact on the viability of such clauses. Thus, the presentation rule's basis in mandatory legislation in Scandinavian law means that there is only very limited room for contractually exempting the carrier of liability for misdelivery. Under English law the effectiveness of such clauses is a matter left to the court's construction of the clauses. As the analysis of Maersk Line's bill of lading clauses – which is meant as an example – has shown there are many uncertainties as to the effectiveness of the clauses and therefore also many ways for the courts to limit the effect of such clauses. However, with the express mention of misdelivery or delivery without production of a bill of lading at least a much greater chance exists that a court will hold that the exemption clause is apt to cover liability for misdelivery.

7 Delivery clauses and the presentation rule

In Chapter 3, part 10, the law relating to goods which are not claimed at the port of destination by a person presenting the bill of lading was described. As explained there, the Merchant Shipping Acts of the Scandinavian countries contain a non-mandatory rule which under certain conditions gives the carrier the option to warehouse such goods which inter alia has as a consequence that the mandatory period of responsibility ends. Under English law until some 20 years ago the matter was subject to statute law, but that statute was repealed and instead the issue was left to contract and to the common law which also under certain conditions allows the carrier to land the goods and put them into storage at the expense of the cargo owner.

Under both Scandinavian and English law the matter is thus subject to freedom of contract and that freedom is widely used in the standard terms of bills of lading. Accordingly, most bills of lading, at least in the liner trade, contain a "delivery clause" which under some heading or other purports to regulate various issues regarding the actual delivery of the goods. The content of these clauses vary quite a lot, but they tend to place an obligation on the consignee (or often using the wider term "Merchant" identifying several parties on the cargo side) to take delivery of the goods either as soon as the ship is ready to discharge or within a certain time period, and to give the carrier various liberties in relation to the goods if the consignee does not take delivery as specified, such as unpacking the goods, storing them, or selling them to cover costs and claims. It is further very often set out that taking such steps "shall constitute due delivery" or similar wording.

In this part it will be examined what the effects of such clauses are on the carrier's obligation only to deliver the goods against presentation of the bill of lading. Other consequences of the clauses, e.g. as to liability for cargo damage, will not be dealt with here.

An initial distinction must be made between situations where a holder of a bill of lading claims delivery of goods which have been sold[140] in accordance with the clause in question and situations where the goods are delivered from the storage to a receiver without presentation of a bill of lading. In the latter situation it may also be relevant to distinguish between situations where the carrier has knowledge of the delivery or even has authorised it and situations where the carrier is unaware that the delivery is being made.

7.1 English law

There is very little case law concerning these types of clauses and the issue of misdelivery. In fact, there does not seem to be any reported English case that deals directly with the issue.[141]

The issue came up in the High Court of Hong Kong in the *Center Optical* case.[142] The bill of lading in question contained a delivery clause which if the Merchant did not take delivery at the correct time and place gave the carrier the right to "without notice" store the goods and "[s]uch storage shall constitute due delivery hereunder, and thereupon the liability of the Carrier in respect of the Goods or that part thereof shall cease".[143] The goods were stored and later released from storage without presentation of the original bills of lading. Stone J. refused to hold that the plain wording of the delivery clause was sufficiently clear to impinge upon the cardinal principle requiring delivery to be made only against an original bill of lading. Thus, the learned judge declined to find that the clause was "sufficient to empower the carrier intentionally to deliver the goods without notice to anyone he wishes".[144]

Professor Gaskell has stated that the receiver could be in breach of the delivery clause if it does not take delivery as specified, but that "[s]till, it would seem that a court is unlikely to hold that this breach was a cause of loss where the carrier puts the cargo into storage and later delivers without production of a bill".[145] Cooke *et al.* have also questioned whether English

140 If the goods have not been sold, but instead been e.g. destroyed, it is a matter of non-delivery rather than misdelivery.

141 In *Motis Exports Ltd. v. Dampskibsselskabet af 1912 A/S*, [2000] 1 Lloyd's Rep. 211, p. 217, para 7, Mance L.J. only stated in relation to the delivery clause that "[w]hile it is unnecessary to express a definite view on the scope of this clause, its focus is at least the delivery obligation".

142 *Center Optical (Hong Kong) Ltd. v. Jardine Transport Services (China) Ltd. and Pronto Cargo Corp.*, [2001] 2 Lloyd's Rep. 678.

143 Set out in extenso ibid., para 49.

144 Ibid., para 56.

145 Gaskell, *Bills of Lading: Law and Contracts*, p. 449. The passage was cited with approval by Stone J. in *Center Optical (Hong Kong) Ltd. v. Jardine Transport Services (China) Ltd. and Pronto Cargo Corp.*, [2001] 2 Lloyd's Rep. 678, para 55.

courts would find that clauses of this kind provide an agreed method of delivery which would bring the bailment of the goods to an end.[146] In that context, it may also be relevant that the Court of Appeal in the *East West* case found that the carrier was in breach of its duty in bailment by virtue of their negligence in failing to arrange for the third party with whom they stored the goods to only deliver the goods against presentation of a bill of lading.[147]

Having noted in the preceding parts that at least in theory the carrier's liability for misdelivery can be excluded, but that it requires very clear language, the question is whether delivery clauses in contexts where the cargo side is in breach of its obligations should be treated less strictly when assessing whether the clause relieves the carrier of liability for delivering the goods without production of a bill of lading. As can be seen, this does not seem to be generally accepted. However, the question is one of construction and that construction must be made in the context of the contract as a whole. In that context, Gaskell suggests that courts might be less hostile to a clause which acts as a cesser of liability clause after a specific period where the cargo side has had a chance to collect the goods than one that stipulates such cessation directly upon discharge of the goods.[148]

7.2 Scandinavian law

Under Scandinavian law, the question was at issue in the Danish Maritime and Commercial Court case reported in ND 1995.109.[149] There, containers were carried to Abidjan. The carrier's agent notified the "notify party" (the buyer) of their arrival, but delivery was not claimed. The carrier therefore put the containers into storage with a stevedoring company from where they were delivered without presentation of an original bill of lading. The shipper (the partly unpaid seller) claimed damages for the misdelivery and the carrier sought to rely on a delivery clause in very similar terms to the one in the *Center Optical* case referred above. The Maritime and Commercial Court stated that the clauses derogated significantly from the rules on bills of lading in the Merchant Shipping Act. Such derogations had to be in clear and unambiguous terms. The Court found that the shipper could not be bound by complicated exemption clauses found on the back of the bill of lading derogating from the Merchant Shipping Act's requirement as to notification of the shipper about the storing of the goods. The court thus awarded the shipper damages.

146 Julian Cooke et al., *Voyage Charters*, 4th ed. (Abingdon: Informa Law from Routledge, 2014), para 10.24.
147 *East West Corp. v. DKBS 1912*, [2003] Q.B. 1509, paras 61, 68, and 86.
148 Gaskell, *Bills of Lading: Law and Contracts*, p. 438, fn 185.
149 The case is also mentioned *supra* at fn 105.

When the consignee does not take delivery of the goods at the correct time and place, the Merchant Shipping Acts §§ 271 and 272 gives the carrier the right to store the goods and set a reasonable time for their collection. When that time has passed the carrier can sell as much of the goods as necessary to cover the carrier's costs and claims it may have. It seems perfectly clear that a carrier who does so cannot subsequently be met with a claim for misdelivery of the sold goods by a holder of the bill of lading. As mentioned, §§ 271 and 272 are non-mandatory and the parties are thus free to agree on other terms, but as the above-mentioned case shows derogations must be made in clear terms. If the delivery clause is in sufficiently clear terms it seems a natural inference that a carrier who has sold part of the goods pursuant to the procedure in said clause will also be discharged of its delivery obligation for those goods. As the above-mentioned case shows, it must, however, be expected that courts will have a strong inclination to imply into the delivery clause the Merchant Shipping Acts' requirements that notification of the storing of the goods must be made, that such storing must be under "safe-keeping", and that the carrier must show due diligence in the sale of the goods.

§§ 271 and 272 do not give the carrier the right to sell more goods than is necessary to cover costs and claims; nor do they give the carrier a general right to deliver the goods to someone else without production of the bill of lading. Putting the goods into storage ends the carrier's period of responsibility pursuant to § 274 meaning that the carrier will not be liable for damage to the goods after such storing. However, the obligation to deliver only against presentation of a bill of lading stems from the mandatory § 302[150] and the liability for breaching this obligation is developed in case law. It may be argued that §§ 271 and 272 do not alter this obligation or the liability save to the limited extent set out in the preceding paragraph. This would mean that a delivery clause to the extent it purported to relieve the carrier of liability for delivering the goods without presentation of a bill of lading after they had been stored would run contrary to the mandatory rules on delivery and thus be void.

On the other hand it must be said that the underlying intention of §§ 271 and 272 is to lessen the obligations on the carrier in a situation where the cargo side is in breach of its obligations. It is for that reason that the rules allow the carrier to store the goods under "safe-keeping". "Safe-keeping" must entail both that it is ensured that delivery will not be made without presentation of a bill of lading and that notification of the storing is given to the shipper.[151] It may be that the carrier will in such

150 As supplemented by analogous application of the rules on negotiable instruments of debt, see *supra* Chapter 3, part 2.1 and 4.1.

151 Erling Selvig in ND 1995 pp. xix–xx in a short commentary to the abovementioned case. Selvig seems to accept in principle that clauses can modify the misdelivery liability developed in case law.

circumstances be free of liability if the goods are anyhow misdelivered, e.g. by employees of a stevedoring company with whom the carrier has stored the goods. If this interpretation is accepted, it would leave more room for delivery clauses to be operable in, but it is submitted that they could not derogate too far from the two requirements just specified and any derogation must be in very clear terms.[152]

A firm conclusion cannot be drawn as to which of the two alternatives is the correct understanding. Either will, however, leave difficult questions as to how far the liability for misdelivery can be excepted even when the cargo side is in breach of its obligation to take delivery of the goods.

7.3 Summing up

Under both Scandinavian and English law there seems to be a disinclination to accept that "delivery clauses" in the terms mentioned above give the carrier a right to deliver the goods without presentation of a bill of lading despite the cargo side being in breach of its obligations under the clause.

It is interesting that both the Danish and the Hong Kong courts in the above-mentioned cases seemed to place substantial emphasis on the fact that the carrier took the relevant steps without giving notice to the shipper and found that under such circumstances the carrier could not rely on the delivery clause despite said clause expressly stated "without notice". Also, it was mentioned that the delivery without presentation of a bill was deliberate. It may be that courts would be more inclined to accept that the carrier can be relieved of liability in a situation where the delivery is undeliberate, e.g. where delivery is made against a forged bill of lading.

Under English law the issue is one of construction. Under Scandinavian law another question is whether the liability for misdelivery can be derogated from through a delivery clause or that is an issue which lies outside the non-mandatory scope of the Merchant Shipping Acts' §§ 271 and 272.

Until more case law emerges on these issues, the effect of delivery clauses on the carrier's obligation only to deliver the goods against presentation of a bill of lading is somewhat uncertain.[153]

8 Conclusion

The possibility of relieving the carrier of liability for misdelivery through exemption clauses in the bill of lading is an issue where the effects of the different bases for the presentation rule in English and Scandinavian law are most clearly seen. In Scandinavian law, the mandatory regulation of the

152 Selvig, ibid., states that "unusually clear language" will be required to modify the misdelivery liability.

153 Cases on situations where the goods are put into storage can often also be further complicated by questions of agency.

requirement only to deliver against presentation of a bill of lading leaves very little room for contractual exemption of liability for misdelivery. In English law, the matter is one of construction, but here the courts have shown great reluctance to accept that exemption clauses are apt to cover liability for misdelivery unless they are in very clear terms. In that regard, it is interesting that several carriers have changed their bill of lading terms and conditions to specifically mention misdelivery or even delivery without presentation of the bill of lading. It remains to be seen whether these clauses will be accepted by the courts as being able to relieve the carrier of liability for misdelivery.

5 Rotterdam Rules and delivery of goods

1 Introduction to the Rotterdam Rules

On 11 December 2008, the United Nations' General Assembly adopted a new Convention entitled United Nations Convention on Contracts for the International Carriage of Goods Wholly or Partly by Sea.[1] As the government of the Netherlands had offered to host a signing ceremony in Rotterdam on 23 September 2009, the General Assembly authorized such ceremony and recommended that the Convention be known as the Rotterdam Rules. To date, the Rotterdam Rules have been signed by 25 countries and ratified by three.[2] The Rules require 20 ratifications to enter into force.[3] In Scandinavia, both Norway and Denmark have in close consultations with each other conducted the preparatory work and issued official reports on the possible implementation of the Rotterdam Rules.[4] In Denmark, this work led to the passing in 2013 of legislation implementing the Rules into Danish law.[5] Denmark has, however, not yet ratified the Convention and the act implementing the Rules will only be put into force when the Rules enter into force.

The adoption of the Rotterdam Rules concluded over a decade of work on the preparation of the convention.[6] The initiative was taken in what

1 Resolution 63/122. The Convention is contained in an annex to the resolution.

2 As per 2 May 2016. The three countries that have ratified are Spain, Togo, and Congo.

3 Article 94. Equal to ratification is acceptance, approval, or accession.

4 In Norway: NOU 2012:10. In Denmark: Betænkning no. 1536/2013 (4. Betænkning afgivet af Sølovsudvalget).

5 Act no. 618 of 12 June 2013. An English translation of the Act is available at www.dma.dk/SiteCollectionDocuments/Legislation/Acts/2013/L-618-12062013-ændring%20af%20søloven%20og%20forskelige%20andre%20love.pdf. The relevant part of the Act is no. 9 (p. 10 et seq.)

6 For a general introduction to the history of the convention, see e.g. (amongst several others) Michael F. Sturley, "Transport Law for the twenty-first century: an introduction to the preparation, philosphy, and potential impact of the Rotterdam Rules", in *A New Convention for the Carriage of Goods by Sea – The Rotterdam Rules*, ed. D. Rhidian Thomas (Lawtext Publishing Limited, 2009), and José Angelo Estrella Faria, "Uniform Law for International Transport at UNCITRAL: New Times, New Players, and New Rules", *Texas International Law Journal* 44 (2009).

must be characterised as a – at the time somewhat surprising – cooperation between the United Nations Commission on International Trade Law (UNCITRAL) and the Comité Maritime International (CMI), a non-governmental organisation with a century-long history of working for international unification of maritime law.

In 1996, UNCITRAL in the context of its work on Electronic Data Interchange (EDI) which led to the adoption of the Model Law on Electronic Commerce[7] had found that it was an obstacle to the use of electronic documentation in maritime transport that both international conventions and national law on maritime transportation were fragmentary and left significant gaps. It was therefore decided that UNCITRAL should gather information, opinions and ideas regarding the problems in practice in close collaboration with industry representatives, including the CMI.[8] The CMI took on the task with vigour and in December 2001 delivered a Draft Instrument on Transport Law to UNCITRAL.[9] In the meantime, UNCITRAL had in July 2001 decided to establish a working group to consider the issues and that the UNCITRAL Secretariat should prepare a preliminary working document containing drafts of possible solutions for a future legislative instrument.[10] For that purpose Working Group III, which had in the 1970s been used for the negotiation of the Hamburg Rules, was revived and the Secretariat converted the CMI Draft Instrument into the aforementioned preliminary working document.[11]

Working Group III first convened in April 2002 and over the following six years met twice a year in formal two-week sessions before finally in January 2008 submitting a final draft convention to the Commission, i.e. the head body of UNCITRAL.[12] The Commission thoroughly reviewed the draft over nine days at its forty-first session in June and July 2008 before submitting it to the General Assembly for adoption.[13] The Commission was in the review careful not to upset the delicate compromises reached in the Working Group, but some changes were made, including most prominently a substantial change of the rules on delivery of the goods. Throughout the negotiations in the Working Group and at the forty-first Commission Session, very extensive and detailed reports of the negotiations were made and approved by the Working Group and Commission respectively. These reports must be considered travaux preparatoires of the final convention.[14]

7 *Infra* Chapter 6, part 2.
8 UNCITRAL, A/51/17, para 210-15.
9 CMI Yearbook (2001), p. 532.
10 UNCITRAL, A/56/17, para 319-45.
11 UNCITRAL, A/CN.9/WG.III/WP.21.
12 UNCITRAL, A/CN.9/645.
13 UNCITRAL, A/63/17, para 12-298 and annex I.
14 The interpretative value of the reports is discussed *supra* Chapter 1, part 2.3.

The end result, the Rotterdam Rules, is a very comprehensive instrument of no less than 96 articles. It builds on many of the notions and principles of the Hague-Visby and Hamburg Rules and codifies certain standard practices of the trade but also introduces completely new rules and notions. In the context of this book five issues are of particular relevance: the scope of application, the regulation of documentary issues, the introduction of regulation of the right of control over the goods en route, the introduction of regulation of the delivery of the goods, and the introduction of regulation of electronic transport records.[15]

With regard to the scope of application, it is worth noting that the Rotterdam Rules' application is not dependent upon the issuance of a specific type of transport document, articles 5–7. Thereby the Rules depart from the method of the Hague and Hague-Visby Rules and builds on the principle of the Hamburg Rules. Whether a bill of lading, a sea waybill or no transport document at all is issued, the basic liability scheme will be the same. The issuance of a bill of lading will, of course, have other important legal ramifications.

Not only is the application not dependent on the issuance of a bill of lading – nowhere in the Rules is there any mention of bills of lading by that name. Thus, the Rules do not use the common names of the documents used in practice but instead use the generic term transport document. This in turn is qualified using two parameters, namely negotiability (in the sense transferability) and whether the document must be surrendered to obtain delivery of the goods. So qualified, the transport documents fall into four groups which respectively correspond to sea waybills, straight bills of lading, ordinary bills of lading (order or bearer) and a new type of document; a negotiable transport document which does not (under certain conditions) have to be surrendered to obtain delivery.[16] In this chapter the main focus will be on the treatment of negotiable transport documents with and without a statement that the document need not be surrendered in order to obtain delivery as these two types correspond to bills of lading with a clause seeking to alter the delivery obligation and traditional order or bearer bills of lading respectively.

The conventions currently in force do not regulate the issue of who controls the goods en route. In practice, this has caused considerable problems, e.g. in connection with the exercise of a right of stoppage *in transitu* which the seller of the goods might have under the sales contract. The

15 The problems associated with the use of electronic bills of lading is dealt with *infra* in Chapter 6 and the Rotterdam Rules' regulation of electronic transport records is the subject of Chapter 7. Some issues specific to the application of the Rotterdam Rules' regulation of the delivery of the goods onto electronic transport records is examined in this chapter, *infra* part 5.7.

16 For further analysis of the terminology regarding transport documents see Anders Møllmann, "From bills of lading to transport documents – the role of transport documents under the Rotterdam Rules", *Journal of International Maritime Law* 17, no. 1 (2011).

Rotterdam Rules include regulation of these problems under the heading of "right of control" which introduces an entity, "the controlling party", who is the party which at any given time is able to exercise the right of control. Because of the detailed regulation of how the right of control is transferred, it is also seen as an attempt at providing an alternative to using negotiable transport documents and, thus, as one way of solving some of the problems associated with delivery where the bill of lading is not presented.[17]

As a novelty, the Rotterdam Rules introduce detailed regulation of the delivery process. This regulation is the main subject of this chapter.

2 Introduction of rules on delivery of goods

As stated above, one of the original reasons for beginning the work that led to the Rotterdam Rules was that in order to be able to produce international rules facilitating the use of electronic transport documentation, it was necessary to regulate in more detail the rights and obligations of the parties. Under the current international conventions on the carriage of goods, many aspects of these rights and obligations are not regulated and instead follow from the issuance of a paper bill of lading.

One of the aspects that has not previously been addressed in the conventions is the delivery of the goods. This is now regulated in detail in Chapter 9 of the Rotterdam Rules which has been called "ambitious" and in the same breath has been deemed to "raise more difficult problems of interpretation than perhaps any other part of the Convention".[18]

In the context of this book, it is particularly interesting that from the very first draft of the convention, a rule was introduced regulating the situation where the original bill of lading (negotiable transport document in the terms of the Rules) cannot be presented at the destination.[19]

It is also worth noting that the chapter was substantially changed during the very final stages of the negotiations. Thus, the rules turned out to be more controversial than the final negotiations in the Working Group had indicated.

3 Overview

Chapter 9 consists of articles 43–49. They fall under three groups: one regarding the obligation to accept delivery and to acknowledge receipt (articles 43–44); one regarding goods remaining undelivered (article 48), and one regarding the actual delivery of the goods (articles 45–47). The

17 See the mention of this possibility *infra* Chapter 7 at fn 28.

18 Anthony Diamond, "The Rotterdam Rules", *Lloyd's Maritime and Commercial Law Quarterly* (2009): 509.

19 UNCITRAL, A/CN.9/WG.III/WP.21, para 160 et seq.

two former groups apply irrespective of which transport document, if any, has been issued, while the latter group is highly dependent on the relevant transport document. Finally, article 49 simply states that the Rules do not affect any right of retention of the goods that may exist pursuant to the contract of carriage or applicable law.

In the following, the three groups will be analysed. Given the theme of this book, particular focus will be given to the rules regarding delivery where a negotiable transport document or negotiable electronic transport record has been issued. It will also be analysed what other effects flow from the fact that delivery is now an obligation regulated in the convention rather than by national law, particularly with respect to limitation of liability and possible P&I cover for misdelivery claims.

The regulation of (paper) transport documents and electronic transport records are parallel. The following analysis will simply refer to transport documents but it applies equally to electronic transport records unless specifically stated. Certain aspects which are specific to the use of electronic transport records will be examined below in part 5.7.

4 Obligations to accept and acknowledge receipt of the goods

4.1 Identity of the consignee

The obligations to accept and acknowledge receipt of the goods rest on the consignee (subject to further conditions). The term consignee is defined in article 1(11) as "a person entitled to delivery of the goods under a contract of carriage or a transport document or electronic transport record".[20] This definition, however, does not clearly specify how one must establish who is entitled to delivery.

The starting point must be that the consignee is the person whom the shipper, i.e. the contractual partner of the carrier, has designated as the person to whom the carrier must deliver the goods.[21] This designation may however require recourse to the rules on delivery under certain types of transport documents. It is not necessarily the party named in the "consignee box" of the transport document.[22] Thus, the controlling party may have replaced the consignee with someone else or, if a negotiable

20 Treitel and Reynolds, *Carver on Bills of Lading*, p. 9f, express that it is a little "puzzling" that the definition refers to both the contract of carriage and to transport documents or electronic transport records. The background for the wording can be seen in UNCITRAL, A/CN.9/510, para 75.

21 Michael F. Sturley, Tomotaka Fujita, and Gertjan van der Ziel, *The Rotterdam Rules* (London: Sweet & Maxwell, 2010), para 8.004.

22 Debattista in Yvonne Baatz et al., *The Rotterdam Rules: A Practical Annotation* (London: Informa, 2009), para 43-04. Debattista notes that this fact may "cause some surprise in the market", at para 1-12.

transport document has been issued, the person being the holder may have changed by a transfer of that document, duly indorsed if necessary.

Establishing the identity of the consignee thus involves construction of the contract of carriage, transport document or electronic transport record in question held up against the material rules on the delivery of the goods and possibly the rules on the right of control. The construction of the contract, document, or record may involve principles of the applicable law of the contract as to who is entitled to delivery, but only insofar as these principles do not contradict the specific provisions of the Rotterdam Rules.[23]

4.2 Definition of delivery

Although delivery of the goods is for the first time included in an international cargo convention, the concept of delivery is in fact not a defined term in the Rules.

In practice, delivery of the goods can happen in many different ways. It may often include the physical handing over of the goods from the carrier to the consignee, but more often it will be a handing over of the goods to an agent or customs or other authorities. Also from a legal viewpoint it is difficult to define delivery.[24] This is why an attempt to define the term has not been made in the Rules.

Instead, the Rules define the carrier's period of responsibility for the goods, art. 12, and set out rules as to how the carrier must act when the period of responsibility has ended, but the goods remain under the carrier's supervision because the consignee has not taken them over, art. 48. These rules make an exact definition of the term delivery unnecessary.[25]

Chapter 9 must therefore be viewed as mainly setting out to whom the carrier must deliver in order to discharge its obligations and thus avoid incurring liability for misdelivery.

23 See however Diamond, "The Rotterdam Rules", p. 509. Diamond seems to take a different starting point in that he suggests that who is entitled to delivery must be ascertained applying the proper law of the contract "supplemented by the terms of the Convention where relevant". This may amount to the same as suggested in the text above. However, as a comment to Debattista, see preceding fn, Diamond in footnote 115 states that he does not think that articles 45-47 are relevant for identifying the "consignee". It is difficult to see why the rules stating the conditions under which the carrier must deliver the goods are always irrelevant, particularly in relation to negotiable transport documents where it is article 47 which positively establishes that it is the holder who is entitled to claim delivery.

24 Gertjan van der Ziel, "Delivery of the Goods", in *The Rotterdam Rules 2008*, ed. Alexander von Ziegler, Johan Schelin, and Stefano Zunarelli (Dordrecht: Kluwer Law International, 2010), p. 190. Sturley, Fujita, and van der Ziel, *The Rotterdam Rules*, para 8.011 et seq. (same author).

25 Van der Ziel phrases it that the "Convention circumvents the potential problem", ibid.

4.3 Obligation to accept delivery and acknowledge receipt

Article 43[26] places an obligation on the consignee "that demands delivery of the goods under the contract of carriage" to accept delivery of the goods.

In the original draft, the Rules would place such obligation to accept delivery on the consignee "that exercises any of its rights under the contract of carriage".[27] It was not until the forty-first Commission Session, i.e. the very final round of negotiations prior to adoption of the Convention by the General Assembly, that the condition that the consignee must demand delivery for the obligation to arise was introduced.[28] The change was made despite the objection that the intention of article 43 was to respond to the problem of consignees who wish to avoid delivery of the goods simply by refusing to claim them.[29]

The final draft which the Working Group submitted to the Commission had altered the original wording of the condition by removing the words "any of" so that the obligation to accept delivery was placed on "the consignee that exercises its rights under the contract of carriage".[30] It was particularly the vagueness of the phrase "its rights" that was objected to and which led to the decision to alter the rule to its final wording.[31]

The negotiations show the difficulty of setting an acceptable and clear threshold for when the consignee assumes obligations under the negotiable transport document.[32] On the one hand, CISG sets out that a buyer who wants to reject goods must take delivery of them from the carrier, but does so on behalf of the seller[33] and it could be said to be in line with the

26 Article 43 reads; "When the goods have arrived at their destination, the consignee that demands delivery of the goods under the contract of carriage shall accept delivery of the goods at the time or within the time period and at the location agreed in the contract of carriage or, failing such agreement, at the time and location which, having regard to the terms of the contract, the customs, usages or practices of the trade and the circumstances of the carriage, delivery could reasonably be expected."

27 UNCITRAL, A/CN.9/WG.III/WP.21, art. 10.1.

28 The article had been subject to extended debate and multiple suggestions throughout the negotiations in the Working Group. In the final draft submitted by the Working Group to the Commission the phrase read "the consignee who exercises its rights under the contract of carriage", see the annex to UNCITRAL, A/CN.9/645, draft article 45.

29 UNCITRAL, A/63/17, para 139-41.

30 The decision to remove the words "any of" was made at the Working Group's twentieth session, UNCITRAL, A/CN.9/642, para 22-23. The concern was that the term was too broad and consequently the threshold for a consignee to be obliged to accept delivery was too low.

31 UNCITRAL, A/63/17, para 139-41.

32 On this issue in general see e.g. Simon Baughen, "Charterparty bills of lading – cargo interests' liabilities to the shipowner", in *The Evolving Law and Practice of Voyage Charterparties*, ed. D. Rhidian Thomas (London: Informa, 2009), and Frank Smeele, "The bill of lading contracts under European national laws (civil law approaches to explaining the legal position of the consignee under bills of lading)", ibid.

33 United Nations Convention on Contracts for the International Sale of Goods, article 86(2).

underlying principle of that rule to set a very low threshold for the obligation to accept delivery under the contract of carriage. On the other hand, setting the threshold too low might mean that (necessary and important) parties in the trading chain who have no interest in receiving the goods, such as financing banks under a letter of credit, might become obliged to accept delivery simply by being the holder of the negotiable transport document and might incur liability for breaching this obligation. Further, an unclearly defined threshold would be in neither party's interest. In addition, the subject of transfer of contractual obligations and liabilities is a very controversial one as doctrinal views are strongly held by many states and dealing with the subject in a transport law convention may very well have wider implications on the legal system in general of a state.

Under article 43, for an obligation on the consignee to accept delivery of the goods to arise, the consignee must, thus, demand delivery. "Demand" must be interpreted relatively broadly so that actions which would not in ordinary communication be called a demand, but rather an indication that the consignee wishes to take delivery of the goods, constitutes a "demand" in the terms of article 43. Accordingly, a response by the consignee to a notice of arrival indicating that the consignee will take delivery when the goods arrive must constitute a "demand".[34] On the other hand, requesting samples of the goods will not constitute a "demand [of] delivery".[35]

The result is that it is for the consignee itself to trigger the obligation by demanding delivery. If the consignee does not do so then no obligation to accept delivery arises under article 43. In this sense, article 43 does not solve the problem it was initially meant to.

One situation where the rule may be relevant is when the consignee under the contract of carriage has a certain time period in which to physically collect the goods from the terminal at the port of destination and the consignee does not do so within the agreed time. If the consignee has given an indication which qualifies as a "demand" then the consignee will be in breach of its obligation under article 43 for the period until collection of the goods exceeding the agreed period.[36]

The consequence of a consignee's breach of article 43 is not exhaustively dealt with in the Rules. Article 48 sets out how the carrier may deal with goods that remain undelivered, but the Rules do not contain regulation of a potential liability of the consignee for breach of article 43. If such liability

34 Sturley, Fujita, and van der Ziel, *The Rotterdam Rules*, Illustration 8-1, p. 245.

35 This can be inferred from the discussion leading to the change of wording of article 43, UNCITRAL, A/63/17, para 139-41. The Rotterdam Rules do not regulate whether the consignee has a right to examine the goods before demanding delivery thereof.

36 Sturley, Fujita, and van der Ziel, *The Rotterdam Rules*, para 8.020. With regard to time and place of delivery, see *infra* part 4.4.

should arise, it must be on the basis of the otherwise applicable law.[37] The applicable law will thus determine important questions such as the basis of liability, causation, remoteness and types of loss.

4.4 Time and location of delivery

When the consignee has demanded delivery, article 43 goes on to set out the time and location where the consignee is obliged to accept delivery. The consignee must accept delivery at the time or within the time period and at the place agreed in the contract of carriage. When a negotiable transport document, i.e. a bill of lading, has been issued and transferred to a third party this must refer to the contract of carriage as contained in or evidenced by the transport document.[38]

Quite often the contract of carriage will not contain a precise stipulation as to the time or place of delivery.[39] In those cases delivery must be accepted at the time and location when "delivery could reasonably be expected".[40] When this could reasonably be expected must be established on the basis of the terms of the contract, the customs, usages, or practices of the trade and the circumstances of the carriage.[41] This leaves ample room for a rather flexible test of the concrete circumstances in which an important factor should probably be when the consignee knew or ought to have known about the arrival of the goods.[42]

4.5 Obligation to acknowledge receipt

Article 44[43] sets out an obligation on the consignee to acknowledge receipt of the goods at the request of the carrier or the performing party that delivers the goods. Such acknowledgement must be in the manner which is customary at the place of delivery. Article 44 further establishes that if the consignee breaches this obligation, the carrier may refuse delivery and may

37 van der Ziel, "Delivery of the Goods", p. 193, states that the consignee may be held liable under article 30 "provided that the applicable national law has extended the application of Article 30 to consignees as well". It is, of course, open to a national legislature to make such extension, but there is no encouragement in the Rules themselves to do so, and making such rule by extending the application of article 30 does not change the nature of the rule; it is still a national law rule on the liability of the consignee.

38 Debattista in Baatz *et al.*, *The Rotterdam Rules: A Practical Annotation*, para 43-07.

39 Although Diamond, "The Rotterdam Rules", p. 510, foresees that carriers will insert in their standard terms that delivery is to be taken within a short period of time.

40 Article 43 in fine.

41 Ibid.

42 Diamond, "The Rotterdam Rules", p. 510.

43 Article 44 reads; "On request of the carrier or the performing party that delivers the goods, the consignee shall acknowledge receipt of the goods from the carrier or the performing party in the manner that is customary at the place of delivery. The carrier may refuse delivery if the consignee refuses to acknowledge such receipt."

then avail itself of the options set out in article 48 as to how to deal with the goods. As with article 43, article 44 does not deal with the potential liability of the consignee for refusing to acknowledge receipt.

The question is what the article obligates the consignee to acknowledge, i.e. whether it is a simple acknowledgement of the goods having been delivered or whether an acknowledgement of the order and condition of the goods may be demanded. The article only sets out that the receipt must be made in the manner which is customary at the place of delivery. In the literature, the meaning of the article has been interpreted from opposite starting points. On the one hand it has been stated that the article is uncontroversial as it follows standard industry practice[44] and that "[o]f course the consignee need acknowledge only what it in fact receives".[45] On the other hand it has been stated that there is nothing in the article to prevent the carrier from requiring a receipt stating that the goods are in good order and condition and that the carrier may refuse to deliver the goods if the consignee refuses to give such receipt.[46] A "clean" receipt, that is a receipt stating that the goods are in good order and condition, might put the consignee in a difficult evidential position in a subsequent claim for damage to or loss of the goods.

First, it must be noted that delivery of the goods is one of the main obligations of the carrier[47] and that delivery ends the period of responsibility of the carrier for the goods.[48] Consequently, it is of great importance for the carrier to obtain proof that it has delivered the goods. This is also so under the current regimes which is why it is standard practice for carriers to request a receipt. Article 44 must be seen in this light. While article 44 does not specifically prohibit the carrier from demanding that the consignee acknowledges the order and condition of the goods, it does not either give any indication that the carrier can demand such acknowledgement.[49]

The latter interpretation above[50] seems to be based on an understanding that it is almost entirely at the carrier's discretion to deny delivery because the acknowledgement by the consignee does not fulfil the demands of the carrier. It is, however, submitted that this is not the case.

The evidential consequences of the acknowledgement must be assessed in conjunction with an analysis of article 23. Debattista compares article 44 with the Hague-Visby Rules, article III, rule 6, regarding notice of loss of or damage to the goods. However, the relevant rule in the Rotterdam Rules

44 van der Ziel, "Delivery of the Goods", p. 193, and Sturley, Fujita, and van der Ziel, *The Rotterdam Rules*, para 8.021 (including the same author).

45 *The Rotterdam Rules*, para 8.023, fn 40.

46 Debattista in Baatz *et al.*, *The Rotterdam Rules: A Practical Annotation*, para 44-02 et seq. Diamond, "The Rotterdam Rules", p. 510f, seems to be in line with this starting point

47 Article 11.

48 Article 12(1).

49 Diamond, "The Rotterdam Rules", p. 510f, accepts this much

50 At fn 46.

regarding notice of loss or damage is article 23. Article 23 creates a presumption that the carrier has delivered the goods according to their description in the contract particulars unless a notice in writing to the contrary is given to the carrier before or at the time of delivery or within seven working days of the delivery if the loss or damage is not apparent.[51] This closely corresponds to the rule in the Hague-Visby Rules except that the time for giving notice of non-apparent loss and damage is longer.[52]

A presumption of the goods being in the order and condition as described in the transport document, thus, arises whether or not the consignee signs a "clean" receipt for the goods, i.e. a receipt stating that the goods are in good order and condition, unless the consignee gives notice of loss or damage. With article 23 being the special rule setting out the consequence of a notice not being given, it is submitted that a "clean" receipt given by the consignee should not create a stronger presumption in favour of the carrier than a simple acknowledgement of receipt of the goods when no notice of loss or damage is given.[53] Further, a notice of loss or damage which was not apparent at delivery given within the time frame set out in article 23 should displace any presumption or *prima facie* evidential value that a "clean" receipt had created. Article 23 and 44 read in conjunction further supports that a carrier cannot on the basis of article 44 deny delivering the goods to a consignee who refuses to give a "clean" receipt if the consignee wants to give notice of loss or damage under article 23.[54]

In conclusion, article 44 seems to simply oblige the consignee to acknowledge receipt of the goods and the evidential value of this receipt only goes to the fact that delivery of the goods has taken place.

5 Structure and content of the rules on delivery

From the very first draft submitted for negotiation in UNCITRAL, the draft convention contained rules attempting to provide a solution for the problem that consignees do not turn up to receive the goods or are not able to present the bill of lading.[55] This was extended to also cover carriages under

51 For an analysis of the effect of article 23, see e.g. Anders Møllmann, "Compensation for Damage", in *The United Nations Convention on Contracts for the International Carriage of Goods Wholly or Partly by Sea – An Appraisal of the "Rotterdam Rules"*, ed. Meltem Deniz Güner-Ösbek (Heidelberg: Springer, 2011), p. 203f.

52 Michael Tsimplis in Baatz *et al.*, *The Rotterdam Rules: A Practical Annotation*, para 23-06, makes the same observation.

53 If the consignee can show that the "clean" receipt was only given under the threat of denying delivery, no effect should be given to such receipt in respect of the condition of the goods at delivery. This would be a matter for the otherwise applicable law to decide, but it is submitted that most jurisdictions could solve this question either under the law of evidence or contract law, e.g. invalidation on the basis of non-violent coercion.

54 For the same view see Francesco Berlingieri, "A Review of some Recent Analyses of the Rotterdam Rules", *Il Diritto Maritimo* (2009): 1012.

55 UNCITRAL, A/CN.9/WG.III/WP.21, section 10.

other transport documents where the problem of consignees not showing up was also perceived to exist. The result was that two separate ways for the carrier to discharge his obligation to deliver the goods were developed. One which may be labelled the "ordinary way" and which is in essence a codification of the current law. And one which may be labelled the "extraordinary way" and which is the attempt to find a solution to the aforementioned problem.

The rules are set out in one article for carriages where no transport document or a non-negotiable transport document has been issued (article 45); one article for carriages where a non-negotiable transport document that requires surrender is issued (article 46); and one for carriages where a negotiable transport document has been issued (article 47). Each of these articles contains both the ordinary and the "extraordinary way" of delivery.

The basic idea of the "extraordinary way" is that if the consignee does not take delivery at the time and place of delivery then the carrier can ask for instructions about to whom to deliver from certain specified parties in a specified order. Such a procedure is, of course, most controversial in relation to transport documents that are traditionally considered to represent the goods and thus be "the key to the floating warehouse", i.e. negotiable bills of lading and to a certain extent also straight or recta bills. The "extraordinary way" is an extra possibility for the carrier. It does not prejudice the carrier's other options as to how to deal with undeliverable goods which is regulated in article 48.[56]

In the following, the rules for delivery of goods transported under a non-negotiable transport document or where no transport document has been issued will be briefly explained followed by an in-depth analysis of the rules for delivery of goods carried under a non-negotiable transport document that requires surrender and negotiable transport documents.

5.1 Delivery when a non-negotiable or no transport document is issued

Article 45[57] regulates delivery when a non-negotiable or no transport document has been issued. The wording of the chapeau of the article sets

56 Articles 45(c), 46(b), and the chapeau of 47(2).

57 Article 45 reads; "When neither a negotiable transport document nor a negotiable electronic transport record has been issued:

(*a*) The carrier shall deliver the goods to the consignee at the time and location referred to in article 43. The carrier may refuse delivery if the person claiming to be the consignee does not properly identify itself as the consignee on the request of the carrier;

(*b*) If the name and address of the consignee are not referred to in the contract particulars, the controlling party shall prior to or upon the arrival of the goods at the place of destination advise the carrier of such name and address;

(*c*) Without prejudice to article 48, paragraph 1, if the goods are not deliverable because (i) the consignee, after having received a notice of arrival, does not, at the time or

out that it applies to carriages where neither a negotiable transport document nor a negotiable electronic transport record has been issued, but in positive terms this means that a non-negotiable or no transport document has been issued. In terms of documents in use today the most common situations would be carriages under sea waybills or where a simple document which does not fulfil the definition of a transport document[58] is issued, inter alia a ferry ticket.

The ordinary way is set out in paragraphs (a) and (b). The carrier must deliver the goods to the consignee, but may refuse to do so if the person claiming to be consignee does not properly identify itself at the request of the carrier, paragraph (a). If the contract particulars do not include the name and address of the consignee then the controlling party[59] must supply this information to the carrier prior to or upon the arrival of the goods at the place of destination, paragraph (b).

It must be noted that there is no obligation on the carrier to require the consignee to identify itself as consignee and it has been suggested that the carrier is better off by simply refraining from asking for identification thereby avoiding a situation where the alleged consignee will not or cannot identify itself as the consignee. Also, the wording as to the consequence of a failure to properly identify itself is in permissive language in that the carrier "may" refuse to deliver in such circumstances. However, the obligation on the carrier is to deliver the goods to the consignee who is defined as a person entitled to delivery.[60] The risk of delivering to someone not entitled to delivery is therefore on the carrier and it is on this background that article 45(a) obliges the consignee to reply to the request of the carrier to identify itself and affords the carrier the option to deny delivery if the consignee does not fulfil this obligation. If the carrier feels confident that the person claiming delivery is the consignee, it does not breach its

within the time period referred to in article 43, claim delivery of the goods from the carrier after their arrival at the place of destination, (ii) the carrier refuses delivery because the person claiming to be the consignee does not properly identify itself as the consignee, or (iii) the carrier is, after reasonable effort, unable to locate the consignee in order to request delivery instructions, the carrier may so advise the controlling party and request instructions in respect of the delivery of the goods. If, after reasonable effort, the carrier is unable to locate the controlling party, the carrier may so advise the shipper and request instructions in respect of the delivery of the goods. If, after reasonable effort, the carrier is unable to locate the shipper, the carrier may so advise the documentary shipper and request instructions in respect of the delivery of the goods;

(*d*) The carrier that delivers the goods upon instruction of the controlling party, the shipper or the documentary shipper pursuant to subparagraph (*c*) of this article is discharged from its obligations to deliver the goods under the contract of carriage."

58 Article 1(14).

59 The identity of which is established pursuant to article 51(1).

60 Articles 45(a) and 1(11).

obligations simply by not requesting identification, but this decision of the carrier is at its own peril.[61]

The carrier may avail itself of the "extraordinary way" if the goods are not deliverable for one of three reasons, article 45(c); 1. The consignee after having received a notice of arrival does not claim delivery of the goods at the correct time; 2. The carrier refuses delivery because the alleged consignee does not properly identify itself as consignee; 3. The carrier is after reasonable effort unable to locate the consignee.

In relation to number 1, it is worth noting that the Rotterdam Rules do not contain a general obligation on the carrier to give a notice of arrival, but if the carrier wishes to avail itself of the "extraordinary way" because the consignee does not claim delivery at the correct time, the carrier must first give a notice of arrival. As will be shown, the carrier must also give notice before dealing with undeliverable goods under article 48.[62]

If the "extraordinary way" is available to the carrier then it may request instructions in respect of the delivery of the goods from the controlling party. The identity of the controlling party is established in article 51(1). The controlling party is the shipper (i.e. the contractual partner of the carrier, article 1(8)) unless the shipper at the conclusion of the contract of carriage has designated the consignee, the documentary shipper[63] or another person as the controlling party, paragraph (a), or the right of control has been transferred and the carrier has been notified of the transfer, paragraph (b).

If the carrier cannot after reasonable effort locate the controlling party, it may instead ask for instructions from the shipper, and if the carrier is after reasonable effort unable to locate the shipper then it may request instructions from the documentary shipper, article 45(c).

When the carrier receives such instructions in respect of the delivery of the goods and follows them then the carrier is discharged from its obligations to deliver the goods under the contract of carriage, article 45(d). Consequently, if the carrier follows the "extraordinary way" correctly, it can deliver the goods to someone other than the consignee without exposing itself to a claim for misdelivery. Thereby the carrier avoids the problems consequential upon a consignee not taking delivery of the goods.

The procedure raises several questions. When has the carrier shown "reasonable effort" in locating the various parties? Are the named parties obliged to give instructions and what are the consequences of a party not giving instructions? Is the carrier obliged to follow instructions if it receives

61 Sturley, Fujita, and van der Ziel, *The Rotterdam Rules*, para 8.027. Debattista in Baatz *et al.*, *The Rotterdam Rules: A Practical Annotation*, para 45-05, supports this interpretation, yet at para 45-11 he seems to suggest that the carrier may avoid a claim for misdelivery by not asking for identification.

62 *Infra* part 5.4.

63 As defined in article 1(9).

them? Can the party giving instructions be held liable? Can the carrier request instructions from the next party in line if the first party refuses to give instructions? These questions will be analysed in the following sections in relation to non-negotiable transport documents that require surrender and negotiable transport documents.

5.2 Delivery when a non-negotiable transport document that requires surrender is issued

Article 46[64] applies "[w]hen a non-negotiable transport document [...] that indicates that it shall be surrendered in order to obtain delivery of the goods" has been issued. In relation to the documents currently in use, the article is supposed to cover straight bills of lading, i.e. bills that are to a named consignee without the addition of "to order" or similar wording, and recta bills of lading, i.e. bills that have a recta clause stating "not to order" or similar wording.

When such document is issued, the carrier must deliver the goods to the consignee at the correct time and location, cf. article 43, upon two conditions. At the request of the carrier, the consignee must properly identify itself and the consignee must surrender the transport document, article 46(a). The consequence of the consignee not fulfilling the former

64 Article 46 reads; "When a non-negotiable transport document has been issued that indicates that it shall be surrendered in order to obtain delivery of the goods:

(*a*) The carrier shall deliver the goods at the time and location referred to in article 43 to the consignee upon the consignee properly identifying itself on the request of the carrier and surrender of the non-negotiable document. The carrier may refuse delivery if the person claiming to be the consignee fails to properly identify itself on the request of the carrier, and shall refuse delivery if the non-negotiable document is not surrendered. If more than one original of the non-negotiable document has been issued, the surrender of one original will suffice and the other originals cease to have any effect or validity;

(*b*) Without prejudice to article 48, paragraph 1, if the goods are not deliverable because (i) the consignee, after having received a notice of arrival, does not, at the time or within the time period referred to in article 43, claim delivery of the goods from the carrier after their arrival at the place of destination, (ii) the carrier refuses delivery because the person claiming to be the consignee does not properly identify itself as the consignee or does not surrender the document, or (iii) the carrier is, after reasonable effort, unable to locate the consignee in order to request delivery instructions, the carrier may so advise the shipper and request instructions in respect of the delivery of the goods. If, after reasonable effort, the carrier is unable to locate the shipper, the carrier may so advise the documentary shipper and request instructions in respect of the delivery of the goods;

(*c*) The carrier that delivers the goods upon instruction of the shipper or the documentary shipper pursuant to subparagraph (*b*) of this article is discharged from its obligation to deliver the goods under the contract of carriage, irrespective of whether the non-negotiable transport document has been surrendered to it."

condition is that the carrier may refuse delivery while the consequence of not fulfilling the latter condition is that the carrier must refuse delivery.

The aim of the article is to harmonise at the international level the use of straight and recta bills of lading. This aim is only partly achieved because the definition of the type of document leaves a wide discretion to the national legislatures and courts to decide whether a given document in fact falls under this category.[65] This is a result of the choice of wording of the article whereby the document must "indicate" that it shall be surrendered. The wording was chosen specifically to give flexibility to accommodate the continuation of the practice in various jurisdictions as to what wording is required to establish that the transport document must be surrendered to obtain delivery of the goods.[66] National differences with respect to the clarity with which the document must "indicate" that it must be surrendered in order to obtain delivery of the goods may, thus, continue even after the entry into force of the Rotterdam Rules. While the Rules do not fully harmonise when a document falls into the category of a non-negotiable document that requires surrender, the Rules do to a large extent set out the legal effect of using such a document. One important aspect of this is the rule in article 46(a) that the document must be surrendered and the carrier must refuse delivery if it is not.[67]

Article 46(a) further sets out the rule that if more than one original of the non-negotiable transport document has been issued then the surrender of one original will suffice in order to obtain delivery of the goods and the other originals will then cease to have any effect or validity. Contrary to the rule relating to negotiable transport documents, article 46 does not specify that the number of originals or the fact that more than one original

65 Møllmann, "From bills of lading to transport documents – the role of transport documents under the Rotterdam Rules", p. 52 et seq. Sturley, Fujita, and van der Ziel, *The Rotterdam Rules*, para 8.041, seem to interpret art. 46 on the basis of the intention of harmonisation such that it is not enough for a document to be called a "bill of lading" to fall under that article. Neither the wording of article 46 nor the travaux preparatoires seem to warrant that contention.

66 The proposal to include regulation of this type of document was made by the government of the Netherlands in UNCITRAL, A/CN.9/WG.III/WP.68 where the term "indicates" was used. After discussion at the seventeenth session of the Working Group, cf. A/CN.9/594 para 208-215, the alternatives "provides" and "specifies" were added in square brackets in draft article 47 of what would become the second to last consolidated draft convention, A/CN.9/WG.III/WP.81. The term "specifies" was deleted at the twentieth session, cf. A/CN.9/642 para 29-35, and finally the term "indicates" was chosen at the twenty-first session, cf. A/CN.9/645 para 154–156.

67 As described in Chapter 3, part 3, this question is still the subject of some uncertainty in English law while under Scandinavian law it is clear that the document must be surrendered. By contrast, under US law a straight bill does not have to be surrendered to obtain delivery, USC § 80110(b), previously the Federal Bills of Lading Act 1916 (the Pomerene Act), section 9. A straight bill including a clause that the bill must be surrendered to obtain delivery would have to be surrendered, but as a matter of contract rather than by law.

has been issued must be stated in the transport document. The rule must be understood to operate even if the number of originals is not stated. It is not a matter that is left to the otherwise applicable law. This can be explained by the fact that the document is considered a non-negotiable document under the Rules even though the surrender of the document is required. Thus, the document is only a representative of the goods in the hands of the named consignee.

The "extraordinary way" of delivery of the goods closely mirrors that which applies under article 45 to carriages where a non-negotiable or no transport document has been issued.[68] The conditions for the "extraordinary way" to be available to the carrier are the same with the addition of the situation where the carrier refuses delivery on the grounds that the alleged consignee does not surrender the transport document, article 46(b).

When the "extraordinary way" is available to the carrier then it may request instructions in respect of the delivery of the goods from the shipper and if after reasonable effort the carrier is unable to locate the shipper then from the documentary shipper. If the carrier follows the instructions then it is discharged from its obligations to deliver the goods under the contract of carriage despite the fact that the non-negotiable transport document requiring surrender has in fact not been surrendered, article 46(c).

One may note that the carrier shall not seek instructions from the controlling party. That is a result of article 51(2) whereby the controlling party is the shipper unless it has transferred the right of control to the consignee named in the document by transferring the document to that person. The "extraordinary way" only becomes relevant if the consignee does not claim delivery, cannot be found, does not properly identify itself, or does not surrender the document and in these circumstances it would not make sense to direct the carrier to the controlling party because that party would be the consignee who has not fulfilled the conditions to obtain delivery in the "ordinary way" or the shipper.

A related aspect regarding the type of transport document dealt with in article 46 is that it has previously been discussed whether straight bills of lading needed to be indorsed when transferred from the shipper to the named consignee. The Rotterdam Rules have solved this uncertainty setting out that a non-negotiable transport document indicating that it shall be surrendered need not be so indorsed, article 51(2).

5.3 Delivery when a negotiable transport document is issued

The by far most controversial part of the chapter on delivery of the goods is that relating to delivery of goods for which a negotiable transport

68 *Supra* part 5.1.

document has been issued, i.e. article 47. The idea of an "extraordinary way" of delivery whereby the carrier is discharged from its obligation to deliver the goods under the contract of carriage despite the transport document not being surrendered runs contrary to some of the core notions associated with the use of bills of lading. A compromise therefore had to be struck during the negotiations for an "extraordinary way" also in relation to negotiable transport documents to be acceptable. Eventually, such compromise was reached in the form of a "contractual opt-in" meaning that the "extraordinary way" will only be applicable to documents which contain a "warning" that they may be subject to the "extraordinary way".

The "ordinary way" is much less controversial, yet holds some issues which may give rise to controversy.

5.3.1 The "ordinary way"

The "ordinary way" is set out in article 47(1).[69] Pursuant to this article, the holder of the negotiable transport document is entitled to claim delivery after they have arrived at the place of destination and the carrier shall then deliver the goods on the condition that the holder surrenders the transport document, paragraph (a)(i). If the transport document is an order document (as opposed to a bearer document or an order document indorsed in blank) then the holder must also properly identify itself, ibid. If either of the conditions is not fulfilled then the carrier must refuse delivery, paragraph (b).

69 Article 47(1) reads; "1. When a negotiable transport document or a negotiable electronic transport record has been issued:

(*a*) The holder of the negotiable transport document or negotiable electronic transport record is entitled to claim delivery of the goods from the carrier after they have arrived at the place of destination, in which event the carrier shall deliver the goods at the time and location referred to in article 43 to the holder:
  (i) Upon surrender of the negotiable transport document and, if the holder is one of the persons referred to in article 1, subparagraph 10 (*a*) (i), upon the holder properly identifying itself; or
  (ii) Upon demonstration by the holder, in accordance with the procedures referred to in article 9, paragraph 1, that it is the holder of the negotiable electronic transport record;

(*b*) The carrier shall refuse delivery if the requirements of subparagraph (*a*) (i) or (*a*) (ii) of this paragraph are not met;

(*c*) If more than one original of the negotiable transport document has been issued, and the number of originals is stated in that document, the surrender of one original will suffice and the other originals cease to have any effect or validity. When a negotiable electronic transport record has been used, such electronic transport record ceases to have any effect or validity upon delivery to the holder in accordance with the procedures required by article 9, paragraph 1."

The holder is a defined term, article 1(10). When the negotiable transport document in question is a bearer document or an order document indorsed in blank, the holder is simply the bearer thereof, paragraph (a)(ii). If the document is an order document then the holder is the person identified in it as the shipper or the consignee or the person to which it has been duly indorsed, paragraph (a)(i).

Article 47 also deals with the situation where the transport document has been issued in a set. Accordingly, if more than one original has been issued, the surrender of one original will suffice to obtain delivery of the goods as long as the number of originals is stated in the document, article 47(1)(c). This only applies to delivery at the agreed place of destination. If the holder wishes to obtain delivery en route, it must claim so using the right of control, article 50(1)(b), and in order to exercise the right of control, all originals of the transport document must be produced, article 51(3)(c). These rules mirror the current law of both England and the Scandinavian countries. The Rules are silent as to what the consequence is of the number of originals not being stated in the transport document. This question is therefore left to the otherwise applicable law and the Rules do not place the risk of the number of originals not being stated on either party.

While article 47(1) (and Chapter 9 as a whole) sets out the delivery obligation of the carrier, the Rotterdam Rules do not regulate the basis of a potential liability for the carrier's breach of this obligation.[70] It is difficult to exactly draw the line between the two and thus establish to what degree national law should supplement article 47. This is of importance in respect of e.g. to which extent the carrier must check the validity of indorsements on the transport document.

As stated, it is the holder who is entitled to claim delivery and the definition of holder in respect of an order document must have the document "duly endorsed" to it, article 1(10)(a). Although these articles are in absolute terms, it is submitted, that it cannot be inferred that the Rules place the risk of forged or unauthorised indorsements solely on the carrier.[71] The placement of that risk can be said to be part of the assessment of the potential liability of the carrier for a breach of the obligation to deliver to the consignee and thus fall under the otherwise applicable law.

70 See *infra* part 5.5.1.

71 Contra perhaps Sturley, Fujita, and van der Ziel, *The Rotterdam Rules*, para 10.017 et seq., who state that "it is essential to have the correct endorsement. An endorsement by the wrong person is ineffective to transfer rights under the document." The statement is, however, made in the context of the transfer of rights under article 57 and it is not certain (even though the authors in Chapter 8 on delivery of the goods, fn 101, refer to the discussion in para 10.017) that the authors claim that the same is the case in relation to the delivery of the goods, e.g. when it comes to the question of whether the carrier obtains a good discharge if it delivers the goods to someone who appears to be the indorsee, but where one of the indorsements turn out to be false.

National law regarding the risk of false or unauthorised indorsements can, thus, most likely continue to apply under the Rotterdam Rules.[72]

Whereas article 47(1) does not mention anything about the carrier checking the validity of the indorsements, it does set out that the carrier may request the holder of an order document to properly identify itself and specifies that the carrier shall refuse delivery if the holder does not comply with such request, subparagraphs (a)(i) and (b). The purpose of the identification is to ensure that the person claiming to be the holder is the person to whom the document is last indorsed. This would indicate that it is for the carrier to ensure that the person to whom it delivers is the person to whom the transport document is last indorsed and if it chooses not to require identification of that person, it does so at its own peril.[73]

5.3.2 The "extraordinary way" – introduction

As mentioned above, the "extraordinary way" is only available when the document contains a "warning" that it may be subject to such a way. Accordingly, article 47(2),[74] which sets out the "extraordinary way",

72 See *supra* Chapter 3, part 4, regarding the question under English and Scandinavian law. In this relation it is interesting that in both Norway and Denmark the committees preparing proposals for legislation implementing the Rotterdam Rules have suggested that "negotiable transport documents" should not be given negotiability senso strictu even though bills of lading under the present legislation have this characteristic, see *supra* Chapter 3, part 2.1, cf. NOU 2012: 10, Chapter 11, and Sølovsudvalget, "Betænkning 1536/2013", p. 49. This may have the effect that the current law regarding the risk of invalid indorsements, which builds to a large extent on the law applicable to negotiable instruments of debt, may be called into question. See on this risk *supra* Chapter 3, part 4.1.

73 Sturley, Fujita, and van der Ziel, *The Rotterdam Rules*, para 8.051. The situation is the same when a non-negotiable transport document is used, see *supra* section 5.1.

74 Article 47(2) reads; "2. Without prejudice to article 48, paragraph 1, if the negotiable transport document or the negotiable electronic transport record expressly states that the goods may be delivered without the surrender of the transport document or the electronic transport record, the following rules apply:

(*a*) If the goods are not deliverable because (i) the holder, after having received a notice of arrival, does not, at the time or within the time period referred to in article 43, claim delivery of the goods from the carrier after their arrival at the place of destination, (ii) the carrier refuses delivery because the person claiming to be a holder does not properly identify itself as one of the persons referred to in article 1, subparagraph 10 (*a*) (i), or (iii) the carrier is, after reasonable effort, unable to locate the holder in order to request delivery instructions, the carrier may so advise the shipper and request instructions in respect of the delivery of the goods. If, after reasonable effort, the carrier is unable to locate the shipper, the carrier may so advise the documentary shipper and request instructions in respect of the delivery of the goods;

(*b*) The carrier that delivers the goods upon instruction of the shipper or the documentary shipper in accordance with subparagraph 2 (*a*) of this article is discharged from its obligation to deliver the goods under the contract of carriage to the holder,

pursuant to the chapeau only applies "if the negotiable transport document [...] expressly states that the goods may be delivered without the surrender of the transport document".

If the negotiable transport document fulfils the prerequisite for the "extraordinary way", the carrier may avail itself of this way if the goods are undeliverable because either the holder after having received a notice of arrival does not claim delivery, because the carrier refuses delivery as a result of the alleged holder failing to properly identify itself, or because the carrier after reasonable effort cannot locate the holder to request delivery instructions, article 47(2)(a). In such circumstances, the carrier may ask the shipper for instructions as to the delivery of the goods and if after reasonable efforts the carrier cannot locate the shipper, it may instead ask the documentary shipper for instructions, ibid.

While the circumstances in which the carrier may avail itself of the "extraordinary way" are much the same under the various transport documents, the consequences for the carrier of following such instructions are much more complex in the case of negotiable transport documents.

As a starting point, the carrier who delivers according to instructions given under paragraph (a) is discharged from its obligation to deliver the goods under the contract of carriage, paragraph (c). However, if a person becomes the holder of the transport document after delivery has taken place pursuant to the "extraordinary way" and said person did not have and could not reasonably have had knowledge of the delivery when becoming a holder then that person acquires the rights incorporated in the transport document, including the right to delivery, paragraph (e). In these circumstances, the carrier is thus not discharged from its obligation to deliver the

irrespective of whether the negotiable transport document has been surrendered to it, or the person claiming delivery under a negotiable electronic transport record has demonstrated, in accordance with the procedures referred to in article 9, paragraph 1, that it is the holder;

(*c*) The person giving instructions under subparagraph 2 (*a*) of this article shall indemnify the carrier against loss arising from its being held liable to the holder under subparagraph 2 (*e*) of this article. The carrier may refuse to follow those instructions if the person fails to provide adequate security as the carrier may reasonably request;

(*d*) A person that becomes a holder of the negotiable transport document or the negotiable electronic transport record after the carrier has delivered the goods pursuant to subparagraph 2 (*b*) of this article, but pursuant to contractual or other arrangements made before such delivery acquires rights against the carrier under the contract of carriage, other than the right to claim delivery of the goods;

(*e*) Notwithstanding subparagraphs 2 (*b*) and 2 (*d*) of this article, a holder that becomes a holder after such delivery, and that did not have and could not reasonably have had knowledge of such delivery at the time it became a holder, acquires the rights incorporated in the negotiable transport document or negotiable electronic transport record. When the contract particulars state the expected time of arrival of the goods, or indicate how to obtain information as to whether the goods have been delivered, it is presumed that the holder at the time that it became a holder had or could reasonably have had knowledge of the delivery of the goods."

goods under the contract of carriage, but the carrier is given a statutory indemnity against the person giving the instruction regarding delivery and the carrier may ask for security as a condition for following the instructions, paragraph (c).

Further, it must be noted that the negotiable transport document contains rights even after delivery pursuant to the "extraordinary way" has taken place. If a person has acquired the transport document under contractual arrangements made before the delivery, but actually obtains the document after the delivery then that person acquires rights under the contract of carriage against the carrier other than the right to claim delivery, paragraph (d).

5.3.3 Eligible documents

The first question that arises is which documents are eligible for the "extraordinary way", i.e. what must the wording or content of the "warning" be.

The chapeau of article 47(2) states that it applies to a "negotiable transport document [...that] expressly states that the goods may be delivered without the surrender of the transport document". The underlying discussions of the change from an unconditional access to the "extraordinary way" as contained in the final proposal from the Working Group to the "contractual opt-in" decided by the Commission are not very well illuminated in the travaux preparatoires as the discussions mainly took place in informal consultations.[75]

The word "expressly" must in this regard be given some importance. It is not difficult to draft a clause which would clearly fulfil the condition in the chapeau of article 47(2).[76] It is more difficult when it comes to clauses which are not drafted with the specific aim of fulfilling the condition in the chapeau or clauses which are incorporated by reference into the transport document.

As for incorporation, it is relevant to consider whether a delivery clause in a charterparty obliging the owner to deliver the goods without the presentation of the negotiable transport document (possibly coupled with an indemnity from the charterer) may validly be incorporated by reference into a negotiable transport document issued under the charterparty, i.e. a tramp bill of lading. In this respect it is worth noting that the introduction of the word "expressly" in the chapeau of article 47(2) was made as a

75 UNCITRAL, A/63/17, para 152.

76 Sturley, Fujita, and van der Ziel, *The Rotterdam Rules*, para 8.083, Illustration 8-22, suggest the following example: "One original transport document must be surrendered, duly endorsed, in exchange of the goods. When no original is presented at the place of destination, the carrier has the option to invoke article 47(2) of the Rotterdam Rules with the result that the goods may be delivered without the surrender of this transport document."

reaction to this very concern.[77] It is submitted that "expressly" thus excludes the possibility of incorporating a delivery clause merely by reference to a charterparty.[78]

This is further supported by the fact that the clause must be said to be very burdensome for a consignee. In this respect the Rules' treatment of another clause which is traditionally seen as burdensome, namely an arbitration clause, is of interest. The Rules allow for the incorporation of an arbitration agreement into a transport document in non-liner transportation, article 76.[79] However, two conditions for the incorporation to be valid are set out; 1. the transport document must identify the charterparty, and 2. the incorporation must specify the clause in the charterparty which contains the terms of the arbitration agreement. There are thus quite strict conditions for the arbitration agreement to be binding on the consignee.

The underlying principle of this decision would seem to also apply to the incorporation of a delivery clause into a negotiable transport document which combined with the term "expressly" in article 47(2) and the travaux preparatoires related to that word invites the conclusion that a delivery clause in a negotiable transport document cannot be made by a mere incorporation of the terms of a charterparty. Unlike in the case of an arbitration agreement, this conclusion is not dependent on whether the consignee is a party to the charterparty because the protection comprised in the requirement of a delivery clause is of a possible subsequent holder who may acquire the negotiable transport document.

The next question is whether a clause which is not drafted as diligently to match the Rotterdam Rules as the one in footnote 76 or is not drafted with the Rotterdam Rules in mind at all, e.g. an existing delivery clause, will fulfil the requirement in the chapeau of article 47(2).[80] The question is important because the consequence of the clause falling under article 47(2) or not determines whether the carrier may deliver without the surrender of the document and be discharged of its delivery obligation. Thus, the value of the document to the holder turns on this issue and it is

77 UNCITRAL, A/63/17, para 161.

78 Diamond, "The Rotterdam Rules", 518f, states that it is "not clear" whether an incorporation would satisfy the requirement, but he does not refer to the travaux on this point.

79 As a starting point, the Rotterdam Rules do not apply to non-liner transportation, article 6(2), but the Rules nevertheless apply as between the carrier and the consignee, controlling party or holder that is not an original party to the charterparty, article 7. It is in this relationship the incorporation of an arbitration agreement in the charterparty into the transport document is valid in certain circumstances under article 76.

80 Debattista in Baatz *et al.*, *The Rotterdam Rules: A Practical Annotation*, para 47-15 et seq., suggests that a carrier may follow the procedure in article 47(2) and be discharged of its delivery obligation even if the transport document does not contain an express statement that the goods may be delivered without the surrender of the document. It is very difficult to follow this reasoning which goes directly against the wording of the chapeau of article 47(2).

important both for the holder and the carrier to be able to ascertain their legal position when the document is issued.

First, it must be noted that there is no requirement that the clause must refer to the Rotterdam Rules. The requirement is that the document expressly states that the goods may be delivered without the surrender of the document. Based on this wording, the (limited) travaux preparatoires on this point and the underlying intention of warning any potential acquirer of the negotiable transport document, it is submitted that the essential requirement is that the document in reasonably clear words and with direct mention of the transport document states that the surrender of the document is not in all circumstances necessary for an effective delivery to take place or for a misdelivery claim to be barred.

Professor Røsæg has suggested that a clause in the Maersk Line terms and conditions[81] would constitute a delivery clause which "article 47(2) will supplement" which must be understood to mean that the clause in his view would fulfil the requirement of the chapeau of said article.[82]

Clause 22.2 reads;

> The Merchant shall take delivery of the Goods within the time provided for in the Carrier's applicable Tariff. If the Merchant fails to do so, the Carrier may without notice unpack the Goods if packed in containers and/or store the Goods ashore, afloat, in the open or under cover at the sole risk of the Merchant. Such storage shall constitute due delivery hereunder, and thereupon all liability whatsoever of the Carrier in respect of the Goods or that part thereof shall cease and the costs of such storage shall forthwith upon demand be paid by the Merchant to the Carrier.[83]

It is submitted that this clause would not, however, fulfil the requirement in article 47(2). The clause deals with the carrier's remedies in relation to the goods when the consignee does not take delivery, but these remedies do not include delivering the goods to someone else and the clause does not at all mention that the surrender of the bill of lading is unnecessary. Rather, the remedies resemble those regulated in article 48 of the Rotterdam Rules, i.e. to store the goods or sell them to cover incurred expenses. The term that "[s]uch storage shall constitute due delivery" must be seen as a term regulating the carrier's period of responsibility rather than a term giving the carrier a right to deliver without the surrender of the bill of lading. Such change in the carrier's responsibility for the goods when the goods are stored is also set out in article 48(5).

81 The terms and conditions are available at www.maerskline.com.

82 Erik Røsæg, "New procedures for bills of lading in the Rotterdam Rules", *Journal of International Maritime Law* 17, no. 3 (2011): 182.

83 See on this type of clause *supra* Chapter 4, part 7.

By contrast, the terms and conditions applied by Maersk Line/Safmarine in an export trade from Western Africa in 2010 included a clause on the carrier's responsibility for port to port shipments which did specifically mention the bill of lading not being presented.

Clause IV (1) reads;

> where the carriage called for by this Bill of lading is a Port to Port Shipment then, whatever the custom of the port and the freight tariff applicable, the Carrier is deemed to take possession of the Goods on loading on the vessel and to deliver same on discharge from the vessel and the Carrier shall not be liable for loss or damage to the Goods during the period before loading on or discharge from the vessel, howsoever such loss or damage arises *and even if an original of the Bill of lading is not presented or accomplished by the Merchant or his agent on discharge from the vessel.* (italics added)

As can be seen, the clause specifically mentions the situation that an original bill of lading is not presented to obtain delivery and the clause aims to exclude any liability after discharge of the goods from the vessel which would prima facie include a claim for misdelivery.[84] This clause would probably be sufficiently clear to fulfil the requirement of article 47(2). The consequence thereof is that the carrier would have to follow the procedures of article 47(2) in order to obtain a discharge of its delivery obligation and, thus, not that the clause is given full effect according to its wording.

Obviously, the Rotterdam Rules will not from the time they enter into force be an all-encompassing, globally enacted system. The result will, thus, be that in some states not parties to the Rotterdam Rules the abovementioned clause will be valid according to its content; in some states it will be invalid and in states parties to the Rules the clause will mean that the carrier may avail itself of the "extraordinary way" as set out in article 47(2).

Another problem that may arise in relation to the delivery clause is that the front of the transport document may contain a statement that the transport document must be surrendered to obtain delivery while the standard terms on the reverse include a delivery clause stating that the goods may be delivered without the surrender of the document, i.e. seemingly contradictory terms. Such situations are classical problems of construction of bills of lading. With respect to the Rotterdam Rules, article 47, however, such clauses should not be considered contradictory. Article 47 is structured such that article 47(1) is the main rule while article 47(2) is an exception when the ordinary procedure in subsection 1 is not possible. Thus, the normal procedure in subsection 1, where the transport document must be

84 See on the construction of exemption clauses in relation to liability for misdelivery *supra* Chapter 4, part 5 and 6.

presented and surrendered to obtain delivery of the goods, is an important part of giving the transport document its legitimation function or function as document of title depending on the preferred terminology, i.e. its function of identifying its holder as the person entitled to delivery.[85] It is clear from the travaux preparatoires that the intention of the procedure in subsection 2 was not to take away the transport document's legitimation function or its negotiable character. The requirement in the chapeau of subsection 2 for a clause expressly stating that the goods may be delivered without the surrender of the document must be seen as a warning that the procedure in subsection 2 is available under the circumstances described therein and not as a total exclusion of the main procedure in subsection 1. The starting point is, thus, that the transport document must be surrendered to obtain delivery, but if for one of the reasons set out in subsection 2(a) the goods are not deliverable then the carrier may deliver the goods according to the procedure set out in subsection 2 and it is this possibility the required delivery clause warns of. This interpretation of article 47 means that a clause requiring the surrender of the document to obtain delivery and a clause stating that the goods may be delivered without the surrender of the document shall not – in relation to the Rotterdam Rules – be construed as contradictory.[86]

The fact that the chapeau of article 47(2) requires the statement to be express may also have a bearing on the clarity with which the statement must appear in the transport document. There is nothing in the Rules to support that the statement cannot be part of the standard terms and conditions or indeed of a standard form bill of lading or other transport document. It will be for the national courts to interpret whether a statement in the transport document fulfils the requirement in article 47(2) and national case law on the clarity with which burdensome clauses in a transport document must appear to be binding may thus come into play.[87] As it is of utmost importance to the parties to be able to rely on the document falling into the intended category and that the result should not depend on national differences, it must be urged that a uniform international interpretation is sought, cf. also the principle in article 2.

Having established the prerequisite for the procedure in article 47(2) to be available, it is obviously of great importance who decides whether a

85 Sturley, Fujita, and van der Ziel, *The Rotterdam Rules*, para 8.082.

86 A document with the described content may, however, cause problems under a documentary credit, where the bank is normally not obliged to check the terms on the back of the bill of lading, UCP 600, article 20(a)(v). The bank may therefore end up paying against a document which does not fulfil the terms of the sales contract or letter of credit.

87 See e.g. the principle that burdensome terms must stand out distinctly, developed under English law in *Thornton v. Shoe Lane Parking Ltd.*, [1971] 2 QB 163, and *Interfoto Picture Library Ltd. v. Stiletto Visual Programmes Ltd.*, [1989] QB 433.

clause fulfilling the requirement in the chapeau of said article shall be included in the transport document. The subject of issuance of the transport document is regulated in article 35.[88] The main rule is that it is the shipper who decides which document the carrier must issue, but this is subject to exceptions.

First, the carrier and shipper may have agreed not to use a transport document at all or not to use a negotiable one. Second, it may be the custom, usage or practice of the trade not to use a transport document or not to use a negotiable one.

The choice of the shipper is, however, between a non-negotiable and an appropriate negotiable transport document, article 35(a) and (b). Article 35 does not mention the possibility of a delivery clause being inserted in the negotiable transport document. The insertion of such a clause does not alter the status of the transport document as negotiable in terms of the Rotterdam Rules which suggests that the carrier fulfils its obligation under article 35 if it issues, at the shipper's request for a negotiable transport document, a negotiable transport document with an express statement that the goods may be delivered without the surrender of the document. However, article 35 speaks of "an appropriate negotiable transport document" and it may be asked whether the word "appropriate" changes the position.

The travaux preparatoires do not show the intended meaning of the term "appropriate", but most likely it refers to whether a "received-for-shipment" or a "shipped" transport document should be issued.[89] One may argue, though, that "appropriate" refers both to the appropriateness for the carriage in question and to the appropriateness in relation to the shipper's needs.[90] If a shipper asks for a negotiable transport document that must be surrendered to obtain delivery of the goods then a transport

88 Article 35 reads; "Unless the shipper and the carrier have agreed not to use a transport document or an electronic transport record, or it is the custom, usage or practice of the trade not to use one, upon delivery of the goods for carriage to the carrier or performing party, the shipper or, if the shipper consents, the documentary shipper, is entitled to obtain from the carrier, at the shipper's option:

(*a*) A non-negotiable transport document or, subject to article 8, subparagraph (*a*), a non-negotiable electronic transport record; or

(*b*) An appropriate negotiable transport document or, subject to article 8, subparagraph (*a*), a negotiable electronic transport record, unless the shipper and the carrier have agreed not to use a negotiable transport document or negotiable electronic transport record, or it is the custom, usage or practice of the trade not to use one".

89 Tomotaka Fujita, "Transport Documents and Electronic Transport Records", in *The Rotterdam Rules 2008*, ed. Alexander von Ziegler, Johan Schelin, and Stefano Zunarelli (Dordrecht: Kluwer Law International, 2010), p. 164, seems to only prescribe this meaning to the term "appropriate".

90 Møllmann, "From bills of lading to transport documents – the role of transport documents under the Rotterdam Rules", p. 55.

document with a clause stating that the goods may be delivered without the surrender of the document (even with specific reference to the procedure in article 47(2)) would not, it is submitted, constitute an "appropriate negotiable transport document" under article 35(b). If the shipper has only requested a negotiable transport document then a document containing a delivery clause may well be "appropriate".[91] From a business perspective, the carrier will obviously normally want to fulfil the wishes of its customer and in the trades where the article 47(2) procedure is most relevant, i.e. the bulk and especially bulk oil trades, it will probably be the shipper side, i.e. the parties to the sales contract and the financing banks who will decide whether a delivery clause should be inserted – or at least is acceptable.[92] However, if it is a key point in the contract of sale or letter of credit, then the shipper would be wise to make it a condition when entering into the contract of carriage that the transport document must not contain a statement that the goods may be delivered without the surrender of the document.

5.3.4 The voluntary nature and continuing exposure

If the transport document fulfils the requirement in the chapeau of article 47(2) then the carrier may avail itself of the procedure set out in that subsection if one of the circumstances set out in subparagraph (a) occurs. The operative word is "may" which shows that this is an option available for the carrier to use at its discretion. The carrier may instead avail itself of the

91 The question is disputed. Francesco Berlingieri et al., "The Rotterdam Rules – An Attempt to Clarify Certain Concerns that have Emerged", (2009), p. 21, state quite bluntly that "there does not appear to be any doubt that the shipper would be entitled to refuse a negotiable transport document that contains the statement indicated in article 47(2) [...]". This is based on the fact that article 35 entitles the shipper to demand a negotiable transport document. However, the statement indicated in article 47(2) does not alter the document's status as negotiable which the authors also write at p. 22. Diamond, "The Rotterdam Rules", p. 518, fn 126, on the other hand, simply states that the shipper has no right to refuse such a document. Diamond does not assess the (possible) effect of the term "appropriate" in article 35.

92 Berlingieri *et al.*, "The Rotterdam Rules – An Attempt to Clarify Certain Concerns that have Emerged", p. 21f. Here the authors state that it is for the parties to the sales contract to decide, but this is based on the assumption that a shipper can refuse a negotiable transport document with a statement as mentioned in the chapeau of article 47(2), see the preceding fn. Diamond, "The Rotterdam Rules", p. 518, fn 126, questions this and states that he suspects "that in many, if not most, cases, the decision will be taken by the carrier alone". That is probably correct in the container trade – at least in relation to small shippers. However, in the container trade, the remedies of article 48 are probably more convenient to the carrier than the procedure of article 47(2) which demands that the carrier takes various steps that are not necessary under article 48. Miriam Goldby, *Electronic Documents in Maritime Trade* (Oxford: Oxford University Press, 2013), p. 170f, assumes, like here, that carriers will not insert an article 47(2)-clause if it is unacceptable to banks, commodity traders, or insurers.

remedies in article 48 or it may do both, e.g. by storing the goods but continue to seek delivery instructions from the shipper.

If the carrier chooses to follow the procedure in article 47(2), it must first advise the shipper and request delivery instructions, subparagraph (a). "If, after reasonable effort, the carrier is unable to locate the shipper" then the carrier can instead ask the documentary shipper, ibid. This raises two questions; one, what is the standard of "reasonable effort", and two, can the carrier also ask the documentary shipper for instructions if the carrier locates the shipper, but the shipper refuses to give instructions.

With respect to the standard of the carrier's effort, it seems obvious that the assessment will depend on the individual circumstances. However, the standard, it is submitted, should be set at a fairly high level. The instructions that the carrier is seeking pertain to the crucial question of who gets the goods and the shipper and documentary shipper may not have the same interests in this respect. Thus, in an f.o.b. sale the shipper will normally be the buyer while the documentary shipper is the seller. Allowing the carrier to seek instructions from the documentary shipper as soon as the shipper "doesn't answer the phone" would therefore be a serious step.

If the carrier locates the shipper and requests delivery instructions, but the shipper is unable to give such instructions or simply refuses to do so (see immediately below as to whether the shipper is obligated to provide instructions) then the carrier may wish to request instructions from the documentary shipper. It must, however, be regarded as uncertain whether the carrier would be allowed to do so. The wording of article 47(2)(a) sets out that the carrier may request instructions from the documentary shipper "[i]f [...] the carrier is *unable to locate* the shipper" (italics added) and does not mention the situation that the shipper cannot or will not give instructions. On the other hand, the intention of the rule is to give the carrier the possibility to obtain instructions from the party who is presumably in the best position to know who is entitled to the goods, e.g. because the shipper has kept track of the string sales of the goods en route. This leads Sturley, Fujita and van der Ziel to clearly state that the carrier can ask the next party in line if the first one does not provide instructions.[93] Given that the parties may have different interests, some caution should, however, be exercised. At least if the shipper replies to the carrier's request by stating that the carrier should only deliver against presentation of the transport document, this should bar the carrier from seeking instructions from the documentary shipper. It is also worth noting that article 55 which sets out a hierarchy of parties who shall provide information, instructions and documents to the carrier specifically sets out that the carrier may turn to the shipper if it is unable to locate the controlling party "or [if] the

93 Sturley, Fujita, and van der Ziel, *The Rotterdam Rules*, paras 8.031, 8.032 and 8.035. The statements are made in the context of article 45, but seem to also apply in the context of article 47(2) as the wording is identical.

controlling party is unable to provide adequate information, instructions or documents to the carrier", paragraph 2. As this passage is not included in article 47(2)(a), or articles 45(c) and 46(b), it would seem to support the interpretation that the carrier cannot turn to the documentary shipper if it locates the shipper, but the shipper cannot or will not provide instructions.[94] The conclusion must, however, be said to be uncertain.

An important question is whether the voluntary nature of the procedure also applies to the shipper and documentary shipper. That is, can the shipper and documentary shipper refuse to comply with the request of the carrier to furnish instructions in relation to the delivery of the goods? Article 47(2)(a) does not itself furnish the answer. In previous drafts of the Rules, the shipper was obliged to give instructions, but this obligation was eventually deleted because the shipper or documentary shipper may simply not possess information to form the basis of instructions as to the delivery.[95] However, article 55 places a general obligation on the controlling party, the shipper and the documentary shipper to provide information, instructions or documents relating to the goods which are not otherwise reasonably available to the carrier and that the carrier may reasonably need to perform its obligations under the contract of carriage. Further, article 28 provides that the carrier and shipper shall respond to requests from each other to provide information and instructions required for the proper handling and carriage of the goods if the information is in the requested party's possession or the instructions are within the requested party's reasonable ability to provide.

This has been interpreted by some to set out an obligation on the shipper or documentary shipper to provide instructions as to the delivery when that person is in a position to do so and that the standard for the shipper's reasonable effort in obtaining necessary information to provide instructions should be somewhat higher than that set out in article 28.[96] Others, on the other hand, have simply stated that there is no obligation on the shipper to provide instructions.[97]

While it is clear from the travaux preparatoires that the reason for removing the obligation on the shipper and documentary shipper to give

94 This may also rely on a simple lack of drafting consistency. The fact that the next sentence of paragraph 2 sets out that the carrier may turn to the documentary shipper if it cannot locate the shipper without including the quoted passage and without any difference being seemingly intended would support that it is a lack of consistency. That inconsistency may, however, also be claimed to exist simply within paragraph 2 and not between article 55 and 47. Ibid., para 9.053 and Illustration 9-21, seem to interpret article 55(2) as if there were no difference of drafting between the various steps from one party to the next.

95 UNCITRAL, A/63/17, para 153.

96 Sturley, Fujita, and van der Ziel, *The Rotterdam Rules*, para 8.097 et seq. van der Ziel, "Delivery of the Goods", p. 211f.

97 Diamond, "The Rotterdam Rules", p. 519. Baughen, "Misdelivery claims under bills of lading and international conventions for the carriage of goods by sea", p. 183.

instructions was based on the fact that these parties may simply not be in a position to give proper instructions, the removal of the obligation was not limited to such situations. This deliberate change of article 47(2)(a) would seem to suggest that the imposition of an obligation through articles 28 and 55 was not intended even if the obligation imposed by these articles is more limited than the one in previous drafts of article 47(2)(a). Further, article 28 specifically speaks of instructions for the proper *handling and carriage of the goods* which in the language of the Rules otherwise does not include the delivery of the goods, see e.g. article 13. Article 55, on the other hand, speaks of instructions which the carrier may reasonably need to perform *its obligations* under the contract of carriage which include the obligation to deliver the goods, cf. article 13. This article would seem to oblige the shipper to give the carrier information which it may possess regarding the identity and location of the holder of the transport document or who the rightful owner of the goods is whereby it would aid the carrier in fulfilling its delivery obligation according to the ordinary way for negotiable transport documents, i.e. article 47(1).

However, imposing an obligation to give instructions as to the delivery of the goods under article 47(2)(a) is a different matter. By giving instructions, the shipper or documentary shipper becomes subjected to the obligation to indemnify the carrier for loss it may suffer by being held liable to a bona fide acquirer of the transport document under subparagraph (e), cf. subparagraph (c). It may also be envisaged that it may be held liable on other grounds to a holder or acquirer of the document. Even if the shipper has accepted – or has had to accept, cf. the discussion at fn 88 et seq. – a statement in the negotiable transport document that the goods may be delivered without surrender of the document, the shipper may not wish to partake in the "extraordinary way" under the given circumstances because these do not in the shipper's opinion warrant deviating from the ordinary procedure. An obligation on the shipper or documentary shipper to give instructions would on this basis require a fairly clear foundation and, it is submitted, that the Rules do not provide such clear foundation. Even if an obligation was accepted in the circumstances where the shipper is in a position to give instructions, a very wide margin of discretion should be accepted for the shipper to decide whether it has the necessary basis on which to give instructions.

In many cases, the cargo side, and thus the shipper, will have an interest in giving instructions at the request of the carrier. The question then arises, whether the carrier is obliged to follow such instructions. The answer is a straightforward "no".[98] The procedure in article 47(2) is completely

98 If the carrier has demanded security from the person giving instructions under subparagraph (c) and such security has been provided, the carrier may at that time be estopped from refusing to follow the instructions. This must however be based on national law and does not follow directly from the Rotterdam Rules.

voluntary for the carrier. If the carrier knows or ought to know that the instructions are wrong, i.e. that someone else has a better right to the goods, the carrier may even be obliged not to follow the instructions.[99] The carrier will, of course, only obtain a discharge of its delivery obligation if it follows the instructions correctly, article 47(2)(b). If it delivers the goods to someone other than the person to whom it is instructed, it will incur an ordinary liability for misdelivery.[100]

Although the relationship between the person claiming delivery without fulfilling article 47(1) and the shipper or documentary shipper falls wholly outside the ambit of the Rotterdam Rules, it is difficult to see any grounds under the otherwise applicable law for a claim from the person claiming delivery against the shipper or documentary shipper for not giving instructions when the Rules do not place a clearer obligation on these parties to give instructions and no such obligation exists under the current law. If, on the other hand, the shipper or documentary shipper does comply with the request of the carrier and gives instructions as to the delivery then that person may expose itself to a liability towards the rightful owner or consignee of the goods. The Rotterdam Rules only deal with the liability-related issues which flow from giving instructions by establishing a statutory indemnity from the party giving instructions towards the carrier, subparagraph (c). In this respect it should also be noted that article 4 making any convention-based defence available to the shipper or documentary shipper applicable irrespective of the basis of the claim would not be of any avail to the party giving instructions – or refusing to do so – as the Rules do not provide any defence in these circumstances.[101] As these liability issues do not involve the carrier and are not regulated directly in the Rotterdam Rules, it falls outside the scope of this book to analyse these issues further.

99 Sturley, Fujita, and van der Ziel, *The Rotterdam Rules*, para 8.100, fn 92, who base this on the carrier's general duty of bona fide implementation of contractual obligations as also expressed in article 2.

100 Debattista in Baatz *et al.*, *The Rotterdam Rules: A Practical Annotation*, para 47-19. However, at para 47-24, Debattista seems to suggest that if the carrier refuses to follow the instructions given because the instructing person does not provide security as demanded by the carrier under subparagraph (c) then it should still be discharged of its delivery obligation. However, if the carrier refuses to follow the instructions then the proper way forward for the carrier is to take steps pursuant to article 48. If it delivers to someone other than the person to whom it was instructed then article 47(2)(b) will not give the carrier a good discharge and it will be liable to a misdelivery claim as if it had not received instructions at all.

101 If one, contrary to the analysis above, construes articles 28 and 55 to impose an obligation on the shipper and documentary shipper to give delivery instructions at the request of the carrier, the party refusing to give such instructions may rely on the defences that can be deduced from these articles, e.g. that the information was otherwise reasonably available to the carrier or that the instructions were not within the requested party's reasonable ability to provide.

The discharge which the carrier obtains under subparagraph (b) is not absolute. Subparagraph (e) contains an exception whereby a holder can still have a right to delivery while subparagraph (d) sets out that the holder may have other rights than the right to claim delivery.

The right to still claim delivery is conferred on the person who becomes a holder of the transport document after delivery pursuant to the "extraordinary way" has taken place and who is in good faith about that delivery having taken place, i.e. "that did not have and could not reasonably have had knowledge of such delivery", subparagraph (e). The good faith must be present at the time when the person becomes the holder. It is this continuing exposure for which subparagraph (c) gives the carrier a statutory indemnity against the instructing person (shipper or documentary shipper) and for which the carrier can request a security. This is meant to uphold the legitimation function of the negotiable transport document.[102]

Subparagraph (e) sets up a presumption that the holder had or could reasonably have had knowledge of the delivery if the transport document either states the expected time of arrival of the goods or indicate how to obtain information as to whether the goods have been delivered. This must be seen in conjunction with the fact that the transport document must contain an express statement that the goods may be delivered without the surrender of the document. The combined effect is that the holder is fairly warned and must then show diligence in assuring that it is not acquiring a transport document covering goods which have already been delivered. It is however only a presumption and an acquirer in good faith can therefore still rely on the content of the negotiable document.

Subparagraph (d) applies in the situation where a person has acquired the transport document prior to the delivery of the goods, but only becomes the holder, that is receives the document, after delivery has taken place, i.e. typically the situation where the document has not made it through the chain of buyers and/or banks before the goods arrive at the destination. In such circumstances, the holder obtains other rights under the contract of carriage than the right to claim delivery. The holder can thus, inter alia, use the document as proof of the carrier's receipt of the goods, cf. article 41 (b).

102 Sturley, Fujita, and van der Ziel, *The Rotterdam Rules*, para 8.095.

103 Article 48 reads; "1. For the purposes of this article, goods shall be deemed to have remained undelivered only if, after their arrival at the place of destination:

(*a*) The consignee does not accept delivery of the goods pursuant to this chapter at the time and location referred to in article 43;

(*b*) The controlling party, the holder, the shipper or the documentary shipper cannot be found or does not give the carrier adequate instructions pursuant to articles 45, 46 and 47;

(*c*) The carrier is entitled or required to refuse delivery pursuant to articles 44, 45, 46 and 47;

(*d*) The carrier is not allowed to deliver the goods to the consignee pursuant to the law or regulations of the place at which delivery is requested; or

(*e*) The goods are otherwise undeliverable by the carrier.

5.4 Remedies other than delivery, article 48

Article 48[103] contains the more "classical" remedies for the carrier when it is unable to deliver the goods due to reasons on the cargo side. The article consists of a non-exhaustive list of steps the carrier may take, a non-exhaustive list of the situations in which the steps may be taken and a rule on the effect on the carrier's responsibility for the goods after such steps are taken.

The steps that the carrier may take are "such action in respect of the goods as circumstances may reasonably require", subparagraph 2. This is then exemplified by three specific actions, namely to store the goods, to unpack or move the goods and to cause the goods to be sold or destroyed.

The steps may be taken "when the goods have remained undelivered". This is deemed to be the case when the consignee does not accept delivery, when the party who may give instructions under "the extraordinary way" cannot be located or does not give adequate instructions, when the carrier is entitled or required to refuse delivery, when the carrier is not allowed to deliver the goods pursuant to local law or regulations or when the "goods are otherwise undeliverable by the carrier", subparagraph 1. The last situation, obviously, makes the list non-exhaustive.

2. Without prejudice to any other rights that the carrier may have against the shipper, controlling party or consignee, if the goods have remained undelivered, the carrier may, at the risk and expense of the person entitled to the goods, take such action in respect of the goods as circumstances may reasonably require, including:
   (*a*) To store the goods at any suitable place;
   (*b*) To unpack the goods if they are packed in containers or vehicles, or to act otherwise in respect of the goods, including by moving them; and
   (*c*) To cause the goods to be sold or destroyed in accordance with the practices or pursuant to the law or regulations of the place where the goods are located at the time.
3. The carrier may exercise the rights under paragraph 2 of this article only after it has given reasonable notice of the intended action under paragraph 2 of this article to the person stated in the contract particulars as the person, if any, to be notified of the arrival of the goods at the place of destination, and to one of the following persons in the order indicated, if known to the carrier: the consignee, the controlling party or the shipper.
4. If the goods are sold pursuant to subparagraph 2 (*c*) of this article, the carrier shall hold the proceeds of the sale for the benefit of the person entitled to the goods, subject to the deduction of any costs incurred by the carrier and any other amounts that are due to the carrier in connection with the carriage of those goods.
5. The carrier shall not be liable for loss of or damage to goods that occurs during the time that they remain undelivered pursuant to this article unless the claimant proves that such loss or damage resulted from the failure by the carrier to take steps that would have been reasonable in the circumstances to preserve the goods and that the carrier knew or ought to have known that the loss or damage to the goods would result from its failure to take such steps."

If the carrier takes such steps in a situation where it is warranted then its liability for loss of or damage to the goods is severely limited as compared to its liability which applies to the period of responsibility under article 17. Pursuant to subparagraph 5, the carrier will only be liable for loss of or damage to the goods that occurs during the time they remain undelivered if the carrier failed to take steps that would have been reasonable in the circumstances to preserve the goods and the loss or damage was a result thereof. Further, the carrier must have known or ought to have known that its failure to take such steps would result in the loss or damage.

The steps that may be taken by the carrier are very severe for the owners of the cargo and the article therefore contains certain safeguards for the cargo side. First of all, the circumstances must reasonably require the particular steps to be taken. Before taking any of these steps, the carrier must give reasonable notice of the steps it intends to take, subparagraph 3. Such notice must be given to the notify party, if one is named in the transport document, and to either the consignee, the controlling party or the shipper, in that order and only if known to the carrier.

Finally, subparagraph 4 sets out that if the carrier causes the goods to be sold then it must hold the proceeds of the sale for the benefit of the person entitled to the goods. However, the carrier may deduct any costs it has incurred as well as other sums due in connection with the carriage of the goods in question, e.g. freight or container demurrage.

Article 48 deals with undeliverable goods in a much more detailed manner than the current law of both the Scandinavian countries and England but it is based on the same main principles. It is the cargo side who is at fault by not receiving the goods and the carrier must therefore be given a way to dispose of the goods while at the same time respecting and safeguarding the interests of the cargo owner. Adoption of the Rotterdam Rules will, thus, bring regulation of this situation back into statute law and will in both England and Scandinavia result in a much more comprehensive regulation of both the steps that may be taken, the situations in which they may be taken, the liability of the carrier when they are taken and the safeguards of the cargo owner's interests. This will also mean that this issue will be harmonised in the states that ratify the Rules.

5.5 Other effects of the rules on delivery

5.5.1 Calculation of compensation, limitation of liability, and time bar

With the Rotterdam Rules regulating the delivery of the goods, thus making this issue convention based, it is worth exploring which other effects this may have on the treatment of a breach of the obligation to deliver the goods.

While the obligation to deliver the goods is regulated in the Rules, the potential liability for breaching that obligation is not. Article 17, which is the main rule on the basis of liability for the carrier, applies to "loss of or damage to the goods, as well as for delay in delivery", subparagraph 1. That does not include a claim for misdelivery.[104] Instead, a liability for breach of the obligation to deliver the goods must be based on the otherwise applicable law.

In the same vein, the rule on calculation of compensation, article 22, applies to "loss of or damage to the goods".[105] If liability is established then the compensation payable by the carrier must also be calculated according to the otherwise applicable law.

Despite the fact that the basis of liability and calculation of compensation must be based on the otherwise applicable law then the obligation to deliver which is breached is an obligation set out in the Rules, cf. articles 11 and 13 as well as Chapter 9. The limitation of the carrier's liability is regulated in Chapter 12. The main rule, article 59,[106] applies to "the carrier's liability for breaches of its obligations under this Convention", subparagraph 1. This undoubtedly also includes liability for breaches of the carrier's obligation to deliver the goods.[107] That is a major change from the current law – of most jurisdictions – where the liability for misdelivery is an unlimited one.[108]

104 This is implicit in the discussion referred in UNCITRAL, A/CN.9/594, para 118-20. See also Møllmann, "Compensation for Damage", pp 202 and 06. The conclusion is, however, not completely undisputed as the discussion in relation to the applicability of the Hague-Visby Rules to misdelivery claims seems to continue in relation to the Rotterdam Rules even if the wording of article 17 is narrower than that in the Hague-Visby Rules article IV, rule 5. Thus, Sturley, Fujita, and van der Ziel, *The Rotterdam Rules*, para 8.002, only state that "[o]ne might argue that the basis for the carrier's liability for misdelivery must be found in otherwise applicable law", even if that does seem to also be their conclusion. See also Baughen, "Misdelivery claims under bills of lading and international conventions for the carriage of goods by sea", p. 185.

105 If one, contrary to what is stated in the text, construes article 17 to also cover liability for misdelivery then article 22 will also apply in relation to the calculation of the damages. "Misdelivery claims under bills of lading and international conventions for the carriage of goods by sea", pp 186 and 89, discusses the implications thereof.

106 Article 59(1) and (2) read; "1. Subject to articles 60 and 61, paragraph 1, the carrier's liability for breaches of its obligations under this Convention is limited to 875 units of account per package or other shipping unit, or 3 units of account per kilogram of the gross weight of the goods that are the subject of the claim or dispute, whichever amount is the higher, except when the value of the goods has been declared by the shipper and included in the contract particulars, or when a higher amount than the amount of limitation of liability set out in this article has been agreed upon between the carrier and the shipper.
2. When goods are carried in or on a container, pallet or similar article of transport used to consolidate goods, or in or on a vehicle, the packages or shipping units enumerated in the contract particulars as packed in or on such article of transport or vehicle are deemed packages or shipping units. If not so enumerated, the goods in or on such article of transport or vehicle are deemed one shipping unit."

107 UNCITRAL, A/CN.9/552, para 41-42. A/CN.9/642, para 152-53 and 65. And especially A/CN.9/645, para 189-90. See also Møllmann, "Compensation for Damage", p. 207.

108 *Supra* Chapter 3, part 13.1.2 and 13.2.2.

The limits of liability are 875 SDR per package and 3 SDR per kilo of the gross weight of the goods, article 59(1). It is worth noting that if the goods are packed in a container, but the number of packages is stated in the transport document, then the stated number will be applicable when calculating the limit of liability, article 59(2). If, for instance, the transport document states that the goods are "1 container said to contain 50 bicycles" then the limit of liability will be 50 × 875 SDR. The limits are thus quite a lot higher than those contained in the Hague, Hague-Visby and Hamburg Rules, but claims in respect of high value, not extremely heavy goods may become subject to limitation. With the scope of application of the limits of liability being broader in the Rotterdam Rules than in the current conventions so that they also apply to claims for misdelivery then it is, of course, a worse position for a claimant even though the limits are higher (in terms of amount).

Another important consequence of the obligation to deliver the goods being an "obligation under the [Rules]" is that breaches of that obligation become subject to Chapter 13 on time for suit. Thus, as a general rule, judicial or arbitral proceedings for a claim for misdelivery must be instituted within two years, article 62(1). The uncertainty under English law as to the application of the time bar in the Hague-Visby Rules to misdelivery claims would therefore not continue under the Rotterdam Rules.

5.5.2 P&I coverage for misdelivery

The International Group of P&I Clubs has not taken a stance on whether the potential introduction of the Rotterdam Rules will affect the clubs' coverage (or rather refusal thereof) of claims for delivery without presentation of an original bill of lading. It is unlikely that the Group will take a stance until it is clear that the Rotterdam Rules will enter into force. Any attempt to address the issue is therefore speculative.

Anthony Diamond has stated that he thinks the P&I Clubs will continue to decline coverage for delivery without surrender of an original bill of lading.[109] In relation to ordinary bills of lading, i.e. that do not contain any statement that delivery may be made without the surrender of the bill of lading, this assessment seems reasonably safe to make. The Rotterdam Rules bring the delivery obligation within the obligations governed by the Rules and as a consequence claims for misdelivery are as a starting point subject to the time bar and limitation of liability set out in the Rules. However, delivering the goods without presentation of an original bill of lading is still a breach of a fundamental obligation under the contract of carriage, normally done intentionally by the carrier. The fact that such breach is for some intents brought within the ambit of the

109 Diamond, "The Rotterdam Rules", p. 521.

Rules does not warrant a change in the P&I Clubs' attitude towards this type of misdelivery.

Diamond's remark is, however, made in the context of article 47(2). It is respectfully submitted that it would be reasonable that the P&I Clubs extended coverage to include the residual exposure of the carrier when it delivers in accordance with article 47(2). First, it is a very narrow exposure under article 47(2)(e) and the potential liability is subject to limitation and time bar under the Rotterdam Rules. Second, and more important, the carrier is following a completely legal procedure. Thus, the carrier is not committing an unlawful act, but is rather acting in a manner envisaged and condoned by the legislature. The fact that a residual liability has been kept on the carrier to protect a transferee in good faith cannot be seen as a disavowal of the use of the procedure that should render such liability uninsurable. Furthermore, the clubs would normally have a right of recourse against the party giving the delivery instruction under the statutory indemnity afforded to the carrier in article 47(2)(c).

What the position of the P&I Clubs will be, of course, remains to be seen.

5.6 Is art 47(2) the solution?

At the beginning of this chapter, Anthony Diamond was quoted for calling the Rotterdam Rules' chapter on delivery ambitious, but also raising more difficult problems of interpretation than perhaps any other part of the Convention. After analysis of article 47 he concludes "with some regret that, owing to the many hazards involved in invoking art 47.2, it is unlikely to provide a solution to the problem of delivery without surrender of an original bill of lading".[110] This is, perhaps, too pessimistic.

The procedure is not a gift wrapped solution for the industry to start using immediately. It requires changing some standard procedures in relation to the handling of transport documents which has an impact on both banking procedures and contracts for the international sale of goods. It should therefore rather be seen as an opportunity for the trades where delivery against letters of indemnity is the rule rather than the exception to develop a lawful and more cost efficient way of dealing with the situation that delivery is desirable before the bill of lading is available at the destination. This requires that the parties involved in those trades – and their

110 Ibid. For a very critical assessment of the rule, see Caslav Pejovic, "Article 47(2) of the Rotterdam Rules: The Solution of Old Problems or a New Confusion?", in *The Hamburg Lectures on Maritime Affairs 2011–2013*, ed. Jürgen Basedow, Ulrich Magnus, and Rüdiger Wolfrum (Heidelberg: Springer, 2015). Professor Pejovic's critique seems a little inconsistent, though. First he criticises virtually every aspect of article 47(2) and the effects he claims it will have on the characteristics of bills of lading. Then, at p. 190, however, he criticises that the solution is only available when a clause to that effect is present in the bill of lading, and finally he states that article 47(2) "probably will not cause many problems in practice", ibid.

industry organisations – reconsider their practices and develop standard forms and procedures which apply the article 47(2) procedure. Article 47(2) can thus only be a solution to the problem if it is embraced by the industry, but if it is, then it must be seen as the necessary foundation for the industry to develop a practicable solution.

In this process, unforeseen adverse effects of article 47(2) may be discovered which could impede the development of a practicable solution. For instance, if the financing bank places importance on the security interest it gets in the goods represented by the transport document, it may be a problem if national law does not accept that the possession of (all originals of) the transport document with a delivery clause pursuant to article 47(2) constitutes perfection of the pledge because delivery may be obtained without the presentation of the document. Also, of a more indirect nature, it could impede the banks' interest in finding a practicable solution if transport documents with a delivery clause must be included at a reduced rate in relation to the solvency obligations of banks under national or regional (EU) financial regulations.[111]

5.7 Special issues relating to negotiable electronic transport records

As stated initially, the treatment of negotiable transport documents and negotiable electronic transport records in relation to the delivery of the goods is parallel. However, a few elements are special to the use of negotiable electronic transport records.

When claiming delivery, the holder of the negotiable electronic transport record must not surrender the transport record as there is no physical record to surrender. Instead, the holder must demonstrate that it is the holder in accordance with the procedures that must be established pursuant to article 9(1) when choosing to use electronic transport records, article 47(1)(a)(ii).[112] The record, however, continues to exist in some form or other, but it ceases to have any effect or validity upon delivery, article 47(1)(c). Again, procedures must be established pursuant to article 9 as to how confirmation must be provided that delivery has taken place and the record therefore has ceased to have effect or validity, subparagraph 1(d).

The "extraordinary way" as set out in article 47(2) is also available when using a negotiable electronic transport record. Even though the use of an electronic transport record enables the transfer of the record to be made instantaneously, situations can easily arise where the record is being held up in the process, e.g. if the record is used in an electronic documentary credit.

111 This issue is mentioned by Røsæg, "New procedures for bills of lading in the Rotterdam Rules", p. 189.
112 About the procedures, see *infra* Chapter 7, part 4.

For article 47(2) to be available to a transport document, the document must expressly state that the goods may be delivered without the surrender of the document, cf. *supra* part 5.3.3. The same applies to negotiable electronic transport records, cf. the chapeau of article 47(2). An electronic transport record, however, never has to be – or indeed is capable of being – surrendered.[113] A statement to that effect would therefore seem highly illogical. The application of the requirement also to electronic transport records must be regarded as a drafting error, but the requirement that the record must contain a "warning" is not. The transport record must therefore contain a "warning" that the goods may be delivered without following the main rule of article 47(1).

Though illogical in a transport record, a statement that the goods may be delivered without the surrender of the record would certainly fulfil the wording of the chapeau of article 47(2) and make the record eligible for the "extraordinary way" regulated in that subparagraph. Bearing in mind the intention of the chapeau that it should warn potential acquirers of the transport document or electronic transport record, it is submitted, that an express statement in the transport record that the goods may be delivered without the person claiming delivery demonstrating that it is the holder of the negotiable electronic transport record should be accepted as fulfilling the requirement of the chapeau thus making the record eligible for the "extraordinary way".[114]

If the goods are delivered pursuant to the "extraordinary way" then the legal effects are the same as when the procedure is followed under a negotiable transport document. However, the continuing exposure of the carrier under article 47(2)(e) must be considered minimal. At least under registry systems it is difficult to imagine that a person could become holder of the electronic transport record without being informed of the fact that delivery has already taken place. Thus, with registry systems a person usually does not become holder until its classification as such has been confirmed by the registrar who would have been notified of the delivery. In this respect, the use of an electronic transport record would seem to better safeguard the carrier and the potential acquirer when availing itself of the "extraordinary way" than the use of a negotiable transport document.

113 In the BOLERO system, *infra* Chapter 6, part 3.4.2, the terminology "surrender" is applied to the action taken by the "holder" of the electronic bill of lading when claiming delivery of the goods, but that, of course, does not entail a physical surrender of the electronic bill of lading, BOLERO Rulebook, rule 3.6.(2) and (3).

114 See also Diamond, "The Rotterdam Rules", 519, who seems to hold that the electronic transport record must refer to the "surrender" of the record and Nicholas Gaskell, "Bills of lading in an electronic age", *Lloyd's Maritime and Commercial Law Quarterly* (2010): p. 281f, who would accept a statement referring to the lack of demonstration that the person claiming delivery is the holder.

6 Summing up

It must be considered a step forward to have this important aspect of any contract of carriage regulated in an international convention. This gives the possibility for a higher degree of unification and consequently predictability for parties involved in international trade and carriage of goods by sea – at least in the long run when some of the uncertainties in the Rules have been settled.

The main rules regarding delivery of the goods are basically a codification of current practices, but the Rules certainly also bring about novelties that will involve major changes to national law of all states that become parties to them, especially the introduction of the "extraordinary way" of delivering pursuant to instructions given by the cargo side.

The general observation above also applies to the law of England and Scandinavia. Thus, the main rules regarding the procedures for delivery under a negotiable transport document are virtually the same as the current rules pertaining to delivery under bills of lading. This does not mean that the current rules regulating bills of lading and which have an indirect or even direct effect on delivery issues will become ineffective. Thus, the Rotterdam Rules do not affect national rules regarding the effects of the documents' negotiable character (*senso strictu*), i.e. the possibility of the transferee getting a better title than its transferor,[115] or the documents' status as a document of title in the common law sense, i.e. capable of transferring ownership in the goods if so intended. Nor do the Rules place the risk of forgeries or other kinds of fraud on either of the parties. As the potential liability for a breach of the delivery obligation as contained in the Rotterdam Rules is to be based on national law, these aspects will have an impact on the liability for misdelivery. The liability for misdelivery thus established on the basis of the applicable national law is subject to limitation of liability under the Rotterdam Rules which is new to both Scandinavian and English law. That limitation is, however, "breakable", i.e. the privilege of limitation is lost, in certain circumstances.[116] It is likely to cause some litigation to assess when that privilege is lost in connection with misdelivery as such claims have not previously been subject to limitation.

The statute based obligation for the consignee to acknowledge receipt of the goods is new to English law but should probably not be seen as too revolutionary as it is already standard practice in the trade and the requirement in the Scandinavian Merchant Shipping Acts does not seem to cause problems in practice. Also, the regulation of the carrier's options in relation to undeliverable goods entail a clarification of the rules in that

115 Both in Norway and Denmark, however, the proposed implementation legislation will do away with the bill of lading's negotiable character senso strictu, *supra* fn 72.

116 Article 61.

situation which should lead to greater international unification and entail appropriate safeguards of the cargo owner's interests in this area which currently is largely left to contract, at least under English law.

Finally, the "extraordinary way", i.e. the procedure in article 47(2) for delivering the goods when the negotiable transport document cannot be presented at the place of destination, is obviously new to both English and Scandinavian law. As stated above, the success of this alternative depends upon how it is embraced by the industry and upon the industry developing proper standard forms and procedures for the use of documents eligible for the "extraordinary way".

6 Electronic documents

1 Introduction

The use of electronic documents[1] in international trade has been a subject ever since computers started becoming a part of business life. Electronic documents have many potential benefits to the business community. Thus, the United Nations Economic Council for Europe (UNECE) in the synopsis for its electronic trade documents project estimated that the use of paper documents in world trade costs US$ 275–550 billion per year.[2] Using electronic alternatives can therefore entail substantial benefits both in terms of transaction speed and ease and of costs.

The benefits of electronic documents are particularly manifest when it comes to bills of lading as it could reduce the processing time of trade documents and eliminate certain risks of mistakes.[3] Thus, of particular interest in relation to the topic of this book, using electronic bills of lading could drastically reduce the time it takes for the bill of lading to go through the transaction process to reach the eventual consignee thereby reducing the risk that the bill of lading only reaches the port of discharge after the goods have arrived. It should also greatly reduce the risk that the bill of lading is lost during the transaction process. Furthermore, the undesirable practice of issuing paper bills of lading in sets of typically three is unlikely to be carried on to the use of electronic bills of lading which in turn should reduce the risk of carriers being met by competing right holders. Also, with proper security in the data systems used, the risk of forgery of electronic

1 Technically speaking, what constitutes an "electronic document" is in fact a file, record or process which is intended to perform the same function as a paper document. One of the legal problems has been whether such file, record or process qualified as a "document" where the law requires a "document" for certain functions. Therefore in legal writings, a different term than "electronic document" has been chosen, e.g. file, record or process. Here, the term "electronic document" will however be preferred as it seems to correspond best with ordinary parlance without creating misunderstandings. For the same reason the term "electronic bill of lading" will be used.

2 The synopsis is available at www.unece.org.

3 Miriam Goldby, "Electronic bills of lading and central registries: what is holding back progress?", *Information & Communications Technology Law* 17, no. 2 (2008): p. 125.

bills of lading should be lower than with paper ones although the use of electronic means opens up to other types of forgeries.

Thus, use of electronic bills of lading could reduce or eliminate several of the problems that the use of paper bills of lading creates in a delivery context as analysed in Chapter 3. However, as will be shown, it has proven to be particularly difficult to transform the paper bill of lading into a suitable electronic alternative.

Using electronic alternatives to paper documents raises a number of legal questions. Contract law – and other aspects of the law relating to international trade – has its roots in a time where a document was a tangible item. It is therefore not certain that contract law will cater satisfactorily for the use of electronic alternatives. This is even more so when it comes to maritime law and especially bills of lading whose legal qualities have developed on the basis of customs and practices of merchants through the centuries.

While using electronic bills of lading could have particular benefits in relation to the issue of delivery of the goods, the challenges to making a change to electronic bills cannot be analysed in a delivery context alone. Instead, the challenges to changing from paper to electronic bills must be looked at as a whole to ensure that the bill of lading can still perform its functions in international trade.[4] In the following, it will first be identified which legal problems the use of electronic documents in general give rise to and how these challenges have been met at the international level. It will then be analysed what further problems arise specifically with the use of electronic bills of lading, including the problems that relate to the delivery of the goods. Along the way it will be pointed out how these problems may be sought overcome and subsequently it will be examined how the solutions currently being offered seek to overcome the problems thus replicating the functions of the paper bill of lading. This chapter should be seen in conjunction with the following chapter which will provide an analysis of the potential impact of the Rotterdam Rules relating to the use of electronic transport documents (or "records" in the terminology of the Rotterdam Rules).

2 The use of electronic documents and legal issues

With contract law having developed in a reality where a document was a paper based item, any change to using electronic alternatives raises questions of the various rules' application to and suitability for such alternatives. Going from paper documents to electronic equivalents is in

4 *Electronic Documents in Maritime Trade* provides a thorough analysis of the use of electronic documents in maritime trade, including documents in the payment process, carriage documents and cargo insurance documents.

essence a change of form. It is therefore no surprise that the legal questions have on the general level revolved around formal requirements in the law; particularly requirements of "writing", "signature" and "document".[5]

The benefits of electronic communication are very strong in dealings between parties who are physically located far from each other and thus in international trade. This means that problems associated with the use of electronic communications should be approached at the international level. Unsurprisingly therefore, questions regarding the possibility of using electronic alternatives to paper documents have given rise to international initiatives, including EU legislation and UNCITRAL instruments, which again have prompted questions in national law of many countries.

At the international level, UNCITRAL first adopted its Model Law on Electronic Commerce in 1996 together with an extensive Guide to Enactment.[6] In 2001, UNCITRAL went on to adopt a model law on the more specific topic of electronic signatures, again with an extensive Guide to Enactment.[7] The two model laws,[8] which have gained substantial acceptance, are based on two basic principles which have become most important in future regulation of electronic documents and their use, namely the principle of functional equivalence and of technology neutrality.[9]

Functional equivalence means that rather than just expanding the scope of current rules to also cover electronic documents, with the consequent inherent problems, the functions performed by form requirements for paper documents are analysed and then rules are made which ensure the same functions for electronic documents. Technology neutrality means that the rules developed should not depend on the use of a particular type of technology but rather can function in relation to any type of communication and storage of information which should also ensure that the rules will function in relation to future technological developments – which will

5 This was, for instance, the scope of the Advice on electronic commerce given by the Law Commission in December 2001, Hugh Beale and Lowri Griffiths, "Electronic commerce: formal requirements in commercial transactions", *Lloyd's Maritime and Commercial Law Quarterly* (2002): p. 468.

6 Often abbreviated MLEC. The model law and guide to enactment are available at www.uncitral.org/uncitral/en/uncitral_texts/electronic_commerce/1996model.html.

7 UNCITRAL Model Law on Electronic Signatures (MLES) available at www.uncitral.org/uncitral/en/uncitral_texts/electronic_commerce/2001Model_signatures.html.

8 In 2005, the model laws were supplemented by a convention, the United Nations Convention on the Use of Electronic Communications in International Contracts (ECC), which was aimed at removing various obstacles to the use of electronic communication. The Convention – which specifically excludes application to bills of lading, art 2(2) – entered into force on 1 March 2013, but has as at April 2016 only been ratified by seven countries.

9 José Angelo Estrella Faria, "Electronic Transport Records", in *The Rotterdam Rules 2008*, ed. Alexander von Ziegler, Johan Schelin, and Stefano Zunarelli (Dordrecht: Kluwer Law International, 2010), p. 53.

inevitably be faster than the developments in international law.[10] These principles were also leading elements when the provisions on electronic documentation in the Rotterdam Rules were made.[11]

In 2011, UNCITRAL decided to reconvene its Working Group on electronic commerce (WG IV) and mandated it to undertake work in the field of electronic transferable records, including what is here called electronic bills of lading. This was decided both with a view to enhancing the generic promotion of electronic communications in international trade and to address some specific issues in relation to the Rotterdam Rules.[12] Working Group IV has since then been working on a Draft Model Law on Electronic Transferable Records and is in the final stages of preparing said model law.[13] As the previous model laws, The Draft Model Law on Electronic Transferable Records is based on the principles of functional equivalence and technology neutrality.[14]

At the EU level, in 1999 a directive was adopted setting out a framework for electronic signatures.[15] That directive inter alia sets out that certain advanced electronic signatures must be recognised in the same manner as a handwritten signature and that an electronic signature must not be denied legal effectiveness simply because it is in electronic form, cf. article 5. As per 1 July 2016, the e-signature directive was superseded by the so-called eIDAS regulation[16] which continues the requirement of recognition of electronic signatures, cf. article 25. In 2000, the EU further adopted the so-called e-commerce directive.[17] That directive included a general provision stating that Member States must ensure that their legal system allows contracts to be concluded by electronic means, cf. article 9. Thus, all Member States were de facto obliged to evaluate their contract law in relation to the use of electronic documents, cf. recital 34.

In the context of bills of lading, it should also be noted that the Comité Maritime International (CMI) early on developed a set of "rules" for the use of electronic bills of lading. This is of particular interest as the initial draft for what became the Rotterdam Rules was prepared by the CMI and

10 Ibid., p. 53, fn 8.
11 *Infra* Chapter 7, part 1.
12 UNCITRAL, A/66/17, para 235 and 38. See *infra* Chapter 7 on the Rotterdam Rules.
13 As at May 2016. The status of the work and the current draft of the model law can be found at UNCITRAL's website, www.uncitral.org.
14 UNCITRAL, A/CN.9/WG.IV/WP.136, para 16.
15 Directive 1999/93/EC of the European Parliament and of the Council of 13 December 1999 on a Community framework for electronic signatures (with later amendments).
16 Regulation (EU) no 910/2014 of the European Parliament and of the Council of 23 July 2014 on electronic identification and trust services for electronic transactions in the internal market and repealing Directive 1999/93/EC.
17 Directive 2000/31/EC of the European Parliament and of the Council of 8 June 2000 on certain legal aspects of information society services, in particular electronic commerce, in the Internal Market (Directive on electronic commerce).

the rules were obviously an important part of the basis for the CMI's extensive work in preparing the draft's e-commerce provisions.

3 Bills of lading

As stated above, it is necessary to take a broader approach than focusing on the delivery of the goods when assessing the possibilities of using electronic bills of lading. The issue of a paper bill of lading triggers important legal consequences both as to the obligations and liability of the carrier and the transferability of rights and obligations under the contract of carriage. These stem in part from the paper bill of lading's status as a negotiable document or as a document of title. Are the same consequences triggered by the issue of an electronic bill of lading? This question is answered fundamentally different under current English and Scandinavian (or rather; Danish) law.

3.1 Scandinavian law

Carriage of goods under bills of lading is regulated in the Merchant Shipping Act Chapter 13.[18] The Scandinavian countries are parties to the Hague-Visby Rules which form the basis of the liability regime. When Chapter 13 was amended in 1994 it was decided to include as much of the Hamburg Rules as possible without breaching the international obligations under the Hague-Visby Rules.[19] In line with this decision the application of Chapter 13 is not dependent on the issue of a bill of lading, § 252. The general rules on liability etc. apply to all contracts for carriage of goods by sea. These are supplemented by specific rules regarding bills of lading regulating documentary issues, liability for misdescription, delivery of the goods, etc. With the application of the general rules on the carrier's liability, including those implementing the Hague-Visby Rules, not being dependent on the issue of a bill of lading at all it is obvious that the use of an electronic bill of lading instead of a paper one will have no bearing on the general obligations and liability of the carrier and shipper.

The specific issues relating to bills of lading are regulated in §§ 292–307. The question is whether these rules also apply to electronic bills and if so, whether they apply in full or only partly (*mutatis mutandis* or by analogy to a certain extent).

The term "bill of lading" is defined in § 292 as a document which 1) is evidence of a contract of carriage by sea and that the carrier has received the goods, and 2) on its face is called a bill of lading (in Danish, Swedish and Norwegian: "konnossement") or contains a provision that the carrier undertakes only to deliver the goods against surrender of the document.[20]

18 See also *supra* Chapter 3, part 3.1.
19 Sølovsudvalget, "Betænkning 1215/1991", p. 33.
20 See also *supra* Chapter 3, part 3.1.

None of the rules in §§ 292–307 indicates that they only apply to paper documents. Also, § 296(3) sets out the requirement that the bill of lading must be signed by the carrier, but then goes on to state that "[t]he signature may be made by mechanical or electronic means". This seems to presuppose that the bill of lading itself can also be electronic, although it could also be understood to only allow for the signature to be made by other means than by hand, but still having to be made onto a paper document, e.g. a signature being printed on the bill of lading from a picture file.

The travaux preparatoires differ on this point between the four countries. The Danish travaux preparatoires specifically state that it is not a condition to fulfil the definition of a bill of lading that a physical document is issued, but that this can be electronically based.[21] A similar statement cannot be found in the Swedish, Norwegian and Finnish travaux preparatoires. In the Swedish travaux preparatoires carriages where electronic alternatives to a transport document are used are mentioned as "documentless carriages" and then it is stated that rules regulating the bill of lading "as an international paper document" is still needed inter alia because this forms the "starting point for a translation into electronic functions".[22] This seems to indicate that only paper documents are regarded as "bills of lading" in relation to Chapter 13 whereas electronic alternatives are not. The Norwegian and Finnish travaux preparatoires do not contain clear indications on the matter, but the Norwegian seem to consider carriages under electronic alternatives as "documentless carriages" and as something different from carriages where a bill of lading is issued.[23]

With the emphasis placed on travaux preparatoires in the interpretation of statutes in Scandinavian law it may be concluded that there is a high degree of likelihood that a Danish court will find that an electronic bill of lading which fulfils the requirements of § 292, i.e. is evidence of a contract of carriage, a receipt for the goods and is either called a bill of lading or contains an undertaking to only deliver against surrender of the bill, constitutes a bill of lading for the purposes of the Act despite the fact that it only exists in electronic form. As a starting point the rules in §§ 292–307 thus apply equally to paper and electronic bills of lading.[24] For Norway, Finland and Sweden the answer is subject to substantial uncertainty.[25] The Danish

21 Sølovsudvalget, "Betænkning 1215/1991", p. 78.
22 SOU 1990:13, p. 161 (my translation).
23 NOU 1993:36, p. 44.
24 Pedersen, *Transportret*, p. 498f.
25 Honka, "New Carriage of Goods by Sea – The Nordic Approach", p. 115f, states that the Nordic Merchant Shipping Acts have not taken electronic data interchange into consideration, but he does not seem to have taken account of the Danish travaux preparatoires. The original Norwegian version of the book: Thor Falkanger and Hans Jacob Bull, *Sjørett*, 7th ed. (Oslo: Sjørettsfondet Akademisk, 2010), p. 320f, also continues to refer to carriages where electronic documentation is used as "documentless carriages" and treats them as apart from carriages under bills of lading or waybills. In the Danish version of

approach is thus not one based on functional equivalence, but a simple extension of the rules to also apply to electronic versions of bills of lading.

As one of the main purposes of this chapter is to show the differences of a statute-based and a more contract-based approach to regulation of bills of lading and its effects on the possibility of replacing paper bills of lading with electronic bills of lading, the following analyses will be based on the Danish approach and, thus, the conclusion that the rules of the Merchant Shipping Act regulating bills of lading apply also to electronic bills of lading. For that reason, references will also mainly be to Danish legislation and travaux preparatoires.

In the following parts, the effects of such application will be examined.

3.1.1 Issuance of the electronic bill of lading

Once the consignor has delivered the goods to the carrier for carriage he can demand the issue of a bill of lading, § 294. With the rules applying equally to paper and electronic bills of lading the question arises whether the consignor may demand an electronic bill. And, does the carrier fulfil its obligation under § 294 if it issues an electronic bill without the consent of the consignor? The answer to both questions seems to be "no". The rule is based on the Hague-Visby Rules article III, rules 3 and 7, and the Hamburg Rules article 14(1) which are generally not considered to comprise electronic bills. Both the wording of the rules in the Merchant Shipping Act and their background firmly suggest that the general starting point that the rules also apply to electronic bills and the specific rules stating this must be seen as a facilitation making it possible for the parties to use electronic documents where they wish to do so. Imposing an obligation on either party to use electronic documents at the choice of the other party would be very burdensome on the parties and would depart from current practices in the trade as well as require technical solutions that many carriers and shippers do not have.[26] A clear rule must therefore be required if either party should be able to unilaterally decide that electronic documents should be used and such a rule does not exist.[27]

the book: Thor Falkanger, Hans Jacob Bull, and Lars Rosenberg Overby, *Søret*, 4th ed. (Copenhagen: Karnov Group, 2013), p. 359f, this section is limited to simply stating that Chapter 13 of the Merchant Shipping Act also applies to such carriages, but without stating whether that includes §§ 292–307.

26 This was of course much more so in 1991 when the rules and travaux preparatoires were formulated.

27 Regarding the same question under the Rotterdam Rules see Møllmann, "From bills of lading to transport documents – the role of transport documents under the Rotterdam Rules", p. 55, and infra Chapter 7, part 2. A shipowner may under a charter party have obliged itself as against the charterer to issue electronic bills of lading for cargoes if requested by the charterer. BIMCO has developed a recommended clause for insertion in charter parties for that purpose; see BIMCO Circular no. 3 of 20 May 2014 available at www.bimco.org.

Under both the international conventions, national transport legislation and associated legislation, e.g. regarding customs and excise, it is required that bills of lading be signed. For the use of electronic documents to be a viable alternative it is therefore a necessary prerequisite that the document can be signed electronically. This in turn requires that legislation is in place which gives to electronic signatures legal status equal to that of a written signature.

The signature requirement is set out in the Merchant Shipping Act § 296, subsection 3. The subsection goes on to explicitly state that the signature can be made "by mechanical or electronic means". The travaux preparatoires explain that the requirement that the bill of lading must be "signed" must not be interpreted narrowly.[28] The maritime legislation thus accepts the use of electronic signatures on bills of lading, but that does not in itself mean that electronic signatures have the necessary legal status. This must be ensured through the general legislation on electronic signatures. In the EU since 1 July 2016 such legal status follows directly from the eIDAS Regulation.[29]

3.1.2 Transfer of rights and obligations under an electronic bill of lading

The role of a bill of lading as the bearer of rights and obligations is based on longstanding customs of the trade coupled with legislation. These traditions, though, regard the use of paper documents and the question therefore is whether the role can be fulfilled by an electronic bill of lading, or put another way, whether rights and obligations may be transferred by transferring the electronic bill.

The rules of the Danish Merchant Shipping Act regulating bills of lading also apply to electronic bills. As a starting point the rules setting out the legal effects of a transfer of a bill of lading or of being a holder of a bill thus also apply to electronic bills.[30] However, as analysed in Chapter 3, part 2.1, these legal effects are a result not only of the rules in the Merchant Shipping Act, but rather of those rules in combination with analogous application of the rules of the Act on Instruments of Debt. Most important the true negotiable nature of a bill of lading, i.e. that a transferee may get a better title than his transferor, must be established using both the Merchant Shipping Act and the Act on Instruments of Debt.

When assessing whether the analogous application of the Act on Instruments of Debt to bills of lading also extends to electronic bills of lading an initial question, bearing in mind that a bill of lading does not fall within the definition of an instrument of debt, is whether the Act on

28 Sølovsudvalget, "Betænkning 1215/1991", pp. 78 and 81.
29 *Supra* fn 16.
30 Pedersen, *Transportret*, p. 511.

Instruments of Debt applies directly to negotiable electronic instruments of debt. The answer is that it only does to a certain extent. The reason for this somewhat unclear answer is that the types of instruments of debt most relevant for electronic form have become subject to specific legislation. Thus, dematerialised securities and digital mortgage deeds are subject to special legislation which establishes the legal effects of their negotiability. However, the registration of property act (regulating digital mortgage deeds) refers back to the Act on Instruments of Debt for some of these effects.[31] It is, thus, not impossible for the rules of the Act on Instruments of Debt to function in relation to dematerialised instruments of debt (in casu digital mortgage deeds), but it apparently only does so in limited circumstances in practice.

With respect to bills of lading, the situation is somewhat different. The Act on Instruments of Debt does not apply directly to bills of lading because bills of lading are not instruments of debt within the meaning of that act. Instead the rules on negotiable instruments of debt and the principles therein supplement the rules of the Merchant Shipping Act by analogy and with the necessary changes. Therefore, it is submitted, that the general applicability of the Act on Instruments of Debt to electronic instruments of debt is not decisive in respect of whether the rules and principles that supplement the Merchant Shipping Act in relation to paper bills of lading will also supplement the same rules in relation to electronic bills of lading. Instead the decisive point should be whether the Merchant Shipping Act envisages the same rules to apply to paper and electronic bills of lading (with the necessary amendments). As stated above at fn 24, that seems to be the case. With some uncertainty it is therefore submitted that the rules of the Act on Instruments of Debt applicable by analogy to paper bills of lading also apply by analogy to electronic bills of lading.

Consequently, the transfer of an electronic bill of lading will have the following main legal effects.[32]

Provided the transferee has relied in good faith on the contract particulars in the electronic bill of lading being correct, proof to the contrary may not be submitted, cf. § 299(3).[33] This includes that if it is not indicated that the consignee shall pay freight, proof may not be submitted that he shall, § 299(2).[34] If the carrier had or should have realized that information in the contract particulars was incorrect and that the bill of lading was therefore

31 Registration of property act, Consolidated Act no. 1075/2014, § 27 a which refers back to the Act on Instruments of Debt §§ 15(1), 16 and 17.

32 The rules mentioned in the following are dealt with as they pertain to paper bills of lading and particularly in relation to the delivery of the goods in Chapter 3, part 2.1. The following account is thus a revision of the consequences of a transfer of a bill of lading and its implications for electronic bills of lading.

33 Implementing the Hague-Visby Rules article III, rule 4.

34 Based on the Hamburg Rules article 16, rule 4.

misleading for the transferee then the carrier will be liable in damages and have no right to limitation of liability, § 300.[35]

A person who has acquired the electronic bill of lading in good faith is not obliged to give it up to the person from whom it has been lost, § 306(2).[36] Thus, even a person from whom the bill of lading has been stolen cannot vindicate (i.e. reclaim) the bill. The use of electronic bills of lading should widely eliminate situations where bills are physically misappropriated such as by theft. However, situations where inter alia an electronic signature is abused may arise. § 306(2) must be taken to mean that in such situations the person who has been deprived of the exclusive control of the electronic bill cannot claim to have the exclusive control of the electronic bill transferred back to him even if this is technically possible, even easy.[37]

Stoppage in transit cannot be exercised against a third party, i.e. someone other than the original buyer of the goods, who has acquired the electronic bill of lading in good faith, § 307(2).

The transferee becomes legitimated as consignee towards the carrier, § 302(1) and *supra* Chapter 3, part 4.1.

These rules derived directly from the Merchant Shipping Act must then be supplemented by those rules and principles of the Act on Instruments of Debt which have analogous application.

Most importantly, §§ 13, 14, 15 and 17 of that Act set out the negotiable nature and effects of a transfer of the instrument. Accordingly, § 13 sets out the essential characteristic of the negotiable instrument of debt, namely that the holder of the instrument is presumed to be entitled to assert the claim. This is the core notion of "legitimation".[38] For bearer documents the simple possession is enough to create the presumption whereas for documents to order the document must either be made out to the person in possession or have been transferred to him by indorsements that appear to be uninterrupted. This rule has analogous application to bills of lading and must be read in combination with the Merchant Shipping Act § 292(3) which states that as between the carrier and a holder who is not the shipper,

35 Corresponding in part to the Hamburg Rules article 17, rule 4.

36 The rule only applies to order and bearer bills of lading. This rule may clash with rules under the available systems requiring the electronic bill of lading to be redelivered if it has been sent to the wrong person. However, the requirement of good faith will probably mean that in most such instances the person having received the electronic bill will not be entitled to it under § 306(2) anyway.

37 § 306(1) contains a rule regulating the priority to the goods in situations where a holder with legitimation transfers different originals of the bill of lading to different transferees, *supra* Chapter 3, part 7.1. In such cases, the person who first receives in good faith his original of the bill obtains the rights to the goods. If, however, someone else in good faith obtains delivery of the goods at the place of destination, said person is not obliged to give up the goods. This rule in theory also applies to electronic bills. However, it is unlikely that electronic bills of lading will be issued in sets.

38 See e.g. Tiberg, "Legal qualities of transport documents", p. 6, who, however, uses the term "ostensible title".

the bill of lading determines the conditions for the carriage and delivery of the goods, and § 302 which states that the holder is legitimated as consignee. Accordingly, the conditions in § 13 for having legitimation must surely be read into the Merchant Shipping Act §§ 292(3) and 302. Further, the case law on § 13, e.g. as to how a string of indorsements must be evaluated, must have an impact on the evaluation of when a transfer of a bill of lading transfers the legitimation to the transferee, see *supra* Chapter 3, part 4.1. In relation to electronic bills of lading the application of the rule requires that the requirements of possession of the document are substituted with exclusive control over the electronic document and electronic indorsements are accepted. Such adjustments seem warranted to fulfil the legislative intention that bills of lading may be in electronic form.

The debtor, i.e. the carrier in the case of bills of lading, can only object to the validity of the bill of lading or the content thereof on the grounds that it is forged, falsified, signed without authority or signed under threat or use of violence, § 17. In Danish legal terminology these are normally referred to as "strong" objections.[39]

§ 15 sets out a number of objections, normally referred to as "weak" objections, which cannot be asserted by the carrier against a third party who has acquired the negotiable document in good faith. These include non-violent coercion, fraud, exploitation, that it would go against common decency to uphold the contract (unconscionability), that the document has been given up without the debtor's acceptance, that the debtor has not received the agreed remuneration, that payment had already taken place before the transfer of the document, or that the obligations under the document had been changed by agreement. Any such objections will be extinguished. These rules can be applied to electronic bills of lading with very minor modifications, viz. that signature must be understood as electronic signature (which also follows directly from the Merchant Shipping Act § 296(3)) and that the giving up of the document must be understood as the passing of exclusive control to someone else.

The relationship between the holder and another who claims to have a right in the instrument of debt is regulated in § 14. In essence, any such right that another person claims to have is extinguished if the transferee has acquired the instrument of debt from a person who had legitimation, cf. § 13, and the transferee has received the instrument of debt in good faith. Thus, for instance an objection from a person that the instrument of debt was stolen from him will be extinguished by a good faith transferee and he will not be entitled to vindicate (i.e. reclaim) the instrument. Of

39 § 17 also mentions invalidity as a result of incapability, that the instrument of debt has been declared null and void through the process known as mortification, *supra* Chapter 3, at and in fn 141, or that the claim has been changed or no longer exists as a result of the legislation on limitation, preclusion or debt-restructuring. These are of less importance in the case of bills of lading.

some importance, § 14 specifies that when a transferor of an instrument to order bases his right on previous transfers the transferee need not check their validity unless specific circumstances give him reason to doubt them. This rule can also be applied to electronic bills of lading with the modification that the transferee's reception of the bill of lading must be understood as obtainment of the exclusive control over the electronic bill of lading. It must be expected that the clarity of electronic indorsements will be greater than indorsements on paper bills of lading thus alleviating some of the problems in practice in this regard.

These rules mean that the transferee can get a better title than the transferor thus giving the document its true negotiable character in a continental European sense.

With the above-mentioned rules facilitating the transfer of legitimation and most often also substantial title by transferring the negotiable document the transferee may suffer a loss if the debtor, i.e. the carrier in a bill of lading setting, acts in breach of its obligations in relation to such legitimation. To enforce his interests the transferee may thus have to initiate legal proceedings. It may, however, be asked whether it has any effect in this regard that the claimant supports its claim on an electronic bill of lading rather than a paper one. Danish procedural law sets very few limits as to the grounds on which one can sue. The Danish Administration of Justice Act § 255 simply states that whoever is the right plaintiff and defendant shall be determined on the basis of the ordinary rules of the legislation.[40] This somewhat unhelpful rule in practice means that anyone with a "legal interest" can sue and get a verdict on the material questions of the case. What constitutes a "legal interest" is interpreted by the courts, but suffice it to say that it gives a wide margin for a potential plaintiff and anyone claiming to have a claim on the basis of a bill of lading or on some other basis against the carrier will certainly be able to sue. It will have no bearing that the bill of lading is an electronic one.

3.1.3 Perfection, mandatory nature and other adjustments

In order for a transferee to safeguard his interests and take advantage of the negotiable effect of the document he will need to perfect the transfer. Both under the Merchant Shipping Act and the Act on Instruments of Debt such perfection includes taking physical possession of the document (in good faith). When using electronic bills of lading such physical possession is not possible as no physical document exists.

Instead, a procedure which performs an equal function as the physical handing over of a paper document must be regarded as perfection when

40 Thor Falkanger, "Cargo damage – who is entitled to sue the maritime carrier?", in *SIMPLY 2010*, ed. Alla Pozdnakova (Oslo: Sjørettsfondet, 2010), discusses the question under Norwegian law.

using electronic bills. Which procedure must be recognised as perfection will depend on the system that is the basis of the paperless document handling.[41] The procedure must, however, provide the same certainty as taking physical possession of a paper document such that it can be said to fulfil the same function. Where a system is used that entails a central bill of lading registry, registration as new holder of the electronic bill will normally be the method for perfection of the transfer.[42]

With each system being defined in an often comprehensive set of rules a risk arises that these set out specific rules which are contrary to those in the Merchant Shipping Act as supplemented by analogous application of the Act on Instruments of Debt. It is therefore of relevance to what degree these rules are mandatory.

As explained in Chapter 3, at fn 20 et seq., in relation to paper bills of lading the relevant rules of the Merchant Shipping Act are mandatory and it was with some uncertainty concluded that the analogous application of the Act on Instruments of Debt is also mandatory. For paper bills of lading the situation is thus that in case of a conflict the rules of the Merchant Shipping Act will prevail, § 254(1). The question is whether the same applies with respect to electronic bills of lading. The answer must be "yes" with some minor exceptions. The presumed intention behind making the rules of the Merchant Shipping Act applicable also to electronic documents was to enable the use of electronic documents as an alternative to paper bills of lading. For electronic documents to be a viable alternative, however, they must afford the same protection as the rules on paper documents regarding the obligations of the parties and the liability regime. Therefore the mandatory rules of the Merchant Shipping Act must prevail in situations where they do not correspond with the terms of an electronic bill of lading or the underlying rules of the system in which the electronic bill functions.[43] The exception is that, as mentioned above, the rules of the Merchant Shipping Act must be adapted as necessary to function with electronic documents. Thus, for instance requirements that the bill of lading must be physically handed over to a transferee[44] will not prevail over a rule in the system for the electronic document that a transfer must be registered to take effect. However, a rule in the system setting out that no perfection is required and that the mere agreement between the transferor and the transferee is enough to e.g. protect the transferee against the transferor's creditors would seem to run contrary to the basic principle of negotiable

41 This is also the method chosen in the Rotterdam Rules, where article 9 prescribes that the use of negotiable electronic transport records shall be subject to procedures which inter alia shall provide for the method for the transfer of that record, *infra* Chapter 7, part 4.

42 See *infra* part 3.4.2.

43 Pedersen, *Transportret*, p. 511.

44 See e.g. § 306(1).

documents embedded in the rule that a transfer of a negotiable paper document must be perfected by its physical handing over. It may thus be argued that this fundamental principle also applies to electronic documents in the sense that the system for the use of the electronic documents must prescribe a perfection which fulfils the same functions as the rules for paper documents.

3.1.4 Delivery of the goods and electronic bills of lading

The delivery of the goods is directly regulated in the Merchant Shipping Act §§ 302–304, *supra* Chapter 3, part 4.1. These rules require that the consignee presents the bill of lading and set out that the consignee can only claim delivery if he deposits the bill and surrenders it duly receipted to the carrier when the goods have been delivered. Obviously, that is not possible when there is no physical document. Therefore the system used must provide for procedures whereby the holder can show that he is in fact the holder entitled to claim delivery and whereby he can "surrender" it to the carrier. It is submitted that these rules must be applied using a functional equivalence approach such that the system must ensure *that* the electronic bill legitimates the holder as consignee, *that* the carrier receives a receipt for the delivery of the goods, and *that* the electronic bill of lading after delivery no longer carries with it a right to demand delivery.[45]

3.2 English law

Contrary to Scandinavian and especially Danish law, under English law many of the fundamental rules of carriage of goods hinge on the issue of a paper bill of lading and the possibilities of applying these rules also to electronic bills of lading have not yet been used.

3.2.1 Liability regime and freedom of contract

The United Kingdom is a party to the Hague-Visby Rules. The enacting legislation is the Carriage of Goods by Sea Act 1971 which came into force in 1977. S. 1(2) gives the Rules the force of law for contracts for the carriage of goods by sea which provide for the issue of a bill of lading or similar document of title, cf. s. 1(4). S. 1(6) further gives the Rules the force of law in relation to other bills of lading and non-negotiable receipts that provide that the Rules shall govern the contract, i.e. that contain a Clause Paramount.

It is highly doubtful whether an electronic bill of lading could fall under

45 How the systems currently available deal with the issue of delivery is examined *infra* part 3.4.2.

the meaning of the term bill of lading in COGSA 1971.[46] The question has yet to make it to the courts. The academic writings seem to be divided. On the one hand, the Law Commission in its advice of December 2001 very clearly stated that an electronic bill of lading is not within the ambit of COGSA 1971.[47] On the other hand, Miriam Goldby submits that the wording of COGSA 1971 is amenable to the inclusion of electronic bills in its application.[48] One might argue that COGSA 1971 should apply if the parties to the contract of carriage had the intention that a bill of lading should be issued.[49] This might be relevant where a system of "remote printing" is used and the damage occurs prior to the actual printing of the paper bill of lading.[50] In situations where the bill of lading is intended to remain electronic throughout its "lifetime", the argument seems less valid. The parties may well have intended that the electronic bill of lading should for all intents be equal to a paper bill of lading. However, if an electronic bill is not in other respects considered a bill of lading within the ambit of COGSA 1971 then the mere intention of the parties to give an electronic bill the same qualities as a paper bill cannot be said to constitute an intention to issue a (paper) bill of lading within the meaning of COGSA 1971.

Until the courts decide otherwise, it must be considered highly doubtful that COGSA 1971 and thereby the Hague-Visby Rules will apply by law to a carriage under an electronic bill of lading. In this respect it is worth noting that when the Hague Rules were adopted, the use of electronic documents was obviously not an issue and likewise, the application of the Hague-Visby Rules to electronic documents was not part of the negotiations of these

46 Beale and Griffiths, "Electronic commerce: formal requirements in commercial transactions", p. 477. Aikens, Lord, and Bools, *Bills of Lading*, para 2.119.

47 Law Commission, "Electronic Commerce: Formal Requirements in Commercial Transactions" (2001), para 4.9. Paul Todd, *Bills of Lading and Bankers' Documentary Credits*, 4th ed. (London: Informa, 2007), para 3.72, also seems to presuppose that an electronic bill will not fall within the term "any bill of lading" as used in COGSA 1971.

48 Miriam Goldby, "The CMI Rules for Electronic Bills of Lading reassessed in the light of current practices", *Lloyd's Maritime and Commercial Law Quarterly* (2008): 64f. Goldby refers to s. 1(6)(a) "any bill of lading" which may imply that she makes a distinction between bills of lading which are mandatorily covered by the Hague-Visby Rules and bills of lading where the Rules have the force of law if there is a Paramount Clause. Such a distinction does not seem warranted simply by the word "any" whose purpose rather seems to be to include straight bills of lading. Also in *Electronic Documents in Maritime Trade*, para 6.14 et seq. Here Goldby, however, bases the assertion directly on s. 1(4) stating that an electronic bill of lading should fall within "bill of lading or any similar document of title". Goldby relies in this respect on the House of Lords' decision in *The Rafaela S.*, see *supra* Chapter 3, part 3.2, at fn 46.

49 COGSA 1971, s. 1(4), and the principle laid down in *Pyrene Co. Ltd. v. Scindia Navigation Co.*, [1954] 2 QB 402, pp. 419–20, (interpreting the Hague Rules art. I(b)) and confirmed in *Parsons Corp. v. CV Scheepvaartonderneming Happy Ranger (The Happy Ranger)*, [2002] 2 Lloyd's Rep. 357, p. 362, (interpreting the Hague-Visby Rules, art. I(b) and COGSA 1971, s. 1(4)).

50 A brief description of remote printing systems is provided *infra* part 3.4.1.

Rules. At the same time it seems safe to say that no international unity on an interpretation of the rules extending their ambit to electronic documents is realistic. Therefore, any decision to apply the Hague-Visby Rules mandatorily to carriages under an electronic bill of lading would have to be a national one and it would thus rest on an interpretation of COGSA 1971, s. 1(4), and not of the Rules themselves. In that interpretation, one might as a matter of policy question whether it should really be possible to avoid the mandatory application of the Hague-Visby regime simply by using an electronic bill of lading rather than a paper one.

Further, it is questionable whether the Hague-Visby Rules may be given the force of law by insertion of a Clause Paramount in the electronic bill of lading. Pursuant to s. 1(6), the Rules shall have the force of law in relation to bills of lading containing a provision that the Rules shall govern the contract and in relation to any receipt which is a non-negotiable document marked as such if the contract expressly provides that the Rules are to govern the contract as if the receipt were a bill of lading. It is, however, questionable whether an electronic bill of lading may qualify as a "non-negotiable document marked as such". Even if an electronic bill will be accepted as being a "document" – and it probably will[51] – then the electronic bill will typically not be marked as non-negotiable as the idea is to create an electronic alternative to the negotiable paper bill of lading.[52] If the Rules were made applicable in this manner it would also mean that the function as conclusive evidence contained in the Hague-Visby Rules, article III, rule 4, second sentence, would not apply, cf. s. 1(6), which would be unacceptable when trying to come up with an electronic alternative to a paper bill of lading.

Instead, the Hague-Visby Rules may be incorporated into the electronic bill of lading by contract, but the Rules will then only have the force of contract rather than force of law. The main consequence of this is that the Rules may be incorporated in part rather than in whole and that express terms of the electronic bill which conflict with the Rules may be found by construction to prevail over the Rules.[53] If the Hague-Visby Rules are not

51 Beale and Griffiths, "Electronic commerce: formal requirements in commercial transactions", pp. 470 and 79.

52 Both BOLERO and ESS-Databridge, see *infra* part 3.4.2, also provide for the use of electronic straight bills of lading. Such bills would be marked as non-negotiable and would contain a receipt for the goods. In the *Rafaela S*, *supra* Chapter 3, at and in fn 46, the House of Lords ruled that a paper straight bill of lading is a bill of lading within s. 1(4) of COGSA 1971, but as with order bills, as described above, it is highly doubtful that s. 1(4) applies to an electronic straight bill. This could create the rather backwards situation that the Paramount Clause in an electronic straight bill of lading could result in the Hague-Visby Rules applying with the force of law pursuant to s. 1(6)(b).

53 Treitel and Reynolds, *Carver on Bills of Lading*, p. 627. The editors with a reference to Dicey and Morris, The Conflict of Laws, also state that as a result of the Rules having the force of law they are an overriding policy of the forum and hence mandatory rules under article 9 of the Rome I regulation, reg. no. 593/2008, meaning that an English court

incorporated into the electronic bill of lading by contract then the carriage will be subject to the liability scheme of the common law.

3.2.2 Transfer of rights and obligations

As is well known, the issue of transfer of rights and obligations in connection with the transfer of bills of lading has vexed the common law for centuries and the attempt to solve it by the Bills of Lading Act 1855 largely failed. Another – and this time successful – attempt was made with the Carriage of Goods by Sea Act 1992.

In essence COGSA 1992 entails that a person who becomes the lawful holder of a bill of lading has all rights of suit under the contract of carriage transferred to and vested in him, s. 2(1), and under certain conditions becomes subject to the same liabilities under the contract as if he had been a party to it, s. 3(1). The Act applies inter alia to negotiable bills of lading, s. 1(1) and (2). However, s. 1(5) and (6) gives the Secretary of State power to make regulations making the Act applicable to electronic documents. Such regulations have not been made to date. The Act, thus, does not apply to electronic bills of lading.[54]

The problem of enforcement of contractual terms by third parties in general is regulated in the Contracts (Rights of Third Parties) Act 1999. However, this Act does not apply to bills of lading, s. 6(5)–(7), and it is expressly stated that this exception includes "a corresponding electronic

must apply the Rules whatever the governing law of the contract, p. 630. This seems to be a simple continuation from the previous edition where the same assertion was made in respect of article 7(2) of the Rome Convention and accordingly the reference is to the fourteenth edition of Dicey and Morris which comments on the Rome Convention. However, Dicey, Morris and Collins maintain the assertion in the fifteenth edition, Lord Collins of Mapesbury, ed. *Dicey, Morris and Collins on The Conflict of Laws*, 15th ed. (London: Sweet & Maxwell, 2012), para 33-111, in relation to article 9 of the Rome I regulation. While the assertion in relation to the Rome Convention may very well be true, it is respectfully submitted that the assertion in relation to the Rome I regulation is at least questionable. Article 9 of the Rome I regulation has limited the ambit of overriding mandatory provisions as compared with the Rome Convention and it seems difficult to argue that the Hague-Visby Rules are "regarded as crucial by a country for safeguarding its public interests, such as its political, social or economic organisation", article 9.

54 Aikens, Lord, and Bools, *Bills of Lading*, para 2.120, suggest that the presence of s. 1(5) and (6) may imply that an electronic bill "is to be treated as a document for the purposes of the Act" which seems to indicate that the authors think the Act applies to such bills. This is supported by a reference to the Law Commission's advice of December 2001. However, in that advice the Law Commission clearly stated that an electronic bill of lading (referred to as "electronic contracts for carriage") is not within the ambit of COGSA 1992, Law Commission, "Electronic Commerce: Formal Requirements in Commercial Transactions", para 4.9. Cf. also Goldby, "The CMI Rules for Electronic Bills of Lading reassessed in the light of current practices", p. 63, and same in *Electronic Documents in Maritime Trade*, para 6.19.

transaction", s. 6(6)(a). Thus, although electronic bills of lading are not covered by COGSA 1992 they are nevertheless excepted from the ambit of the Contracts (Rights of Third Parties) Act 1999.

Consequently, the transfer of rights and obligations under an electronic bill of lading is not regulated by statute, but only by common law.[55] The starting point is, thus, that a holder of an electronic bill of lading who is not the shipper cannot assert rights or be subject to liabilities on the basis of the electronic bill as he is not privy to the contract contained in or evidenced by it. Further, the solutions developed in the common law to partially alleviate the problem prior to COGSA 1992 may be of less avail to electronic bills of lading.

At common law a contract has in some circumstances been implied between the carrier and a holder of a bill of lading claiming delivery of the goods at the discharge port; a so-called *Brandt v. Liverpool* contract.[56] This doctrine is, however, of limited aid as it is only in limited circumstances that a contract will in fact be implied and, what may be worse for the traders in practice, it is far from clear what the requirements to create a contract are.[57] Most importantly it has been established that the parties' conduct must clearly indicate an intention to contract.[58] This means that if the parties do nothing which they would not do if no contract between them was established then that is an indication that they did not intend to contract. Especially if the consignee does not have to pay freight or other charges then a contract will only in extraordinary circumstances be implied as the consignee will have provided no consideration. It is further doubtful that the *Brandt v. Liverpool* doctrine would be applicable to electronic bills of lading. The doctrine was a response to the defect in the law that whereas by custom of merchants a bill of lading is transferable by indorsement and may thereby pass property in and constructive possession of the goods to the indorsee, nevertheless the rights and liabilities represented by the bill of lading did not pass.[59] No such custom making an electronic bill of lading transferable exists. It therefore seems unlikely that a court would find that it is necessary to give business efficacy to the parties' intention to imply a

55 The Bill of Lading Act 1855 was repealed by COGSA 1992, s. 6(2). The Bill of Lading Act 1855 would anyway be of no avail in the case of electronic bills of lading. An electronic bill of lading would almost certainly not fall within the meaning of "bill of lading" in the Act which in the preamble spoke of bills of lading which "by the custom of merchants" are transferable by indorsement. Such custom only applies to paper bills of lading.

56 Named after *Brandt v. Liverpool, Brazil & River Plate Steam Navigation Co. Ltd.*, [1924] 1 K.B. 575, but actually developed earlier. For a review of the authorities, see *The Aramis*, [1989] 1 Lloyd's Rep. 213, pp. 218–224, per Bingham L.J.

57 This was observed by Saville J. in *The Agia Skepi*, [1992] 2 Lloyd's Rep. 467. Aikens, Lord, and Bools, *Bills of Lading*, para 8.23.

58 *The Aramis*, [1989] 1 Lloyd's Rep. 213, p. 224 per Bingham L.J. Aikens, Lord, and Bools, *Bills of Lading*, para 8.21 et seq.

59 I.e. prior to the adoption of COGSA 1992.

contract between the carrier and the consignee. In the least, the doctrine is fraught with enough uncertainties that it would be hazardous to base the use of electronic bills of lading on its application.

The parties to the underlying sale have also had recourse to contractual techniques, especially assignment and novation. Both, however, suffer from the fact that the seller will have to do something extra as compared with the normal procedure of simply transferring the bill of lading duly indorsed and the carrier has to be involved to some degree on each sale which will be especially problematic in string sales. Further, assignment and novation are areas of the law where the material rules differ greatly from country to country and, especially as regards assignment, conflicts of laws issues are particularly complicated.[60] The risk of ending up in a situation where the assignment turns out to be invalid is thus substantial. Still, novation is an essential part of the systems that are currently available.[61]

Another legal vehicle for the transfer of rights and obligations is the principles of bailment. While there is discussion in the legal literature as to whether the transfer of a (paper) bill of lading also transfers rights under the bailment as a result of the principle of an attornment in advance,[62] it seems safe to state that the transfer of an electronic bill of lading will not in and by itself be considered an attornment in advance by the carrier. An actual attornment (in advance) must be required to obtain this effect for electronic bills of lading. This is crucial in attempting to replicate the presentation rule in relation to the delivery of the goods. In this connection it is worth mentioning that if a system is set up using the above-mentioned legal vehicles which gives the transferee the right to immediate possession of the goods then this right may form the basis for a claim in conversion if the carrier delivers the goods to someone else. Thus, the tort of conversion is not tied to the use of (paper) bills of lading, but on an interference with the claimant's possessory or proprietary rights.[63]

When setting up a system for the use of electronic bills of lading it is therefore necessary to contractually regulate as far as possible the legal effects of a transfer of the electronic bill.

3.2.3 Evidentiary effect

One of the three key functions of a (shipped) bill of lading is its role as a receipt for the goods evidencing that the goods have been shipped and their condition at the time of shipment. The evidentiary value of a bill of lading is set out in the Hague-Visby Rules article III, rule 4, according to

60 See e.g. Anders Møllmann, "Security assignment of debts and the conflict of laws", *Lloyd's Maritime and Commercial Law Quarterly* (2011).

61 *Infra* part 3.4.2.

62 *Supra* Chapter 3, part 4.2.

63 *Supra* Chapter 3, part 13.2.1.

which proof to the contrary of the information regarding the goods in the bill of lading shall not be admissible when the bill has been transferred to a third party acting in good faith. The use of this rule is, of course, dependent on the applicability of the Hague-Visby Rules to the electronic bill of lading in question. However, as discussed in part 3.2.1, it is highly questionable that COGSA 1971, and thereby the Hague-Visby Rules, do apply to electronic bills of lading. The parties may incorporate the Rules into their contract of carriage by a Paramount Clause and this would *prima facie* include article III, rule 4.[64] If the Rules are incorporated by a Paramount Clause, then article III, rule 4, must, it is submitted, apply to the electronic bill of lading in the same manner as to a paper bill of lading despite the electronic form. The Paramount Clause must – without a clear expression to the opposite – indicate that the parties have intended for the electronic bill to be treated as a paper bill would in respect of the Rules.[65]

If there is no Paramount Clause in the electronic bill of lading then also this aspect will be subject to the common law.[66] At common law, a carrier will normally, i.e. when the information is not validly qualified, be estopped as against an indorsee of the bill of lading from proving that the information contained in the bill is incorrect.[67] Again however, it may be questioned whether this doctrine which was developed in the context of paper bills of lading will apply to electronic bills. There does not seem to be any reason that it should not.[68] If the parties have chosen to use an electronic bill of lading as an alternative to a paper bill and the indorsee or holder of the electronic bill has relied in good faith on the information given therein then such indorsee or holder should have the same protection as an indorsee or holder of a paper bill of lading. As compared with the statutory rule, the common law principle also has a shortcoming in the *Grant v. Norway*[69] exception. This exception in essence means that the carrier will not be estopped from proving that the goods which the bill of lading represents have never been shipped.[70] The exception, which is

64 Such incorporation will most likely only give the Rules the force of contract, cf. *supra* part 3.2.1, and conflicting terms in the bill of lading may therefore limit the application of the Rules, including article III, rule 4.

65 Goldby, *Electronic Documents in Maritime Trade*, p. 126 et seq., also places emphasis on the parties' intention to treat paper end electronic bills of lading alike, but does so in the assertion that a court should find that COGSA 1971 is applicable to electronic bills.

66 Assuming that COGSA 1971 does not apply directly to electronic bills of lading, see the discussion *supra* part 3.2.1.

67 For a full discussion including references to the authorities see Treitel and Reynolds, *Carver on Bills of Lading*, p. 39ff.

68 Goldby, "The CMI Rules for Electronic Bills of Lading reassessed in the light of current practices", p. 64.

69 (1851) 10 C.B. 665.

70 The ruling is based on principles of agency, i.e. that an indorsee would not be justified to assume that the master had authority to sign a shipped bill of lading when the goods had in fact not been shipped.

clearly unacceptable to the trading community, will apply to electronic bills of lading unless it can be established that it is usual for electronic bills to be (electronically) signed before the goods are laden onboard.[71]

With the uncertainty that the above described circumstances create, one solution may be to combine a Paramount Clause with a clause whereby the carrier undertakes not to raise the electronic nature of the bill of lading as a ground for defeating an estoppel, i.e. the application of article III, rule 4, of the Hague-Visby Rules.[72]

3.2.4 Document of title at common law – passing of property

A paper order bill of lading is a document of title at common law.[73] This is not a term of art, but it is clear that it entails that the transfer of the bill of lading transfers constructive possession of the goods and if so intended can transfer property in the goods. The bill of lading's status as a document of title was established in the common law on the basis of a proven custom of merchants several centuries ago. This status certainly does not extend to electronic bills of lading.

As already mentioned, one way of seeking to obtain functional equivalence is through the use of the principles of bailment and attornment. Through the use of these principles the transfer of constructive possession can be replicated for electronic bills of lading. This requires, however, attornment by the carrier on each transfer which in reality requires setting up a system where all parties involved in the chain of transfers from the original shipper to the eventual consignee are somehow tied together because the carrier must know of all transfers taking place which is a very significant difference from using a paper bill of lading.[74]

The passing of property relies on the intention of the parties to the sales contract.[75] Transferring a paper bill of lading does, thus, not in itself pass property, but rather establishes a presumption that the requisite intention is present.[76] This presumption may be rebutted and any express provision in the sales contract as to the passing of the property will prevail over the presumption.[77] It seems very unlikely that a court will find that the presumption that the transfer of a paper bill of lading also shows intention

71 Goldby, "The CMI Rules for Electronic Bills of Lading reassessed in the light of current practices", p. 64, fn 56. For paper bills of lading the problem has been alleviated by COGSA 1992, s. 4, but as COGSA 1992 does not apply to electronic bills of lading, *Grant v. Norway* is still of relevance to such bills.

72 Ibid., p. 65. See also *infra* part 3.4.2.

73 See *supra* Chapter 3, part 2.2.

74 Goldby, *Electronic Documents in Maritime Trade*, p. 135.

75 Debattista, *Bills of Lading in Export Trade*, p. 107f, stressing the importance of express clauses in sales contracts setting out when property is to pass.

76 Ibid., p. 116 et seq., on the content of such presumption.

77 Goldby, *Electronic Documents in Maritime Trade*, p. 104.

to pass the property in the goods also applies to the transfer of an electronic bill of lading.[78] This emphasises the importance for traders wishing to use electronic documentation to regulate in their sales contract when property is to pass. There does not seem to be anything which should bar that this may occur on the tender of electronic documentation, including an electronic bill of lading.[79] This question, it seems, is better left to the parties to the sales contract to regulate rather than attempting to regulate this aspect when setting up a system for electronic bills of lading.

3.2.5 Delivery of the goods

An electronic bill of lading is not a document of title in the traditional common law sense, nor in the more limited sense that it must be presented to obtain delivery of the goods. Furthermore, the actual obligation to deliver the goods only against presentation of a bill of lading is not regulated by statute and to the extent that COGSA 1992 impacts on the delivery obligation, it does not apply to electronic bills of lading. Consequently, the functional equivalence of an electronic to a paper bill of lading in respect of the delivery of the goods must be obtained by contractual means. It must thus inter alia be established that the carrier must deliver against the "presentation" of the electronic bill, that the carrier is only discharged of its delivery obligation if it delivers against such "presentation" and that the right to delivery ceases to exist once delivery has been made.

3.3 Summing up

Electronic bills of lading are treated very differently in the law in Denmark and England.

In Denmark, electronic bills of lading are in principle treated equally to paper bills and thus the rules of the Merchant Shipping Act regulating bills of lading apply equally which also means that they are mandatory to the same extent as regards paper bills of lading. However, the lack of a paper document makes certain alterations necessary and the application must thus be *mutatis mutandis*. Further, the basic liability scheme based on the Hague-Visby Rules applies irrespective of the issue of a transport document at all and accordingly also in situations where an electronic bill of lading is issued. The rules of the Merchant Shipping Act supplemented with the rules of the Act on Instruments of Debt also put the legal effects of a transfer of an electronic bill of lading on the same footing as the transfer of a paper bill. The legal framework facilitating the use of electronic bills of lading is thus quite extensive.

78 Ibid., p. 136.
79 Ibid., p. 136 et seq.

In England, the legal effects of using an electronic bill of lading differs in virtually every way from using a paper bill of lading as a result of both the common law notion of a bill of lading, its classification as a document of title and of legislation. The Hague-Visby Rules as enacted by COGSA 1971 are not applicable to electronic bills and it is doubtful that the parties can incorporate them in a way so that they are given the force of law. Further, COGSA 1992 does not apply to electronic bills, but they are excluded from the ambit of the Contracts (Rights of Third Parties) Act 1999. Consequently, the transfer of rights and liabilities under an electronic bill is subject only to the common law, but the doctrines developed to alleviate some of the problems relating to the use of paper bills of lading prior to COGSA 1992 are unlikely to be applicable to electronic bills. Electronic bills of lading are thus basically subject to freedom of contract. Under English law, for an electronic bill of lading to be a true alternative to a paper one, it is necessary to establish the basic functions of a bill of lading by contract combined with other techniques, e.g. the principles of bailment.

When deciding to offer the use of electronic bills of lading, a carrier will have to set up a system of its own or to use a system offered by an external provider. Such a system must – like standard paper bill of lading terms – be able to function in an international setting. This will almost always be addressed by an express choice of law, but conflict of laws rules may in certain circumstances lead to a different law applying. It is therefore necessary to take as a starting point "the lowest common denominator" and to as large an extent as possible contractually regulate the issues which are not regulated by statute. Such contractual regulation may, however, in some instances come into conflict with mandatory rules of national law in countries where the legislation on carriage of goods also applies to electronic bills of lading, e.g. in Denmark.

In the following, some of the systems which have so far been set up will be touched upon.

3.4 The available systems

3.4.1 Remote printing systems

The preceding parts have dealt with electronic bills of lading in fully dematerialised form, i.e. which remain electronic throughout the entirety of their "lifetime". As shown, several legal obstacles exist in relation to the use of electronic bills of lading. However, the use of electronic communications and data systems have, as in all other areas of business, long been used in the concluding of contracts of carriage, provision of cargo information, shipping particulars etc. Especially in the liner trade this use has moved farther into the bill of lading transaction in the form of remote printing systems, normally offered by the carrier itself.

In such systems, very simplified and generalised, the cargo particulars are sent by the shipper via the system to the carrier who generates a bill of lading which is sent as a file to the shipper. The shipper can then print the bill of lading, in some instances on the carrier's stationery provided by the carrier, and this printed bill is the "original" bill of lading. Contrary to the situation examined in the preceding parts there is no intention to treat an electronic bill of lading like a paper one. Rather there is at all times in the process an intention that the bill of lading shall become a paper document. In some systems, the bill of lading may, however, be passed on while still in electronic form and not be printed until e.g. it is presented to a bank under a documentary credit. This raises questions similar to some of the ones examined above while the bill of lading is still in electronic form. The answers will to a large extent rely on the particulars of the system and the issue will not be pursued here.[80]

3.4.2 Electronic bills of lading – BOLERO and ESS-Databridge

Two main systems for electronic bills of lading exist that have been set up to overcome the problems under English law associated with the use of electronic bills of lading. These are BOLERO and ESS-Databridge.[81] Both are closed systems meaning that all parties who are to have any dealings with the bill of lading must sign up to the system and agree to be bound by a multipartite contract. It is through this contract that the replication of the bill of lading's functions is made possible.

ESS-Databridge is an electronic shipping document exchange provided by a company trading as essDOCS within its CargoDocs solution.[82] Aside from the electronic bill of lading essDOCS also caters for electronic handling of associated documentation such as certificates of origin, quality, and quantity and manifests. The system is based on the Databridge Services & Users Agreement (DSUA) which is in essence a contract between all users of the system and between each user and essDOCS. The DSUA is kept confidential.

ESS-Databridge does not have a Title Registry. Rather, the electronic bill of lading can be seen as a token-based document which the parties handle

80 For an analysis of such systems see Gaskell, "Bills of lading in an electronic age", especially parts III–V. Goldby, *Electronic Documents in Maritime Trade*, p. 304 et seq., discusses carrier-provided systems and performs an interesting analysis of how American President Lines' system could be turned into a completely dematerialised one and how such a system would fit with the Rotterdam Rules.

81 Recently a third system, named e-title, has appeared. From its website it appears that it is a closed registry system working pursuant to a multipartite contract. The present author has, however, not been able to obtain access to that multipartite contract, The Electronic Title User Agreement, for research purposes and without such access nothing meaningful can be said about the system. It will therefore not be mentioned further.

82 www.essdocs.com.

within the closed system using various authentication and authorisation processes to ensure that at any given time only one party has control over the bill of lading. An important feature of the ESS-Databridge is that the electronic bill of lading visually resembles a paper bill and the handling processes also closely resemble those for paper bills. For instance, indorsements appear on the "back" of the electronic bill of lading when it is transferred.

BOLERO, which stands for Bill of Lading Electronic Registry Organisation, is as the name indicates a registry-based system. It has a considerably longer history than the ESS-Databridge. Like ESS-Databridge it also caters for the electronic handling of associated documentation aside from the electronic bill of lading. The system is governed by the BOLERO Rulebook which is in essence a contract between all users of the system and the users and BOLERO. The Rulebook is freely available on the internet.[83] The creation of and dealing with the electronic bill of lading is done via electronic messages, digitally signed, sent through the BOLERO Exchange (also referred to as the Core Messaging Platform in the Rulebook).

An electronic bill of lading in the BOLERO system is called a Bolero Bill of Lading (BBL). A BBL consists of two parts; a BBL Text and a related Title Registry Record.[84] The BBL Text is the documentary part of the BBL and also a receipt for the goods. This can be in the form of a scanned version of a paper bill of lading which is imported into the BOLERO system via the Core Messaging Platform by the carrier. The carrier also makes a Title Registry Instruction about inter alia the identity of the shipper and holder. The Title Registry will record this information and send the BBL to the first holder. To transfer the BBL the holder must send a message through the Core Messaging Platform which verifies that it is the holder and records the holdership of the transferee in the Title Registry. It is thus the Title Registry that shows who the holder of a BBL is and who has title to the goods.

Both BOLERO and ESS-Databridge thus builds on quite extensive multipartite contracts in the form of the BOLERO Rulebook and the DSUA with further associated documents of a more technical and operational nature. To replicate the functions of a paper bill of lading and to overcome the shortcomings of the law applicable to electronic bills of lading described in the preceding parts the systems apply a number of contractual techniques. The parties undertake not to rely on the fact that the bill of lading or any transaction in relation thereto is in electronic rather than paper form. The electronic bill of lading contains a receipt by the carrier for the goods and under the rules such receipt is to have the same effect as receipts contained in a paper bill of lading. The electronic bill of lading is made subject to any

83 http://resource.bolero.net/bolero-rulebook-access.

84 Bolero Bill of Lading is defined in the Rulebook, rule 1.1.(11); BBL Text in rule 1.1.(6), and Title Registry Record in rule 1.1.(55).

international convention or national law that would have applied mandatorily to the bill of lading had it been a paper one. Each transfer of the electronic bill of lading involves a novation of the contract of carriage and an attornment by the carrier to hold the goods for the benefit of the transferee.

As can be seen, it is an elaborate scheme that is set up to replicate the functions of paper bills of lading to electronic bills (which should not be misunderstood to mean that the actual use of the systems is complicated; on the contrary).[85]

With regard to delivery, under BOLERO the carrier is obliged only to deliver the goods to (or to the order of) the Holder-to-Order or Consignee Holder who duly "surrenders" the BBL.[86] "Surrender" is defined as the "presentation of a Bolero Bill of Lading [...] in accordance with the Operational Rules, in order to obtain delivery of the goods at the end of the carriage".[87] When the Surrender has been recorded in the Title Registry the BBL ceases to be effective as a BBL.[88] Thus, in essence, the party claiming delivery and who has authority to do so in the system by being registered in the Title Registry as Holder-to-Order or Consignee Holder sends a Surrender message through the Core Messaging Platform to the carrier or another party whom the carrier has appointed as Surrender Party. The Rulebook contains no further rules as to how the carrier must identify the person actually claiming delivery at the ship's side. BOLERO has, however, explained that together with the surrender of the BBL the holder will send instructions to the carrier as to whom to release the cargo to, including copy of picture ID.[89] There are no further actions to be taken by either party in relation to the BBL after the "Surrender".

Under the ESS-Databridge the holder of the electronic bill of lading must produce it to the carrier which means that the holder transfers the electronic bill of lading to the carrier within the ESS-Databridge. The holder will at the same time nominate the receiver who will actually take physical delivery of the goods on behalf of the holder. The carrier is obliged to deliver against and only against such production. When the carrier has delivered the goods upon such production, the carrier identifies the electronic bill of lading as "Accomplished" in the ESS-Databridge upon which it ceases to be effective as an electronic bill of lading.

Neither BOLERO nor ESS-Databridge regulates the carrier's liability for misdelivery. With all users of each system being tied to each other by a multipartite contract which prescribes an obligation on the carrier to only

85 Treitel in Bridge, *Benjamin's Sale of Goods*, para 18–247, focuses on the uncertainty and limitations resulting from the use of the various contractual techniques and as a result advocates a legislative solution to the problems of electronic bills of lading.

86 Rule 3.6.(1).

87 Rule 1.1.(51).

88 Rule 3.6.(3).

89 Email from BOLERO to the author of 19 April 2016.

deliver against production/surrender of the electronic bill of lading, a party being a holder[90] under the rules set out in that contract would seem to have a claim for breach of the multipartite contract against the carrier who delivers the goods without such production/surrender. Presupposing that the system set up for novation of the contract of carriage on each transfer of the electronic bill of lading is legally valid, the holder under the rules may also have a claim for breach of the contract of carriage contained in or evidenced by the electronic bill of lading for such misdelivery. Further presupposing that the system set up for attornment by the carrier on each transfer of the electronic bill of lading is legally valid, the holder under the rules may have a claim for breach of bailment or in conversion. Thus, remedies alike to those applicable in relation to paper bills of lading seem to be available to a party who suffers damage as a result of a misdelivery under a BBL or an ESS electronic bill of lading.

3.4.3 P&I cover

Until February 2010, the P&I clubs who comprise the International Group of P&I Clubs all excluded cover for liabilities in respect of the carriage of goods under electronic bills of lading to the extent that the liabilities would not have arisen if paper based documentation had been used. In 2010, the P&I Clubs decided to extend cover for liabilities arising in respect of carriage of goods under electronic bills of lading if the system used had been approved by the International Group of P&I Clubs. Such approval was given to BOLERO and ESS-Databridge.[91] This decision seems to have been based on an assessment by the International Group that the two systems ensure performance of the three functions of a bill of lading underpinning P&I Club cover, viz. as a receipt, as a document of title and as a contract of carriage which incorporates the Hague or Hague-Visby Rules.[92]

3.4.4 Applicability of Danish Merchant Shipping Act to BOLERO and ESS electronic bills of lading

Having established in part 3.1 above that the Danish Merchant Shipping Act's rules on bills of lading also apply to electronic bills of lading that fulfil

90 "Holder" is here used to denote the party who under the respective multipartite contract has the status required to claim delivery of the goods.

91 Similar circulars were published by all P&I clubs comprising the International Group; see e.g. Gard circular no. 10/2010. The current version of the DSUA (version 2013.1) has subsequently been approved; see e.g. Gard circular no. 1/2013. The third system mentioned *supra* in fn 81, e-title, was approved in 2015, see e.g. Gard circular no. 7/2015.

92 See the answer to question 1 in Paperless Trading (Electronic Bills of Lading), Frequently Asked Questions of 20 October 2015, published by the International Group, available e.g. at www.skuld.com/Documents/Topics/Circulars/IG_FAQs_Electronic_BLs_20151020.pdf?epslanguage=en.

the definition of a bill of lading it may be asked whether a BOLERO Bill of Lading and an ESS electronic bill of lading would be subject to these rules presupposing that the contract of carriage is subject to Danish law.[93] § 292 defines the bill of lading as a document which 1) is evidence of a contract of carriage by sea and that the carrier has received the goods, and 2) on its face is called a bill of lading (in Danish, Swedish and Norwegian: "konnossement") or contains a provision that the carrier undertakes only to deliver the goods against surrender of the document. Both the BBL and the ESS electronic bill of lading seem quite clearly to fulfil requirement no. 1. Both would also seem to fulfil requirement no. 2. The electronic document is headed "Bill of Lading"[94] which in itself should be sufficient. Furthermore there is a surrender requirement in order to obtain delivery even though this requirement may be said not to be contained in the document itself, but rather in the multipartite contract setting up the system.

It would thus seem likely that the BBL and the ESS electronic bill of lading would fulfil the definition of a bill of lading in the Danish Merchant Shipping Act. Accordingly §§ 292–307 would be mandatorily applicable to such electronic bills of lading meaning e.g. that if the rules of the Merchant Shipping Act regarding the effects of a transfer of the electronic bill of lading conflict with the rules set out in the relevant multipartite contract, the former would prevail.

Neither in England nor in Scandinavia is there any reported case regarding the use of an electronic bill of lading.

93 Under § 252.

94 Both systems cater for carriers using the system to use their own standard form, but it is reasonable to expect that these will always contain the heading "bill of lading".

7 Rotterdam Rules and electronic transport documents

1 Introduction

The Rotterdam Rules contain rules giving legal effect to electronic documents, thus creating a basis for international unification of this issue. This may be said to be one of the most important aspects of the convention and indeed the initial decision to start up the work which eventually led to the Rotterdam Rules was made in the context of developing rules on electronic commerce in general.[1]

The negotiation of the e-commerce aspects of the Rules took place on the backdrop of UNCITRAL's previous work in the field of e-commerce generally.[2] This meant that both the interrelationship between the Rotterdam Rules and the previous instruments on e-commerce had to be assessed and that the regulation of the subject in the Rotterdam Rules had to be based on the same underlying principles as the previous instruments which had already gained a fairly wide acceptance in the international community.[3]

It is worth noting that the rules of the Rotterdam Rules pertaining to e-commerce, i.e. specifically electronic communication regarding the contract of carriage and electronic transport documents (termed "transport records" in the Rules), shall not be seen as a compromise between carrier and shipper interests. Rather, both carriers and shippers had an interest in facilitating the use of electronic communication and e-commerce and the task was therefore to produce rules which reflected this shared interest.[4] The rules should be read in this context.

The essential aim of these issues is to put on an equal footing information put on paper and given in electronic form, i.e. to obtain media

1 See the introduction to the Rotterdam Rules, *supra* Chapter 5, part 1.
2 Ibid.
3 The status of the instruments can be seen at www.uncitral.org/uncitral/en/uncitral_texts/electronic_commerce.html.
4 Manuel Alba, "Electronic Commerce Provisions in the UNCITRAL Convention on Contracts for the International Carriage of Goods Wholly or Partly by Sea", *Texas International Law Journal* 44 (2009): p. 388.

neutrality. In practice, this largely means removing requirements of form necessitating paper documents and giving the same legal effects to information recorded in electronic form as to paper documents. The policy principles generally accepted as guiding the choice of regulation to achieve the goal are the functional equivalence approach, the non-discrimination principle and the technological neutrality principle.[5] It was on the basis of these principles the provisions of the Rotterdam Rules were drafted.

The perhaps most tangible of these principles is the functional equivalence approach. In essence, it means that electronic communications must be able to fulfil the same functions as paper documents.[6] It requires the analysis and identification of the functions fulfilled by paper documents and an assessment of how to allow for the fulfilment of these functions by electronic communications.

It could be asked why electronic bills of lading could not just follow the general international rules on electronic commerce. The answer is that too much of the law pertaining to bills of lading flow directly from the issuance of a paper bill of lading and is not codified.[7]

Functional equivalence may be achieved in different ways which visually to the parties resemble the use of paper documents more or less. Thus, it may be achieved by using an electronic document which when viewed on a computer screen appears as a document. This e-document can then be transferred by an electronic indorsement which is given the same legal effect as the indorsement of a paper document. In this way, the transaction appears to the parties very much like the traditional paper transaction, only it is performed on computers. It can (to a certain extent) still be said that the document is the carrier of the rights and obligations contained in it. This way of achieving functional equivalence is sometimes called the full equalisation method.[8]

A different approach is to establish some other way than transfer of an electronic document to transfer the rights under the contract of carriage. This means that it is the rights that are transferred rather than the file containing the electronic document as a bearer of these rights. This method is sometimes called the transfer of rights method.[9]

As will be shown in the following, the Rotterdam Rules are based on the full equalisation method, but also to a large extent facilitate the transfer of rights method. For both methods it is, however, necessary that it is clear which rights and obligations are transferred. This is the main reason why the Rotterdam Rules became such a comprehensive instrument. Whereas many of the essential rights and obligations under a contract of carriage

5 Ibid., p. 394, fn. 28.
6 *Supra* Chapter 6, part 2.
7 *Supra* Chapter 5, part 1.
8 Sturley, Fujita, and van der Ziel, *The Rotterdam Rules*, para 3.005.
9 Ibid., para 3.006.

flow directly from the issuance and holding of a paper bill of lading, the same is not the case with an electronic bill of lading.[10] Therefore, in order to create international rules giving functional equivalence to electronic bills of lading effectively required the codification of the rights and obligations which it was the intention to make transferable by electronic means.

The structure of the Rotterdam Rules as pertains to electronic documents is that the rules specific to such electronic documents, i.e. the requirements for their use, are placed in a separate chapter, Chapter 3, while the legal effect of their use is regulated throughout the convention parallel to the regulation of paper transport documents. In addition, several definitions pertaining to electronic communication and electronic documents are included in article 1. It is also worth noting that some of the more general aspects of the use of electronic documents is not regulated in the Rotterdam Rules, but must instead be ascertained on the basis of the general rules regulating e-commerce as such, both at the international and national levels.[11]

2 Basic equivalence of electronic communication and writing and of paper and electronic transport documents

Only some of the communication envisaged in the Rotterdam Rules is subject to form requirements. These requirements are set out in article 3 which requires certain communications to be in writing.[12] The second sentence goes on to state that electronic communications may be used for these purposes provided such use is with the consent of both the sender and receiver of such communication. The consent may be implicit, e.g. by acknowledging receipt or answering using the same mode of communication, which will probably often be the case in practice.[13] This rule must be read in conjunction with article 1(17) which defines electronic communication as "information generated, sent, received or stored by electronic, optical, digital or similar means with the result that the information communicated is accessible so as to be usable for subsequent reference". The definition, thus, contains two parts; one setting out the action and

10 See *supra* Chapter 6, part 3.2 for the situation under English law.

11 Note should also be made of the work being conducted by UNCITRAL in its Working Group IV. The Working Group is (as at May 2016) in the final stages of preparing a Draft Model Law on Electronic Transferable Records which is aimed at inter alia aiding in the implementation of the Rotterdam Rules. See also *supra* Chapter 6, at fn 12. The status of the work and the draft model law can be found at www.uncitral.org.

12 This pertains to the notices, confirmation, consent, agreement, declaration and other communications referred to in articles 19(2); 23(1)–(4); 36(1)(b), (c) and (d); 40(4)(b); 44; 48(3); 51(1)(b); 59(1); 63; 66; 67(2); 75(4); and 80(2) and (5).

13 Sturley, Fujita, and van der Ziel, *The Rotterdam Rules*, para 3.021. Hannu Honka, "General Provisions", in *The Rotterdam Rules 2008*, ed. Alexander von Ziegler, Johan Schelin, and Stefano Zunarelli (Dordrecht: Kluwer Law International, 2010), p. 33.

means and one stating the result, i.e. that the information must be usable for subsequent reference. The two parts correspond to the UNCITRAL Model Law on Electronic Commerce's definition of "data message" and article 6 respectively.[14]

The general equivalence of paper and electronic transport documents is established in article 8. Subparagraph (a) provides that if the carrier and shipper consent then anything that is to be in or on a transport document under the Rules may be recorded in an electronic transport record. Subparagraph (b) states that the issuance, exclusive control, or transfer of an electronic transport record has the same effect as the issuance, possession, or transfer of a paper transport document. Several definitions make these provisions more specific.

First however, it is worth noting that the use of an electronic transport record requires the consent of the shipper and carrier, but not that of other parties with interests in the carriage, e.g. a documentary shipper, the consignee, another indorsee, or a bank who becomes holder of the record as part of a documentary credit. It is difficult to imagine, though, that an electronic transport record can be issued without the consent of the documentary shipper. Also, the article must be seen in conjunction with article 10(2) which provides for the possibility of replacing an already issued negotiable electronic transport record with a negotiable (paper) transport document. However, this requires the consent of both the holder and the carrier.

The requirement of consent is separate to the requirement of consent in article 3 regarding the use of electronic communication. This means that parties may consent to communicating electronically without consenting to the use of an electronic transport record and – in theory – vice versa. The former is probably already the practical reality in most contracts of carriage whereas the latter is highly unlikely to occur and would be highly impractical.

As already mentioned, the Rotterdam Rules do not speak of electronic transport documents but rather use the term electronic transport records. This term is defined in article 1(18) as "information in one or more messages issued by electronic communication under a contract of carriage by a carrier, including information logically associated with the electronic transport record by attachments or otherwise linked to the electronic transport record contemporaneously with or subsequent to its issue by the carrier, so as to become part of the electronic transport record, that: (a) Evidences the carrier's or a performing party's receipt of goods under a contract of carriage; and (b) Evidences or contains a contract of carriage."

This definition closely mirrors the definition of a transport document.[15]

14 Regarding the consequences of not adhering to the form requirements see "General Provisions", p. 33.

15 Alba, "Electronic Commerce Provisions in the UNCITRAL Convention on Contracts for the International Carriage of Goods Wholly or Partly by Sea", p. 397.

Thus, the two conditions as to its content are that the record must constitute a receipt for the carrier's receipt of goods for carriage and evidence or contain a contract of carriage. The difference between a transport document and an electronic transport record is therefore only the form. The result of media neutrality could have been obtained simply by making a comprehensive definition of "document" including both paper and electronic versions. This idea was, however, already at an early stage discarded and instead the two separate definitions were chosen together with separate reference to the two separate types of "document" throughout the substantive rules.[16] As regards the medium, the definition facilitates that the information which together makes up the transport record may be stored in different places. Also, terms may be incorporated into the record by attachment or by a hyperlink to a website where the information is available.[17] For instance, a carrier's standard conditions may be incorporated in such a manner, i.e. by inserting a hyperlink in the electronic transport record.

3 Issuance, exclusive control, and transfer of an electronic transport record

The three key elements used to create general equivalence in article 8(b) are issuance, exclusive control, and transfer of an electronic transport record. Issuance and transfer are defined terms in relation to negotiable electronic transport records, whereas exclusive control is not. Exclusive control is, however, given its content through both the definitions of issuance and transfer and by article 8(b) itself.

Issuance means the issuance of the record in accordance with procedures that ensure that the record is subject to exclusive control from its creation until it ceases to have any effect or validity[18] while transfer means the transfer of exclusive control over the record.[19] Both issuance and transfer of a negotiable electronic transport record, thus, revolves around the notion of exclusive control.

Pursuant to article 8(b), exclusive control of an electronic transport record has the same effect as the possession of a transport document. This means that the person with exclusive control of a negotiable electronic transport record should be able to do the same things with and rely to the same extent on said record as if it were a negotiable (paper) transport document.

16 CMI Yearbook (2001), p. 534. Alba, "Electronic Commerce Provisions in the UNCITRAL Convention on Contracts for the International Carriage of Goods Wholly or Partly by Sea", p. 398.
17 Faria, "Electronic Transport Records", p. 57.
18 Article 1(21). See *infra* part 4. regarding the procedures.
19 Article 1(22).

The notion of exclusive control is heavily influenced by the United States' implementation of MLEC, the Uniform Electronic Transactions Act (UETA), s. 16.[20] Pursuant to this section, a condition for the legal equivalence of electronic records to negotiable instruments is that the record is of such nature that a person may exercise control over it. Control is said to exist when "a system employed for evidencing the transfer of interests in the transferable record reliably establishes [the person claiming control] as the person to whom the transferable record was issued or transferred".[21] Under such conditions, "control" substitutes delivery, indorsement and possession of a negotiable promissory note or negotiable document of title.

The essential element of the notion of exclusive control in the Rotterdam Rules is, thus, that a system is employed that makes it possible to at all times identify *the* person who is entitled to the rights incorporated in the electronic transport record. How the exclusive control is to be established rests on the parties and thus the marketplace.[22]

4 Requirements for the use of negotiable electronic transport records

Article 9 of the Rules sets out the framework for the method by which the equivalence of negotiable electronic transport records, and thus exclusive control, is to be achieved in practice. It establishes that the use of such records shall be subject to procedures that provide for (a) the method for the issuance and the transfer of the record to an intended holder; (b) an assurance that the record retains its integrity; (c) the manner in which the holder is able to demonstrate that it is the holder; and (d) the manner of providing confirmation that delivery to the holder has been effected, or that the record has otherwise ceased to have any effect or validity.

These requirements obviously only create a framework and reflect the notions and practices from the use of paper documents that have been established by the marketplace over a long period of time. Because the use of electronic transport documentation at the time of negotiation and adoption of the Rotterdam Rules was – and despite an increase still is – very limited, such practices had not become well-established for electronic transport documentation. The regulation established by the Rotterdam Rules has therefore been called a "reversed catch-up"; whereas the law relating to negotiable paper bills of lading "caught up" to the practices evolved by the merchants, the Rotterdam Rules seek to provide the

20 Faria, "Electronic Transport Records", p. 58.

21 Ibid., p. 58f. UETA section 16(b).

22 See immediately below. Treitel and Reynolds, *Carver on Bills of Lading*, p. 589, finds that the lack of a definition of "exclusive control" leaving this to "commercial practices and technological developments as yet unknown" leads to lack of certainty which "can only be regretted".

framework for the marketplace to "catch up" by developing systems to fill in this framework.[23] Thus, the Rules provide the legal recognition of electronic transport records and thereby the certainty which makes it possible for the marketplace to develop the necessary technology.[24] A benefit of this approach is also that it is technology neutral and therefore also able to cater for technologies that the industry will develop in the future rather than being tied in with the techniques currently available.[25] One might object that it is a somewhat defensive approach, based as it is on the current paper system's notions and practices rather than seizing the opportunity to "weed out" some of the inexpedient practices of the paper system. The change to electronic documentation practices could then facilitate a modernisation not just of the form but also of the substance. However, the choice can be said to be a consequence of the functional equivalence approach and is an expression of a principle of non-alteration of the pre-existing current law.[26] The latter principle may seem somewhat misleading, though, as the Rotterdam Rules do change the pre-existing law to a certain extent and it is the new rules which the electronic transport record will functionally equate. The approach may also be based on a perception that for the regulation on electronic documentation to be acceptable to the industry, its solutions should not deviate from the paper practices.[27] At the same time, it must be remembered that the Rules do open the possibility for changing the current practices. Thus, the rules on the right of control and transfer thereof give the parties the possibility of setting up a practice which would not require the issue of any transport document or electronic transport record at all. Professor van der Ziel has advocated such a practice proposing a payment term abbreviated CATOC; Cash Against Transfer Of Control.[28]

23 Alba, "Electronic Commerce Provisions in the UNCITRAL Convention on Contracts for the International Carriage of Goods Wholly or Partly by Sea", p. 412.

24 Ibid.

25 David Martin-Clark, "Electronic Documents and The Rotterdam Rules", in *The Carriage of Goods by Sea Under The Rotterdam Rules*, ed. D. Rhidian Thomas (London: Lloyd's List, 2010), p. 292, however, alleges that despite the technology neutrality "article 9 clearly had in mind" the BOLERO Rulebook. Since the adoption of the Rotterdam Rules some further providers of electronic bill of lading solutions have emerged, see *supra* Chapter 6, part 3.4.2, and the carrier-provided systems for remote printing have been further developed and could probably with relative ease be turned into fully dematerialised systems. However, because the Rotterdam Rules are not yet in force these evolutions have still been made with an attempt at overcoming the legal obstacles especially under English law to the use of electronic bills of lading.

26 Alba, "Electronic Commerce Provisions in the UNCITRAL Convention on Contracts for the International Carriage of Goods Wholly or Partly by Sea", p. 394, fn 28.

27 The same perception seems to be underlying the choice by ESS-Databridge to set up their system in such a way that the electronic bill of lading and the handling of it visually resemble the paper practices – apparently with some success.

28 Van der Ziel, "Delivery of the goods, rights of the controlling party and transfer of rights", p. 255ff.

Article 9 gives the parties autonomy to choose what type of system including the level of security to use in their particular transaction. Despite the open language of subsection (a) the parties are not completely free to choose. The definition of issuance sets out that the procedures must ensure that the record is subject to exclusive control throughout its lifetime.[29] The standard of exclusive control must be subject to an objective control to ensure that the equivalence of the negotiable record to a negotiable document is well-founded and gives the parties with interests in the carriage the same certainty. The standard of the objective control should, thus, be the security that the holder of a negotiable paper transport document has as a result of the holder's possession of the document.[30]

How the exclusive control is established and ensured rests on the parties. Currently, it seems, only closed, third party provided systems are able to fulfil this condition. The systems available are "closed" in the sense that the parties must be contractually linked and have accepted the terms and conditions of the system in order to use it.[31] Further, dealings with the electronic bill of lading are made through a central database or registry where the electronic bill of lading is kept. As a result, the use of the systems is presently mainly limited to trades that are dominated by a relatively small number of traders and carriers although attempts are being made at extending the systems into other trades. However, the technology neutrality of the Rotterdam Rules means that the conditions may also be fulfilled without using a registry. Thus, an open, token-based system could be applied providing it has an appropriate level of security ensuring the uniqueness of the electronic record so that at any time one record can be identified as the "original" and can be transferred to a new holder without the use of a central database or registry. Such a technology does not currently seem to be available.

Subsection (b) requires an assurance that the record retains its integrity. This means that a procedure must be established by which it can be proved that the information in the record is unaltered. The underlying purpose is to preserve the information intact and (for the holder) to be able to prove it. How the assurance must be assessed is a rather (computer) technical problem. The issue is touched upon in the MLEC and the principles therein can provide guidance in relation to the issue under the Rotterdam Rules.[32]

Subsection (c) requires that a procedure must set out the manner in which the holder is able to demonstrate that it is the holder. With a paper bill of lading, showing that one is the holder is a matter of physically presenting the document along with further requirements as to indorsements and

29 Article 1(21).

30 Sturley, Fujita, and van der Ziel, *The Rotterdam Rules*, para 3.036.

31 See *supra* Chapter 6, part 3.4.2.

32 Faria, "Electronic Transport Records", p. 67.

identification depending on the type of bill. When using an electronic alternative it becomes more complicated and a procedure must therefore be established as to how one shows that one is the rightful holder of the "original" record. Subsection (c) must be read in conjunction with the definition in article 1(10)(b) which defines "holder" as the person to which a negotiable electronic transport record has been issued or transferred in accordance with the procedures referred to in article 9, paragraph 1. Whereas the definition in article 1(10)(a) of "holder" in respect of a negotiable paper transport document specifies the requirements for a person to be identified as the holder (i.e. that the person is identified in the document as shipper or consignee, or the document is duly indorsed to the person if an order document, and the person is the bearer of the document if a bearer document) subsection (b) again leaves it to the parties to set out how it must be established that a person is the holder of an electronic transport record. This could for instance be through the use of passwords, PINs (personal identification numbers), a key card or combinations thereof.[33] The determining factors for the parties in their choice of method should be the desired level of security, the available technical solutions and the cost thereof.

The procedures shall be referred to in the contract particulars and be "readily ascertainable", cf. article 9(2). The travaux preparatoires show that the intended meaning is that the procedures must be available to parties who have a legitimate interest in knowing them prior to entering a legal commitment based on the validity of the negotiable electronic transport record and that this is intended to function in a manner not dissimilar to the current availability of terms and conditions of bills of lading.[34,35]

5 Digital signature

Article 38 sets out the requirement that a transport document or electronic transport record must be signed by the carrier. Subsection (1) pertains to paper transport documents whereas subsection (2) sets out that an electronic transport record must include the electronic signature of the carrier or a person acting on its behalf which signature shall identify the signatory and indicate the carrier's authorisation of the record.

33 Ibid., p. 68.

34 UNCITRAL, A/CN.9/WG.III/WP.47, fn 34, A/CN.9/576, para 198–99, and A/CN.9/WG.III/WP.81, fn 35.

35 Martin-Clark, "Electronic Documents and The Rotterdam Rules", p. 294, states that both the BOLERO Rulebook and the ESS-Databridge Services and User Agreement seem to fulfil the requirement for procedures in article 9. Gaskell, "Bills of lading in an electronic age", p. 284, seems to agree stating that "it is difficult to see that the Rules will have altered the fundamental basis on which Bolero and ESS-Databridge are currently constructed". See *supra* Chapter 6, part 3.4.2 on the systems.

The lack of certain required contract particulars does not of itself affect the legal character or validity of the transport document or electronic transport record, cf. article 39. This article does not, however, mention the signature or electronic signature and the Rules therefore do not uphold the validity of an unsigned transport document or electronic transport record. Nor do the Rules specify that an unsigned document or record is invalid. Instead the question is left to national law (or other applicable instruments).[36]

The regulation of electronic signatures (and classic signatures) is limited to the above mentioned requirement for transport documents and electronic transport records to be signed. Many important questions regarding the use of electronic signatures are thus left to national law. In fact, "electronic signature" is not even a defined term in the Rules. This is a result of a policy decision not to attempt in the Rotterdam Rules to regulate matters regarding agency[37] and the principle of technology neutrality. The two policies combined leave hardly any room for regulation of signatures; electronic or handwritten. A requirement in national law of a specific level of reliability for an electronic signature to be valid, thus, also applies to the electronic signing of an electronic transport record.[38] However, it must be assumed that a national rule not recognizing validity of electronic signatures at all would be contrary to the Rotterdam Rules as such a rule would in effect completely render the use of electronic transport records impossible.

An effect of the Rules not regulating questions of agency in connection with signatures is that a (electronic) signature which fulfils the requirement in the Rules, article 38, does not necessarily fulfil the requirements of UCP 600 or eUCP.[39] These requirements are set out in UCP 600 articles 19–22. A shipper who has contracted on documentary credit terms would therefore be wise to ensure when contracting with the carrier that the carrier will issue a transport document or electronic transport record that fulfils the requirements of the UCP including the rules on (electronic) signature.

36 Sturley, Fujita, and van der Ziel, *The Rotterdam Rules*, para 7.057. In Fujita, "Transport Documents and Electronic Transport Records", p. 174f, Fujita, however, simply states that the lack of signature would make the transport document void. Filippo Lorenzon in Baatz et al., *The Rotterdam Rules: A Practical Annotation*, p. 111, seems to read article 39 *e contrario* stating that "this requirement is considered necessary for the legal character and validity of the document". As stated in the text above, that is a question for national law, but probably most jurisdictions would not recognise an unsigned transport document as legally valid.

37 UNCITRAL, A/CN.9/616, para 11–12, A/CN.9/621, para 291.

38 Sturley, Fujita, and van der Ziel, *The Rotterdam Rules*, para 7.059.

39 The question was raised during the negotiations whether the Rotterdam Rules should be aligned with the requirements of UCP 600 when it was published. UNCITRAL, however, decided to also in this respect stay with the decision not to regulate any questions of agency, UNCITRAL, A/CN.9/621, para 290–91.

Another important question in relation to electronic signatures which is left to national law is who bears the risk of forgery and abuse or misuse of the electronic signature as well as for lack of authority. This is particularly relevant because the parties when using electronic signatures rely on a third party supplier of a Public Key Infrastructure, a so-called PKI. PKIs often try to contractually limit their potential liability to a relatively low amount. A purchaser of a negotiable electronic transport record that turns out to have a false signature for which the PKI may be responsible may thus find himself in a situation where the PKI's limitation of liability may be far lower than the value of goods represented by the electronic transport record. In such a situation it will again be left to national law to decide whether the PKI can be held liable at all and, if so, whether the limitation of liability is valid.[40]

In the EU Member States, many aspects of the use of electronic signatures were at the time of negotiation of the Rotterdam Rules regulated in the e-Signature directive.[41] The directive has now been superseded by the eIDAS regulation[42] which will apply also to electronic signatures in electronic transport records. Although the Rotterdam Rules do not specify any requirements regarding the electronic signature, it must be assumed that the use of electronic signatures will be an integral part of the procedures which the parties agree pursuant to article 9. Such procedures must thus be made in observance of the rules of the regulation – and other national law which the electronic transport record may become subject to – in order for the procedures to have the intended effect between the parties, i.e. to make the use of a negotiable electronic transport record valid.[43]

6 Substantive rules on content, evidentiary effect and delivery

The required contract particulars are set out in article 36.[44] This rule applies both to transport documents and electronic transport records which, again, ensures the functional equivalence of electronic transport

40 This issue is discussed by Erik Røsæg in Røsæg, "New procedures for bills of lading in the Rotterdam Rules", p. 193f.

41 Directive no. 1999/93 of the European Parliament and of the Council.

42 See *supra* Chapter 6, part 2, at fn 16.

43 It is worth noting that the issue of competency to negotiate and enter into the Rotterdam Rules' regulation of electronic transport records and electronic signatures was not raised during the negotiations. This supports that, at least the EU Member States and the EU Commission, interprets the Rules such that national law regarding electronic signatures supplements (and overrides) the regulation contained in the Rotterdam Rules including the procedures to be established by the parties pursuant to article 9, cf. in this respect also Røsæg, "New procedures for bills of lading in the Rotterdam Rules", p. 193.

44 Contract particulars are defined in article 1(23) as "any information relating to the contract of carriage or to the goods (including terms, notations, signatures and endorsements) that is in a transport document or an electronic transport record".

records. The required information is the typical information regarding the goods, regarding the carrier and its receipt of the goods, and regarding the particular carriage. The rule also partially sets out which of the parties, the carrier or the shipper, who is to provide the information.[45] This is of importance in relation to the evidentiary value of the information in non-negotiable transport documents and electronic transport records.[46]

The evidentiary effect of the contract particulars is regulated in article 41. Pursuant to subsection (b)(i), proof to the contrary in respect of any contract particulars shall not be admissible when the negotiable electronic transport record has been transferred to a third party acting in good faith. Prior to such transfer, the electronic transport record is prima facie evidence of the carrier's receipt of the goods as stated in the contract particulars, subsection (a). The foregoing does not apply to the extent the particulars have been qualified by the carrier.[47] Article 41(b)(i) also applies both to negotiable transport documents and negotiable electronic transport records putting these on an equal footing. The rule in article 41(b)(i) is very similar to the rule in the Hague-Visby Rules article III, rule 4, relating to bills of lading.[48]

The Rotterdam Rules introduce positive regulation of the delivery of the goods.[49] Article 47 applies when a negotiable instrument has been issued, whether it be a transport document or an electronic transport record, once again establishing functional equivalence. For electronic transport records, article 47 must be read in conjunction with article 9(1), cf. article 47(1)(a)(ii), in that the holder must demonstrate that it is the holder pursuant to the procedures which the parties must establish pursuant to article 9(1).

7 Substantive rules on transfer of rights and right of control

The Rotterdam Rules deal in a limited manner with the transfer of rights and in an even more limited way with the assumption of liabilities by holders.[50] Thus, in relation to the transfer of rights, the Rules only regulate the

45 The shipper's obligation to provide information for the compilation of the contract particulars is separately regulated in article 31 which also sets out a guarantee obligation by the shipper for the accuracy of the information.

46 Article 41(c). See Møllmann, "From bills of lading to transport documents – the role of transport documents under the Rotterdam Rules", p. 55f.

47 The conditions for qualifying the contract particulars are set out in article 40.

48 The rule is also similar to that of the Hamburg Rules, article 16(3)(b), except that the additional requirement in the Hamburg Rules that the third party must have acted in reliance on the description in the contract particulars is not regulated. UNCITRAL, A/CN.9/616, para 56.

49 The Rotterdam Rules' regulation of the delivery of the goods is assessed in detail *supra* Chapter 5, and for the specific issues relating to electronic transport records part 5.7.

50 In Chapter 11.

situation where a negotiable transport document or a negotiable electronic transport record has been issued.

With respect to negotiable electronic transport records, article 57(2) contains the important rule that the holder of said record may transfer the rights incorporated in it by transferring the record.[51] However, the way in which such transfer is to be made is not set out. Instead it is stated that the transfer must be made in accordance with the procedures established pursuant to article 9(1). It is, thus, left to the parties to set up the way in which the electronic transport record can be transferred, but the legal effect of such a transfer, i.e. that it transfers the rights incorporated in the record, is established in article 57(2).

Furthermore, the Rotterdam Rules introduce regulation of the right of control while the goods are in transit.[52] These rules regulate the content of the right of control,[53] who the controlling party is and how this status may be transferred,[54] how the carrier shall execute instructions given in pursuance of the right of control[55] as well as further related issues.[56] In this context it is sufficient to mention that when a negotiable electronic transport record has been issued, the holder is the controlling party and the holder may transfer the right of control by transferring the record in accordance with the procedures established pursuant to article 9(1).[57]

These two important aspects which the marketplace has traditionally dealt with through the use of (paper) bills of lading are now dealt with in the Rotterdam Rules.[58] The content of the rights is the same whether a negotiable paper transport document or a negotiable electronic transport record is issued and the rights may in both instances be transferred by transfer of the document/record, but how such transfer must be made is regulated only for paper documents while the parties must establish a system for such transfers within the framework set out in article 9(1).

8 Do the Rotterdam Rules solve the problems?

Do the Rotterdam Rules then solve the basic legal problems currently impeding the use of negotiable electronic transport documents?

51 The "transfer" of a negotiable electronic transport record is defined in article 1(22) as the transfer of exclusive control over the record, see *supra* part 3.
52 In Chapter 10.
53 Article 50.
54 Article 51.
55 Article 52.
56 Articles 53–56.
57 Article 51(4).
58 Chapter 10 also regulates the content and transfer of the right of control for carriages where no negotiable transport document or record is issued. As mentioned *supra* at fn 28, Professor van der Ziel has advocated that this be used to establish payment terms that do not require the issue of a negotiable transport document or record.

As regards the liability system, it is worth noting that the Rotterdam Rules apply mandatorily to contracts for the international carriage of goods by sea irrespective of the issue of a specific type of transport document, article 5. Consequently, the mandatory liability regime will be the same whether a paper or an electronic bill of lading is issued.

Further, the Rules give legal status to electronic transport records on an equal footing with paper transport documents. This is done by establishing a functional equivalence between electronic transport records and paper transport documents. Accordingly, any requirement that information is to be in writing, in a document or signed can also be fulfilled by electronic communication and by using an electronic transport record. Further, the core acts regarding paper documents; issuance, possession, and transfer, are equalled by transactions regarding electronic transport records.

In addition to the general equivalence, the relevant substantive rules involving transport documents are duplicated with the appropriate amendments for the use of electronic transport records. This confers the three basic functions of a bill of lading on the negotiable electronic transport record. Thus, a negotiable electronic transport record is a receipt for the carrier's reception of the goods under a contract of carriage and evidence contrary to the information in this regard may not be produced after the transfer of the record to a third party;[59] the record must evidence or contain a contract of carriage;[60] and the negotiable electronic transport record gives a transferable right to claim delivery.[61]

In conclusion, the Rotterdam Rules solve the basic legal problems impeding the use of negotiable electronic transport documents. However, the practical, technical problems of setting up an infrastructure in which the electronic transport record can be used and which ensures the uniqueness of and exclusive control over the record is left to the parties and, thus, for the marketplace to develop, cf. article 9. The Rules thereby create the legal framework making the use of electronic documentation possible which the marketplace must then fill in for such use to become a reality.[62] If the Rules enter into force and gain widespread application it will, thus, still be necessary for the parties to use an elaborate system, whether carrier or third party provided, but this will only need to ensure the technical aspects of the use of electronic transport records and not also seek to overcome legal obstacles to such use. It is worth noting that the Rules are technology neutral and the procedures to be established can both be

59 Articles 1(18)(a), 8(a), and 41(b).

60 Articles 1(18)(b), and 8(a).

61 Articles 47, 8(b), and 9(1)(a).

62 Gaskell, "Bills of lading in an electronic age", p. 284, concludes that "[t]here is little in the Rules to harm the introduction or continuation of e-commerce, and quite a lot which will be of assistance". Anthony Diamond, "The Rotterdam Rules", p. 502, adopts Gaskell's conclusion.

fulfilled by a registry and a token system – if the technological solutions are available.

Many associated aspects of the electronic communication and documentation provisions of the Rotterdam Rules are also subject to other regulation in international and national laws, cf. especially rules on electronic signatures. Several of the aspects which the parties must regulate in procedures to be established pursuant to article 9 may also be subject to current or future national law. This could inter alia be legislation setting out minimal requirements as to the level of security of the system applied or on limitation of liability for the providers of such systems. Article 9 of the Rotterdam Rules cannot be seen as an impediment for rules regulating in part issues which must be subject to procedures mentioned in said article and there is therefore ample room for national lawmakers – and international or regional (EU) institutions – to supplement the Rotterdam Rules' regulation of e-commerce. UNCITRAL is itself close to completion of one such instrument in the form of the Draft Model Law on Electronic Transferable Records.

8 Concluding remarks

In Chapters 1 and 2 the central role of the bill of lading in international trade was described. This role is a result of the core functions of the bill of lading being recognised virtually universally. At the same time the bill of lading system is under pressure mainly as a result of technological advances and (derived) changes in business practices which challenge especially the "presentation rule". Thus, the public regulation of the use of bills of lading no longer fully corresponds to the realities of business practices.

While the functions of the bill of lading are recognised universally, the bases for affording these functions to the bill of lading in general, and not least in relation to the delivery of the goods, vary extensively, as shown in Chapter 3. Thus, under English law, bills of lading are mainly governed by contract law, but supplemented by common law principles of bailment as well as tort law, while under Scandinavian law the issues are widely regulated by mandatory rules of the Merchant Shipping Acts supplemented by the rules and principles relating to negotiable instruments.

As shown especially in Chapters 4 and 6, the different bases for the rules have immense effects on the possibilities for the industry's attempts at overcoming some of the challenges now inherent in the bill of lading system. Accordingly, the basis in mandatory legislation under Scandinavian law very strongly limits the possibilities for the parties to the bill of lading contracts to contractually regulate the delivery obligation or the liability for breach of this obligation. Under English law there is a much wider possibility for the parties to do so even if the courts have traditionally been reluctant to accept in the absence of very clear words that this is in fact the intention of the parties. In that connection it is an interesting development that several carriers have changed their standard bill of lading terms to expressly refer to misdelivery or even using the term "delivery without production of the bill of lading".

An effect in the opposite direction of the legislation-based approach can be observed in relation to the use of electronic bills of lading. Here the fact that the relevant Danish legislation also applies to electronic bills of lading enables the parties to use such electronic bills of lading with the same legal effects as when using paper bills of lading. This is not possible under

English law where most of the legal effects of using a bill of lading hinge on the issuance of a paper bill of lading and not an electronic version. Instead, elaborate contractual schemes have been set up in attempts at reproducing the functions of the paper bill of lading. This would seem to be a more cumbersome and perhaps risky approach and the legislation-based approach thus seems to aid the parties in seeking to overcome the challenges associated with the use of paper bills of lading by using electronic bills of lading.

With shipping and international trade being global in nature any potential solutions to the challenges in the bill of lading system will have to take into consideration the bases for the rules ensuring the bill of lading functions in all relevant jurisdictions. As the analyses in this book – which have taken on just English and Scandinavian law – have shown, this can be a very difficult task.

An obvious alternative to the industry seeking to find solutions to the perceived problems in practice under the current regimes is to regulate the matters at the international level. Accordingly, the Rotterdam Rules introduce both rules regulating the delivery of the goods and enabling the use of electronic transport records with the same legal effects as using paper transport documents. As shown in Chapters 7 and especially 5 the rules are not without complications and some aspects which change the current rules substantially are quite controversial. Only time will tell whether this convention will be internationally accepted and thus bring international harmonisation of this area of the law.

Annex

Numbering of §s in the Scandinavian Merchant Shipping Acts

Norwegian and Danish	*Swedish and Finnish*
§ 252	13th ch. 2nd §
§ 254	13th ch. 4th §
§ 271	13th ch. 21st §
§ 272	13th ch. 22nd §
§ 292	13th ch. 42nd §
§ 293	13th ch. 43rd §
§ 294	13th ch. 44th §
§ 295	13th ch. 45th §
§ 296	13th ch. 46th §
§ 297	13th ch. 47th §
§ 298	13th ch. 48th §
§ 299	13th ch. 49th §
§ 300	13th ch. 50th §
§ 301	13th ch. 51st §
§ 302	13th ch. 52nd §
§ 303	13th ch. 53rd §
§ 304	13th ch. 54th §
§ 305	13th ch. 55th §
§ 306	13th ch. 56th §
§ 307	13th ch. 57th §

Bibliography

Aikens, Richard, Richard Lord, and Michael Bools. *Bills of Lading*. 2nd ed. Abingdon: Informa Law, 2016.

Alba, Manuel. "Electronic commerce Provisions in the UNCITRAL Convention on Contracts for the International Carriage of Goods Wholly or Partly by Sea". *Texas International Law Journal* 44 (2009): 387–416.

Andersen, Lennart Lynge, Peter Møgelvang-Hansen, and Anders Ørgaard. *Gældsbrevsloven med kommentarer*. 2nd ed. Copenhagen: Thomson, 2007.

Andersen, Lennart Lynge, and Palle Bo Madsen. *Aftaler og mellemmænd*. 6th ed. Copenhagen: Karnov Group, 2012.

Arizon, Felipe, and David Semark. *Maritime Letters of Indemnity*. Abingdon: Informa Law from Routledge, 2014.

Baughen, Simon. "Charterparty bills of lading – cargo interests' liabilities to the shipowner". In *The Evolving Law and Practice of Voyage Charterparties*, edited by D. Rhidian Thomas, 217–50. London: Informa, 2009.

Baughen, Simon. "Bailment or conversion? Misdelivery claims against non-contractual carriers". *Lloyd's Maritime and Commercial Law Quarterly* (2010): 411–30.

Baughen, Simon. "Misdelivery claims under bills of lading and international conventions for the carriage of goods by sea". In *The Carriage of Goods by Sea under the Rotterdam Rules*, edited by D. Rhidian Thomas, 163–90. London: Lloyd's List, 2010.

Beale, Hugh. *Chitty on Contracts*. The Common Law Library. 31st ed. Vol. I, London: Sweet & Maxwell, 2012.

Beale, Hugh and Lowri Griffiths. "Electronic commerce: formal requirements in commercial transactions". *Lloyd's Maritime and Commercial Law Quarterly* (2002): 467–84.

Berlingieri, Francesco. "A Review of some recent analyses of the Rotterdam Rules". *Il Diritto Maritimo* (2009): 955–1036.

Berlingieri, Francesco, Philippe Delebecque, Tomotaka Fujita, Rafael Illiescas, Michael F. Sturley, Gertjan van der Ziel, Alexander von Ziegler, and Stefano Zunarelli. "The Rotterdam Rules – an attempt to clarify certain concerns that have emerged". 2009. Available at www.uncitral.org/pdf/english/texts/transport/rotterdam_rules/ExpertPaper.pdf.

Bools, Michael. *The Bill of Lading – A Document of Title to Goods; An Anglo-American Comparison*. London: LLP, 1997.

Bredholt, Jørgen, Jesper Martens, Jens V. Mathiasen, and Allan Philip. *Søloven med kommentarer*. 4th ed. Copenhagen: Jurist- og Økonomforbundets Forlag, 2012.

Bridge, Michael. *The International Sale of Goods.* 3rd ed.: Oxford University Press, 2013.

Bridge, Michael ed. *Benjamin's Sale of Goods.* 9th ed. London: Sweet & Maxwell, 2014.

Bridge, Michael, Louise Gullifer, Gerard McMeel, and Sarah Worthington. *The Law of Personal Property.* 1st ed. London: Sweet & Maxwell, 2013.

Brækhus, Sjur. "Bortfrakterens ansvar for utlevering av last til ulegitimert mottager". In *Juridiske arbeider fra Sjø og Land,* 337–50. Oslo: Universitetsforlaget, 1968. Originally published in *Arkiv for Sjørett* no. 2 (1955): 141–59.

Baatz, Yvonne, Charles Debattista, Filippo Lorenzon, Andrew Serdy, Hilton Staniland, and Michael Tsimplis. *The Rotterdam Rules: A Practical Annotation.* London: Informa, 2009.

Collins, Lawrence, ed. *Dicey, Morris and Collins on The Conflict of Laws.* 15th ed. London: Sweet & Maxwell, 2012.

Cooke, Julian, Timothy Young, Michael Ashcroft, Andrew Taylor, John D. Kimball, David Martowski, Leroy Lambert, and Michael F. Sturley. *Voyage Charters.* 4th ed. Abingdon: Informa Law from Routledge, 2014.

Debattista, Charles. *Bills of Lading in Export Trade.* 3rd ed. Haywards Heath: Tottel Publishing, 2009.

Diamond, Anthony. "The Hague-Visby Rules". *Lloyd's Maritime and Commercial Law Quarterly* (1978): 225–66.

Diamond, Anthony. "The Rotterdam Rules". *Lloyd's Maritime and Commercial Law Quarterly* (2009): 445–536.

Falkanger, Thor. "Cargo damage – who is entitled to sue the maritime carrier?" In *SIMPLY 2010,* edited by Alla Pozdnakova, 47–64. Oslo: Sjørettsfondet, 2010.

Falkanger, Thor and Hans Jacob Bull. *Sjørett.* 7th ed. Oslo: Sjørettsfondet Akademisk, 2010.

Falkanger, Thor, Hans Jacob Bull, and Lars Rosenberg Overby. *Søret.* 4th ed. Copenhagen: Karnov Group, 2013.

Faria, José Angelo Estrella. "Uniform law for international transport at UNCITRAL: new times, new players, and new rules". *Texas International Law Journal* 44 (2009): 277–319.

Faria, José Angelo Estrella. "Electronic transport records". In *The Rotterdam Rules 2008,* edited by Alexander von Ziegler, Johan Schelin and Stefano Zunarelli, 51–69. Dordrecht: Kluwer Law International, 2010.

Fujita, Tomotaka. "Transport documents and electronic transport records". In *The Rotterdam Rules 2008,* edited by Alexander von Ziegler, Johan Schelin, and Stefano Zunarelli, 161–88. Dordrecht: Kluwer Law International, 2010.

Gaskell, Nicholas. *Bills of Lading: Law and Contracts.* London: LLP, 2000.

Gaskell, Nicholas. "Bills of lading in an electronic age". *Lloyd's Maritime and Commercial Law Quarterly* (2010): 233–84.

Girvin, Stephen. "Bills of lading and straight bills of lading: principles and practice". *Journal of Business Law* (2006): 86–116.

Girvin, Stephen. *Carriage of Goods by Sea.* 2nd ed. Oxford: Oxford University Press, 2011.

Goldby, Miriam. "The CMI Rules for Electronic Bills of Lading reassessed in the light of current practices". *Lloyd's Maritime and Commercial Law Quarterly* (2008): 56–70.

Goldby, Miriam. "Electronic bills of lading and central registries: what is holding back progress?" *Information & Communications Technology Law* 17, no. 2 (2008): 125–49.

Goldby, Miriam. *Electronic Documents in Maritime Trade*. Oxford: Oxford University Press, 2013.

Grönfors, Kurt. *Tolkning av fraktavtal*. Gothenburg: Sjörättsföreningen, 1989.

Grönfors, Kurt and Lars Gorton. *Sjölagens bestämmelser om godsbefordran*. Stockholm: P A Nordstedt & Söners förlag, 1982.

Hagstrøm, Viggo. *Obligasjonsrett*. 2nd ed. Oslo: Universitetsforlaget, 2011.

Hazelwood, Steven J., and David Semark. *P&I Clubs Law and Practice*. London: Lloyd's List, 2010.

Honka, Hannu. "New carriage of goods by sea – The Nordic Approach." In *New Carriage of Goods by Sea*, edited by Hannu Honka, 15–216. Åbo: Institute of Maritime and Commercial Law, Åbo Akademi University, 1997.

Honka, Hannu. "General provisions". In *The Rotterdam Rules 2008*, edited by Alexander von Ziegler, Johan Schelin and Stefano Zunarelli, 27–38. Dordrecht: Kluwer Law International, 2010.

Jantzen, Johs. and Nils Dybwad. *Godsbefordring til Sjøs*. 2nd ed. Oslo: Fabritius & Sønners Forlag, 1952.

Leung, William. "Misdelivery of cargo without production of original Bill of lading: applicability of the mandatory legal regime of Hague-Visby and the one year time bar". *Journal of Maritime Law & Commerce* 39, no. 2 (2008): 205–27.

Lewison, Kim. *The Interpretation of Contracts*. 5th ed. London: Sweet & Maxwell, 2011.

Lookofsky, Joseph. *Consequential Damages in Comparative Perspective*. Copenhagen: Jurist- og Økonomforbundets Forlag, 1989.

Lorenzon, Filippo. *Sassoon on C.I.F. and F.O.B. Contracts*. British Shipping Laws. 5th ed. London: Sweet & Maxwell, 2012.

Lyngsø, Preben. *Gældsbrevsloven*. 3rd ed. Copenhagen: Jurist- og Økonomforbundets Forlag, 1989.

Lyngsø, Preben. *Negotiable Dokumenter*. Copenhagen: Juristforbundets Forlag, 1972.

Martin-Clark, David. "Electronic documents and the Rotterdam Rules". In *The Carriage of Goods by Sea Under The Rotterdam Rules*, edited by D. Rhidian Thomas, 283–94. London: Lloyd's List, 2010.

McGregor, Harvey. *McGregor on Damages*. The Common Law Library. 19th ed. London: Sweet & Maxwell, 2014.

McMeel, Gerard. *The Construction of Contracts – Interpretation, Implication, and Rectification*. 2nd ed. Oxford: Oxford University Press, 2011.

Munk-Hansen, Carsten. *Ansvarsregulering i overdragelsesaftaler*. Copenhagen: Jurist- og Økonomforbundets Forlag, 2007.

Møllmann, Anders. *Certepartifortolkning – i nordisk og engelsk ret*. Copenhagen: Jurist- og Økonomforbundets Forlag, 2007.

Møllmann, Anders. "Compensation for damage". In *The United Nations Convention on Contracts for the International Carriage of Goods Wholly or Partly by Sea – An Appraisal of the "Rotterdam Rules"*, edited by Meltem Deniz Güner-Ösbek, 201–9. Heidelberg: Springer, 2011.

Møllmann, Anders. "From bills of lading to transport documents – the role of transport documents under the Rotterdam Rules." *Journal of International Maritime Law* 17, no. 1 (2011): 50–7.

Møllmann, Anders. "Security assignment of debts and the conflict of laws". *Lloyd's Maritime and Commercial Law Quarterly* (2011): 262–74.

Pedersen, Per Vestergaard. *Transportret.* Copenhagen: Thomson, 2008.

Peel, Edwin. *Treitel's The Law of Contract.* 13th ed. London: Sweet & Maxwell, 2011.

Pejovic, Caslav. "Article 47(2) of the Rotterdam Rules: the solution of old problems or a new Confusion?" In *The Hamburg Lectures on Maritime Affairs 2011–2013*, edited by Jürgen Basedow, Ulrich Magnus and Rüdiger Wolfrum, 177–97. Heidelberg: Springer, 2015.

Petersen, J. Günther. *Ansvarsfraskrivelse.* Copenhagen: Ejnar Munksgaards Forlag, 1957.

Ramberg, Jan. *International Commercial Contracts.* 4th ed.: Norstedts Juridik, 2011.

Rogers, W.V.H., and M.G. Clarke. *The Unfair Contract Terms Act 1977.* London: Sweet & Maxwell, 1978.

Rosenmeyer, Kjeld. *Transportret.* Copenhagen: Juristforbundets Forlag, 1982.

Røsæg, Erik. "New procedures for bills of lading in the Rotterdam Rules". *Journal of International Maritime Law* 17, no. 3 (2011): 181–94.

Schmidt, Folke, Gösta Wilkens, Kurt Grönfors, and Kaj Pineus. *Huvudlinjer i svensk frakträtt.* 2nd ed. Stockholm: P. A. Nordstedt & Söners Förlag, 1962.

Selvig, Erling. *Unit Limitation of Carrier's Liability.* Oslo: Oslo University Press, 1961.

Selvig, Erling. *Fra kjøpsrettens og transportrettens grenseland.* Oslo: Universitetsforlaget, 1975.

Smeele, Frank. "The bill of lading contracts under European national laws (civil law approaches to explaining the legal position of the consignee under bills of lading)". In *The Evolving Law and Practice of Voyage Charterparties*, edited by D. Rhidian Thomas, 251–80. London: Informa, 2009.

Sturley, Michael F. "Transport Law for the twenty-first century: an introduction to the preparation, philosophy, and potential impact of the Rotterdam Rules". In *A New Convention for the Carriage of Goods by Sea – The Rotterdam Rules*, edited by D. Rhidian Thomas, 1–33. Lawtext Publishing Limited, 2009.

Sturley, Michael F., Tomotaka Fujita, and Gertjan van der Ziel. *The Rotterdam Rules.* London: Sweet & Maxwell, 2010.

The Swedish Maritime Code Sjölagen 1994 – In Swedish and English. Skrifter utgivna av Axel Ax:son Johnsons institut för sjörätt och annan transporträtt. Stockholm: Juristförlaget, 1995.

Tiberg, Hugo. "Legal qualities of transport documents". *Tulane Maritime Law Journal* 23 (1998): 1–44.

Tiberg, Hugo. "Liability for wrongful delivery". In *Cargo Liability in Future Maritime Carriage*, edited by Hugo Tiberg. Svenska Sjörättsföreningen Skrifter 73, 153–77. Stockholm: Jure AB, 1998.

Todd, Paul. "The bill of lading and delivery: the common law actions". *Lloyd's Maritime and Commercial Law Quarterly*, no. 4 (2006): 539–67.

Todd, Paul. "Delivery against forged bill of lading". *Lloyd's Maritime and Commercial Law Quarterly*, no. 4 (1999): 449–56.

Todd, Paul. *Maritime Fraud.* London: LLP, 2003.

Todd, Paul. *Bills of Lading and Bankers' Documentary Credits.* 4th ed. London: Informa, 2007.

Todd, Paul. "Liability for misdelivery: Trafigura v MSC". *Journal of International Maritime Law* 13 (2007): 356–65.

Todd, Paul. "Excluding and limiting liability for misdelivery". *Journal of Business Law*, no. 3 (2010): 243–66.

Todd, Paul. *Maritime Fraud and Piracy.* Maritime and Transport Law Library. 2nd ed.

London: Lloyd's List, 2010.

Treitel, Sir Guenter, and F.M.B. Reynolds. *Carver on Bills of Lading*. British Shipping Laws. 3rd ed. London: Sweet & Maxwell, 2011.

Ulfbeck, Vibe. *Kontrakters relativitet*. Copenhagen: Thomson, 2000.

Ulfbeck, Vibe. "Fortolkning af ansvarsfraskrivelser". In *Avtalslagen 90 år*, edited by Boel Flodgren, Lars Gorton, Eva Lindell-Frantz and Per Samuelsson, 481–98. Stockholm: Norstedts Juridik AB, 2005.

Ussing, Henry. *Køb*. 4th ed. (7th print run(1985)) Copenhagen: Jurist- og Økonomforbundets Forlag, 1967.

van der Ziel, Gertjan. "Delivery of the goods, rights of the controlling party and transfer of rights". In *A New Convention for the Carriage of Goods by Sea – The Rotterdam Rules*, edited by D. Rhidian Thomas, 242–57. Lawtext Publishng Limited, 2009.

van der Ziel, Gertjan. "Delivery of the Goods". In *The Rotterdam Rules 2008*, edited by Alexander von Ziegler, Johan Schelin and Stefano Zunarelli, 189–218. Dordrecht: Kluwer Law International, 2010.

von Eyben, B., P. Mortensen, and I. Sørensen. *Lærebog i obligationsret II, Personskifte i skyldforhold, Fordringers ophør, Hæftelsesformer*. 2nd ed. Copenhagen: Thomson Reuters, 2005.

von Eyben, Bo, Peter Mortensen, and Ivan Sørensen. *Lærebog i Obligatiosnret II – Personskifte i skyldforhold, Fordringers ophør, Hæftelsesformer*. 4th ed. Copenhagen: Karnov Group, 2014.

Walin, Gösta, and Johnny Herre. *Lagen om skuldebrev m.m. En kommentar*. 3rd ed. Stockholm: Norstedts Juridik, 2011.

Yates, David. *Exclusion Clauses in Contracts*. 2nd ed. London: Sweet & Maxwell, 1982.

Index

For Product Safety Concerns and Information please contact our EU representative GPSR@taylorandfrancis.com Taylor & Francis Verlag GmbH, Kaufingerstraße 24, 80331 München, Germany